Conference of the North American Chapter of the Association for Computational Linguistics: Human Language Technologies (NAACL HLT 2018)

Student Research Workshop

New Orleans, Louisiana, USA

1 – 6 June 2018

ISBN: 978-1-5108-6349-1

Printed from e-media with permission by:

Curran Associates, Inc.
57 Morehouse Lane
Red Hook, NY 12571

Some format issues inherent in the e-media version may also appear in this print version.

Printed by Curran Associates, Inc. (2018)

For permission requests, please contact the Association for Computational Linguistics
at the address below.

Association for Computational Linguistics
209 N. Eighth Street
Stroudsburg, Pennsylvania 18360

Phone: 1-570-476-8006
Fax: 1-570-476-0860

acl@aclweb.org

Additional copies of this publication are available from:

Curran Associates, Inc.
57 Morehouse Lane
Red Hook, NY 12571 USA
Phone: 845-758-0400
Fax: 845-758-2633
Email: curran@proceedings.com
Web: www.proceedings.com

NAACL HLT 2018

**The 2018 Conference of the
North American Chapter of the
Association for Computational Linguistics:
Human Language Technologies**

Proceedings of the Student Research Workshop

June 2 - June 4, 2018
New Orleans, Louisiana

©2018 The Association for Computational Linguistics

Introduction

Welcome to the NAACL-HLT 2018 Student Research Workshop!

This year's submissions were organized in two tracks: research papers and thesis proposals.

- Research papers may describe completed work, or work in progress with preliminary results. For these papers, the first author must be a current graduate or undergraduate student.

- Thesis proposals are geared towards PhD students who have decided on a thesis topic and wish to get feedback on their proposal and broader ideas for their continuing work.

This year, we received a total of 51 submissions: 43 of these were research papers, and 8 were thesis proposals. We accepted 16 research papers and 4 thesis proposals, resulting in an overall acceptance rate of 39%. The main author of the accepted papers represent a variety of countries: Canada, Estonia, France, Germany, India, Japan (2 papers), Switzerland, UK, USA (11 papers).

Accepted research papers will be presented as posters within the NAACL main conference poster sessions. We will have oral presentations at our SRW oral session on June 2 for all 4 thesis papers to allow students to get feedback about their thesis work, along with 2 research papers selected as outstanding papers.

Following previous editions of the Student Research Workshop, we have offered students the opportunity to get mentoring feedback before submitting their work for review. Each student that requested pre-submission mentorship was assigned to an experienced researcher who read the paper and provided some comments on how to improve the quality of writing and presentation of the student's work. A total of 21 students participated in the mentorship program. During the workshop itself, we will also provide an in-site mentorship program. Each mentor will meet with their assigned students to provide feedback on their poster or oral presentation, and to discuss their research careers.

We would like to express our gratitude for the financial support from the National Science Foundation (NSF) and the Computing Research Association Computing Community Consortium (CRA-CCC). Thanks to their support, this year's SRW is able to assist students with their registration, travel, and lodging expenses.

We would like to thank the mentors for dedicating their time to help students improve their papers prior to submission, and we thank the members of the program committee for the constructive feedback they have provided for each submitted paper.

This workshop would not have been possible without the help from our faculty advisors, and we thank them for their guidance along this year of workshop preparation. We also thank the organizers of NAACL-HLT 2018 for their continuous support.

Finally, we would like to thank all students who have submitted their work to this edition of the Student Research Workshop. We hope our collective effort will be rewarded in the form of an excellent workshop!

Organizers:

Silvio Ricardo Cordeiro (Aix-Marseille Université)
Shereen Oraby (University of California, Santa Cruz)
Umashanthi Pavalanathan (Georgia Institute of Technology)
Kyeongmin Rim (Brandeis University)

Faculty Advisors:

Swapna Somasundaran (ETS Princeton)
Sam Bowman (New York University)

Program Committee:

Bharat Ram Ambati (Apple Inc)
Rachel Bawden (Université Paris-Sud)
Yonatan Bisk (University of Washington)
Dallas Card (Carnegie Mellon University)
Wanxiang Che (Harbin Institute of Technology)
Monojit Choudhury (Microsoft Research)
Mona Diab (George Washington University)
Jesse Dodge (Carnegie Mellon University)
Bonnie Dorr (Florida Institute for Human-Machine Cognition)
Ahmed Elgohary (University of Maryland, College Park)
Micha Elsner (The Ohio State University)
Noura Farra (Columbia University)
Thomas François (Université catholique de Louvain)
Daniel Fried (University of California, Berkeley)
Debanjan Ghosh (Rutgers University)
Kevin Gimpel (Toyota Technological Institute at Chicago)
Ralph Grishman (New York University)
Alvin Grissom II (Ursinus College)
Jiang Guo (Massachusetts Institute of Technology)
Luheng He (University of Washington)
Jack Hessel (Cornell University)
Dirk Hovy (Bocconi University)
Mohit Iyyer (Allen Institute for Artificial Intelligence)
Yacine Jernite (New York University)
Yangfeng Ji (University of Washington)
Kristiina Jokinen (University of Helsinki)
Daisuke Kawahara (Kyoto University)
Chris Kedzie (Columbia University)
Philipp Koehn (Johns Hopkins University)
Jonathan K. Kummerfeld (University of Michigan)
Maximilian Köper (University of Stuttgart)

Éric Laporte (Université Paris-Est Marne-la-Vallée)
Sarah Ita Levitan (Columbia University)
Jasy Suet Yan Liew (Universiti Sains Malaysia)
Diane Litman (University of Pittsburgh)
Stephanie M. Lukin (US Army Research Laboratory)
Shervin Malmasi (Harvard Medical School)
Diego Marcheggiani (University of Amsterdam)
Daniel Marcu (University of Southern California)
Mitchell Marcus (University of Pennsylvania)
Prashant Mathur (eBay)
Kathy McKeown (Columbia University)
Julie Medero (Harvey Mudd College)
Amita Misra (University of California,Santa Cruz)
Saif M. Mohammad (National Research Council Canada)
Taesun Moon (IBM Research)
Smaranda Muresan (Columbia University)
Karthik Narasimhan (Massachusetts Institute of Technology)
Shashi Narayan (University of Edinburgh)
Graham Neubig (Carnegie Mellon University)
Avinesh P.V.S. (Technische Universität Darmstadt)
Yannick Parmentier (University of Lorraine)
Gerald Penn (University of Toronto)
Massimo Poesio (Queen Mary University of London)
Christopher Potts (Stanford University)
Daniel Preoţiuc-Pietro (University of Pennsylvania)
Emily Prud'hommeaux (Boston College)
Sudha Rao (University Of Maryland, College Park)
Mohammad Sadegh Rasooli (Columbia University)
Michael Roth (Saarland University)
Markus Saers (Hong Kong University of Science and Technology)
David Schlangen (Bielefeld University)
Minjoon Seo (University of Washington)
Kevin Small (Amazon)
Sandeep Soni (Georgia Institute of Technology)
Ian Stewart (Georgia Institute of Technology)
Alane Suhr (Cornell University)
Shyam Upadhyay (University of Pennsylvania)
Sowmya Vajjala (Iowa State University)
Bonnie Webber (University of Edinburgh)
John Wieting (Carnegie Mellon University)
Adina Williams (New York University)
Diyi Yang (Carnegie Mellon University)
Justine Zhang (Cornell University)
Meishan Zhang (Heilongjiang University)
Ran Zhao (Carnegie Mellon University)

Table of Contents

Conference Program

Saturday, June 2

10:30–12:00   **Posters and Demos: Discourse and Pragmatics**

Alignment, Acceptance, and Rejection of Group Identities in Online Political Discourse
Hagyeong Shin and Gabriel Doyle

15:30–17:00   **Posters and Demos: Semantics**

Combining Abstractness and Language-specific Theoretical Indicators for Detecting Non-Literal Usage of Estonian Particle Verbs
Eleri Aedmaa, Maximilian Köper and Sabine Schulte im Walde

Verb Alternations and Their Impact on Frame Induction
Esther Seyffarth

A Generalized Knowledge Hunting Framework for the Winograd Schema Challenge
Ali Emami, Adam Trischler, Kaheer Suleman and Jackie Chi Kit Cheung

Towards Qualitative Word Embeddings Evaluation: Measuring Neighbors Variation
Benedicte Pierrejean and Ludovic Tanguy

A Deeper Look into Dependency-Based Word Embeddings
Sean MacAvaney and Amir Zeldes

15:30–17:00   **Posters and Demos: Sentiment Analysis**

Learning Word Embeddings for Data Sparse and Sentiment Rich Data Sets
Prathusha Kameswara Sarma

17:00–18:30   **Oral Presentations: Student Research Workshop Highlight Papers**

17:00–17:14
Igbo Diacritic Restoration using Embedding Models
Ignatius Ezeani, Mark Hepple, Ikechukwu Onyenwe and Enemouh Chioma

17:15–17:29
Using Classifier Features to Determine Language Transfer on Morphemes
Alexandra Lavrentovich

17:30–17:44
End-to-End Learning of Task-Oriented Dialogs
Bing Liu

17:45–17:59
Towards Generating Personalized Hospitalization Summaries
Sabita Acharya, Barbara Di Eugenio, Andrew Boyd, Richard Cameron, Karen Dunn
Lopez, Pamela Martyn-Nemeth, Carolyn Dickens and Amer Ardati

18:00–18:14
A Generalized Knowledge Hunting Framework for the Winograd Schema Challenge
Ali Emami, Adam Trischler, Kaheer Suleman and Jackie Chi Kit Cheung

18:15–18:30
Alignment, Acceptance, and Rejection of Group Identities in Online Political Discourse
Hagyeong Shin and Gabriel Doyle

10:30–12:00 Posters and Demos: Question Answering

Training a Ranking Function for Open-Domain Question Answering
Phu Mon Htut, Samuel Bowman and Kyunghyun Cho

10:30–12:00 Posters and Demos: Social Media and Computational Social Science

Corpus Creation and Emotion Prediction for Hindi-English Code-Mixed Social Media Text
Deepanshu Vijay, Aditya Bohra, Vinay Singh, Syed Sarfaraz Akhtar and Manish Shrivastava

14:00–15:30 Posters and Demos: Cognitive Modeling and Psycholinguistics

Sensing and Learning Human Annotators Engaged in Narrative Sensemaking
McKenna Tornblad, Luke Lapresi, Christopher Homan, Raymond Ptucha and Cecilia Ovesdotter Alm

14:00–15:30 Posters and Demos: Vision, Robotics and Other Grounding

Generating Image Captions in Arabic using Root-Word Based Recurrent Neural Networks and Deep Neural Networks
Vasu Jindal

Alignment, Acceptance, and Rejection of Group Identities in Online Political Discourse

Hagyeong Shin
Dept. of Linguistics
San Diego State University
San Diego, CA, USA, 92182
`hshin@sdsu.edu`

Gabriel Doyle
Dept. of Linguistics
San Diego State University
San Diego, CA, USA, 92182
`gdoyle@sdsu.edu`

Abstract

Conversation is a joint social process, with participants cooperating to exchange information. This process is helped along through linguistic alignment: participants' adoption of each other's word use. This alignment is robust, appearing many settings, and is nearly always positive. We create an alignment model for examining alignment in Twitter conversations across antagonistic groups. This model finds that some word categories, specifically pronouns used to establish group identity and common ground, are negatively aligned. This negative alignment is observed despite other categories, which are less related to the group dynamics, showing the standard positive alignment. This suggests that alignment is strongly biased toward cooperative alignment, but that different linguistic features can show substantially different behaviors.

1 Introduction

Conversation, whether friendly chit-chat or heated debate, is a jointly negotiated social process, in which interlocutors balance the assertion of one's own identity and ideas against a receptivity to the others. Work in Communication Accommodation Theory has demonstrated that speakers tend to converge their communicative behavior in order to achieve social approval from their in-group members, while they tend to diverge their behavior in a conversation with out-group members, especially when the group dynamics are strained (Giles et al., 1991, 1973).

Linguistic alignment, the use of similar words to one's conversational partner, is one prominent and robust form of this accommodation, and has been detected in a variety of linguistic interactions, ranging from speed dates to the Supreme Court (Danescu-Niculescu-Mizil et al., 2011; Guo et al., 2015; Ireland et al., 2011; Niederhoffer and

Pennebaker, 2002). In particular, this alignment is usually positive, reflecting a widespread willingness to accept and build off of the linguistic structure provided by one's interlocutor; the differences in alignment have generally been of degree, not direction, subtly reflecting group differences in power and interest.

The present work proposes a new model of alignment, SWAM, which adapts the WHAM alignment model (Doyle and Frank, 2016). We examine alignment behaviors in a setting with clear group identities and enmity between the groups but with uncertainty on which group is majority or minority: conversations between supporters of the two major candidates in the 2016 U.S. Presidential election. Unlike previous alignment work, we find some cases of substantial negative alignment, especially on personal pronouns that play a key role in assigning group identity and establishing common ground in the discourse. In addition, within-versus cross-group conversations show divergent patterns of both overall frequency and alignment behaviors on pronouns even when the alignment is positive. These differences contrast with the relatively stable (though still occasionally negative) alignment on word categories that reflect possible rhetorical approaches within the discussions, suggesting that group dynamics within the argument are, in a sense, more contentious than the argument itself.

2 Previous Studies

2.1 Linguistic Alignment

Accommodation in communication happens at many levels, from mimicking a conversation partner's paralinguistic features to choosing which language to use in multilingual societies (Giles et al., 1991). One established approach to assess accommodation in linguistic representation

1

Proceedings of NAACL-HLT 2018: Student Research Workshop, pages 1–8
New Orleans, Louisiana, June 2 - 4, 2018. ©2017 Association for Computational Linguistics

is to look at the usage of function word categories, such as pronouns, prepositions, and articles (Danescu-Niculescu-Mizil et al., 2011; Niederhoffer and Pennebaker, 2002). This approach argues that function words provide the syntactic structure, which can vary somewhat independently of the content words being used. Speakers can express the same thought through different speech styles and reflect their own personality, identity, and emotions (Chung and Pennebaker, 2007).

In this context, we view limit our analysis to convergence in lexical category choices, which can be the consequence of both social and cognitive processes. We call this specific quantification of accommodation "linguistic alignment", but it is closely related to general concepts such as priming and entrainment. This alignment behavior may be the result of social or cognitive processes, or both, though we focus on the social influences here.

2.2 Linguistic Alignment between Groups

Recent models of linguistic alignment have attempted to separate homophily, an inherent similarity in speakers' language use, from adaptive alignment in response to a partner's recent word use (Danescu-Niculescu-Mizil et al., 2011; Doyle et al., 2017). If homophily is not separated from alignment, it is impossible to compare within- and cross-group alignment, since the groups themselves are likely to have different overall word distributions. Both alignment and homophily can be meaningful; Doyle et al. (2017) combine the two to estimate employees' level of inclusion in the workplace.

Separating these factors opens the door to investigate alignment behaviors even in cases where different groups speak in different ways; if homophily is not factored out, cross-group differences will produce alignment underestimates. Thus far, these models of alignment been applied mostly in cases where there is a single salient group that speakers wish to join (Doyle et al., 2017), or where group identities are less salient than dyadic social roles or relationships, such as social power (Danescu-Niculescu-Mizil et al., 2012), engagement (Niederhoffer and Pennebaker, 2002), or attraction (Ireland et al., 2011).

There is some evidence and an intuition that alignment can cross group boundaries, but it has not been measured using such models of adaptive linguistic alignment. Niederhoffer and Pennebaker (2002) pointed out that speakers with negative feelings are likely to coordinate their linguistic style to each other, while speakers who are not engaged to each other at all are less likely to align their linguistic style. Speakers also might actively coordinate their speech to their opponents' in order to persuade them more effectively (Burleson and Fennelly, 1981; Duran and Fusaroli, 2017). If two people with different opinions are talking to each other, they may also align their speech style as a good-faith effort to understand the other's position (Pickering and Garrod, 2004).

However, it is also reasonable to expect that speakers with enmity would diverge their speech style as a way to express their disagreement to each other, especially if they feel disrespected or slighted (Giles et al., 1991). At the same time, if the function word usage can reflect speakers' psychological state (Chung and Pennebaker, 2007), then negative alignment to opponents would be observed as a fair representation of the disagreement between speakers. Supporting this idea, Rosenthal and McKeown (2015) showed that accommodation in word usage could be a feature to improve their model detecting agreement and disagreement between speakers.

In the present work, we consider cross-group alignment on personal pronouns, which can express group identity, as well as on word categories that may indicate different rhetorical approaches to the argument (Pennebaker et al., 2003). Van Swol and Carlson (2017) suggests that the pronoun category can be useful markers of group dynamics in a debate setting, and Schwartz et al. (2013) suggests that it is reasonable to expect the different word usage from different groups. In fact, although we find mostly positive alignment, we do see negative alignment in some cross-group uses, suggesting strong group identities can overrule the general desire to align.

3 Data

3.1 Word categories

This study examines alignment and baseline word use on 8 word categories from Linguistic Inquiry and Word Count (LIWC; Pennebaker et al. (2007)), a common categorization method in alignment research. Details on word categories and example words for each category can be found in Table 1. For example, the first person singular pronoun *I* category counted 12 different forms of

Category	Example	Size
1st singular (*I*)	I, me, mine	12
2nd person (*You*)	you, your, thou	20
1st plural (*We*)	we, us, our	12
3rd plural (*They*)	they, their, they'd	10
Social processes	talk, they, child	455
Cognitive processes	cause, know, ought	730
Positive emotion	love, nice, sweet	406
Negative emotion	hurt, ugly, nasty	499

Table 1: Word categories for linguistic alignment with examples and the number of word tokens in the category.

the *I* pronoun, such as *I, me, mine, myself, I'm,* and *I'd.*

We choose four pronoun categories (*I, you, we, they*) to investigate the relationship between group dynamics and linguistic alignment. We expect that in a conversation between in-group members, *I, we, they* will be observed often. When these pronouns are initially spoken by a speaker, repliers can express their in-group membership while aligning to their usage of the words at the same time. In the conversation with out-group members, *you* usage will be observed more often because it will allow repliers to refer to the speaker while excluding themselves as a part of the speaker's group. In the cross-group conversation, alignment on inclusive *we* indicates that repliers acknowledged and expressed themselves as a member of speakers' in-group. However, alignment on exclusive *they* in cross-group conversation should be interpreted with much more attention. When a replier is aligning their usage of *they* to their out-group member, it likely indicates that both groups are referring to a shared referent, implying enough cooperation to enter an object into common ground (Clark, 1996).

Additionally, four rhetorical word categories are considered. In LIWC, psychological processes are categorized into social processes, cognitive processes, and affective processes, the last of which covers positive and negative emotions. Social and affective process categories are, as their names indicate, the markers of social behavior and emotions. Cognitive process markers include words that reflect causation (*because, hence*), discrepancy (*should, would*), certainty (*always, never*), and inclusion (*and, with*), to name a few. A speaker's baseline usage of rhetorical categories

will present the group-specific speech styles that may be dependent on group identity, reflecting preferred styles of argument. The degree of alignment on rhetorical categories indicates whether speakers maintain their group's discussion style or adapt to the other group.

3.2 Twitter Conversation

The corpus data was built specifically for this research. The population of the data was Twitter conversations about the 2016 presidential election dated from July 27th, 2016 (a day after both parties announced their candidates) to November 7th, 2016 (a day before the election day). Twitter users were divided into two different groups according to their supporting candidates, based on the assumption that all speakers included in the data were partisans and had a single supporting candidate. When the users' supporting candidate was not explicitly shown in their speech, additional information was considered, including previous Tweets, profile statements, and profile pictures. Speakers' political affiliation was first coded by the researcher and the coder's reliability was tested. Two other coders agreed on the researcher's coding of 50 users (25 were coded as Trump supporters and 25 were coded as Clinton supporters) with Fleiss' Kappa score 0.87 ($\kappa = 0.86$, $p < 0.001$) with average 94.4% confidence in their answers.

3.3 Sampling Method

The corpus data was built by a snowball method from seed accounts. Seed accounts spanned major media channels (@cnnbrk; @FoxNews; @NBCNews; @ABC) and the candidates' Twitter accounts (@realDonaldTrump; @HillaryClinton). The original Twitter messages from the seed accounts were not considered as a part of the data, but replies and replies to replies were. The minimal unit of the data was a paired conversation extracted from the comment section. An initial message *a* (single Twitter message, known as a tweet) and the following reply *b* created a pair of the conversation.

3.4 Datasets

In total, four sets of Twitter data were gathered. The first two datasets (TT, CC) consisted of conversations between members of the same group (within-group conversation). The other two datasets (TC, CT) consisted of conversations

Dataset	Message	Reply
TT	I saw a poll where she was up by 8 here and people say that they hate her so who knows	I'm not sure what's going on with that, but #Reality tells a different story. Someone's lying.
	Dems spreading lies again. They are projecting Trump as stupid but voters knows he is not!!	Dems running out of ways to get rid of Trump, so now they will push this BS that he is CRAZY and out of control!!
CC	Jill Stein is more concerned about Hillary than she is about Trump. That tells you all you need to know about this loon. #GreenTownHall	You make a lot of sense. I'm sick of Hillary bashing.
TC	#Libtard you are in for the shock of your life #TRUMPTRAIN	You are if you think he has a chance; have you any idea what the Electoral U map looks like?... Hillary!
	Unbelievable that #TeamHillary thinks America is so stupid we won't notice that moderator is a close Clinton pal	Not America. Just folks like you. #Trumpsuneducated
CT	Fight - not a fight - he was told Mexico won't pay for it. Why should they?	Never expected Mex 2 write us a check. Other ways 2 make them pay for wall. Trump knows how 2 negotiate.

Table 2: Examples of conversation pairs from each dataset (First letter indicates initiator's group, second indicates replier's)

across the groups (cross-group conversation). In the dataset references, Trump supporters' message is represented with T, and Clinton supporters' message is represented with C. The first letter indicates the initiator's group; the second indicates the replier's group. There is an average of 266 unique repliers in each group.

4 SWAM Model

This study adapts the Word-Based Hierarchical Alignment Model (WHAM; Doyle and Frank (2016)) to estimate alignment on different word categories in the Twitter conversations. WHAM defines two key quantities: *baseline* word use, the rate at which someone uses a given word category W when it has not been used in the preceding message, and *alignment*, the relative increase in the probability of words from W being used when the preceding message used a word from W.

Both quantities have been argued to be psychologically meaningful, with baseline usage reflecting internalization of in-group identity, homophily, and enculturation, and alignment reflecting a willingness to adjust one's own behavior to fit another's expectations and framing (Doyle et al., 2017; Giles et al., 1991).

The WHAM framework uses a hierarchy of normal distributions to tie together observations from related messages (e.g., multiple repliers with similar demographics) to improve its robustness when data is sparse or the sociological factors are subtle. This requires the researcher to make statistical assumptions about the structure's effect on alignment behaviors, but can improve signal detection when group dynamics are subtle or group membership is difficult to determine (Doyle et al., 2016).

However, when the group identities are strong and unambiguous, this inference can be excessive, and may even lead to inaccurate estimates, as the more complex optimization process may create a non-convex learning problem. The Bayesian hierarchy in WHAM also aggregates information across groups to improve alignment estimates; in cases where the groups are opposed, one group's behavior may not be predictive of the other's. We propose the Simplified Word-Based Alignment Model (SWAM) for such cases, where group dynamics are expected to provide robust and possibly distinct signals.

WHAM infers two key parameters: η^{align} and η^{base}, the logit-space alignment and baseline values, conditioned on a hierarchy of Gaussian priors.

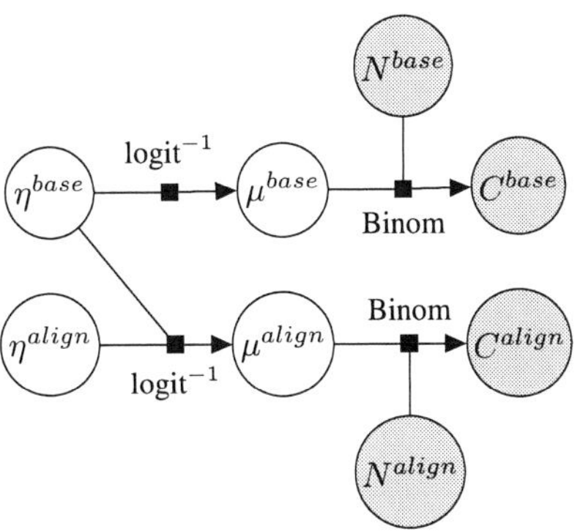

Figure 1: Generative schematic of the Simplified Word-Based Alignment Model (SWAM) used in this study. Hierarchical parameter chains from the WHAM model are eliminated; alignment values are fit independently by word category and conversation group.

SWAM estimates the two parameters directly as:

$$\eta^{base} = \log p(B|notA) \tag{1}$$

$$\eta^{align} = \log \frac{p(B|A)}{p(B|notA)}, \tag{2}$$

where $p(B|A)$ is the probability of a replier using a word category when the initial message contained it, and $p(B|notA)$ is the probability of the replier using it when the initial message did not.

SWAM treats alignment as a change in the log-odds of a given word in the reply belonging to W, depending on whether W appeared in the preceding message. SWAM can be thought of as a midpoint between WHAM and the subtractive alignment model of Danescu-Niculescu-Mizil et al. (2011), with three main differences from the latter model. First, SWAM's baseline is $p(B|notA)$, as opposed to unconditioned $p(B)$ for Danescu-Niculescu-Mizil et al. (2011). Second, SWAM places alignment on log-odds rather than probability, avoiding floor effects in alignment for rare word categories. Third, SWAM calculates by-word alignment rather than by-message, controlling for the effect of varying message/reply lengths. These three differences allow SWAM to retain the improved fit of WHAM (Doyle et al., 2016), while gaining the computational simplicity and group-dynamic agnosticism of Danescu-Niculescu-Mizil et al. (2011).

5 Results

5.1 Pronouns

The results of baseline frequency and alignment values for the four conversation types are presented in Figure 2 and 3, respectively. We analyze each pronoun set in turn.

First of all, baseline usage of *you* shows that *you* was used more often among repliers in the cross-group conversations. However, the alignment pattern for *you* was much stronger in within-group conversations. That is, repliers are generally more likely to use *you* in cross-group settings to refer to out-group members overall, but within the group, one member using *you* encourages the other to use it as well.

You alignment in within-group conversation could reflect rapport-building, a sense that speakers understand each other well enough to talk about each other, and an acceptance of the other's common ground (as in the example for CC in Table 2). On the other hand, *you* alignment in between-group conversations should be interpreted as the result of disagreement to each other (See examples for TC in Table 2). *You* alignment in this case is the action of pointing fingers at each other, which happens at an overall elevated level, regardless of whether the other person has already done so.

Baseline usage of *they* shows the opposite pattern from *you* usage, with higher *they* usage in the in-group conversations. This type of *they* usage can be a reference to out-group members (see the second example for TT in Table 2). By using *they*, repliers can express their membership as a part of the in-group and make assertions about the out-group. It also can reflect acceptance of the interlocutor placing objects in common ground, which can be referred to by pronouns.

They alignment patterns were comparable across the conversation types, except that Trump supporters showed divergence when responding to Clinton supporters. The CT conversation in Table 2 reflects this divergence, with *Mexico* being repeated rather than being replaced by *they*, suggesting Trump supporters reject the elements Clinton supporters attempt to put into common ground.

Moving on to baseline usage of *we*, Trump supporters were most likely to use this pronoun, especially in their in-group conversations, suggesting a strong awareness of and desire for group identity. Contrary to the alignment patterns of *they*, Clin-

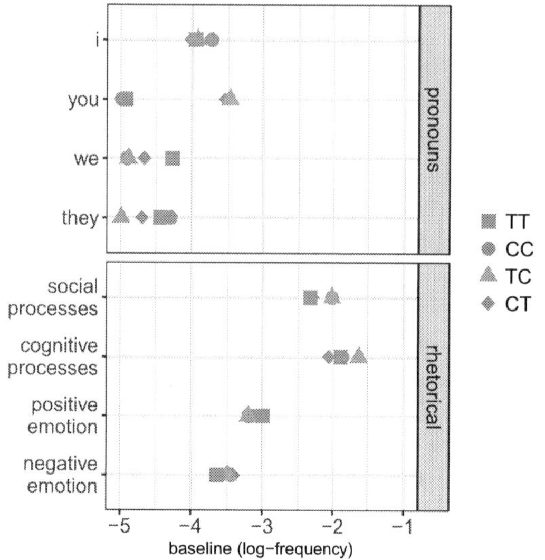
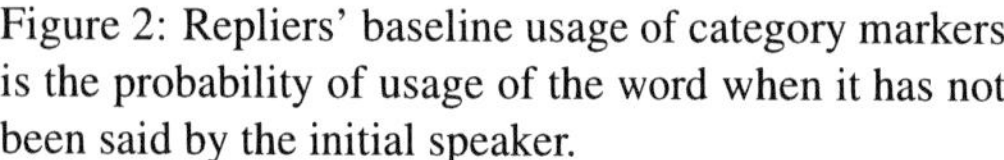
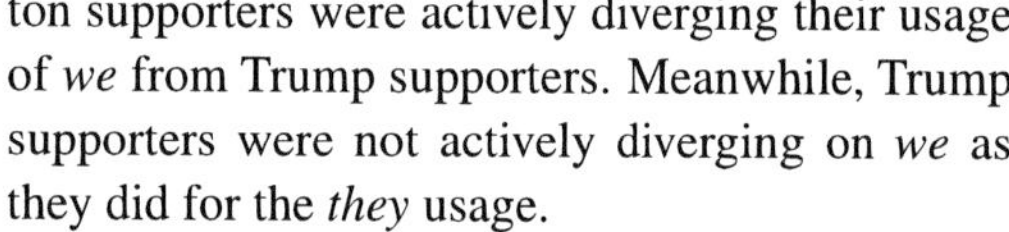
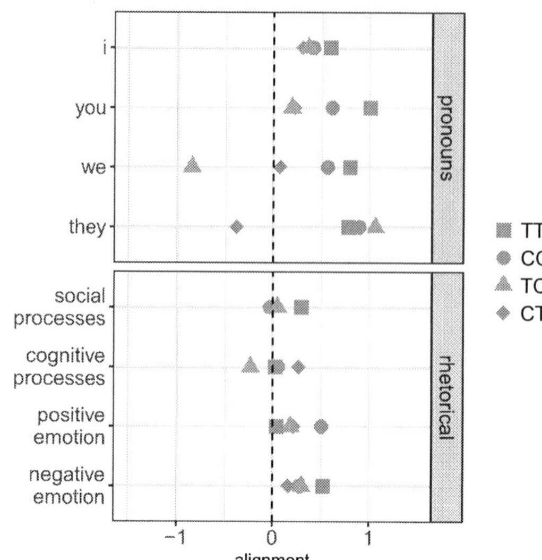

Figure 2: Repliers' baseline usage of category markers is the probability of usage of the word when it has not been said by the initial speaker.

Figure 3: Repliers' alignment on category markers represents the probability of repliers' usage of the word when it has been said by the initial speaker.

ton supporters were actively diverging their usage of *we* from Trump supporters. Meanwhile, Trump supporters were not actively diverging on *we* as they did for the *they* usage.

Claiming in-group membership by using in-group identity marker can be one way of claiming common ground, which indicates that speakers belong to the group who shares specific goals and values (Brown and Levinson, 1987). Therefore, Trump supporters' baseline use and alignment of *we* and *they* suggest that they were accepting and reinforcing common ground with in-group members by using *we*, but rejecting common ground with out-group members by not aligning to *they*. Clinton supporters showed a different way of reflecting their acceptance and rejection. They chose to reject common ground by not aligning to their out-group members' in-group marker *we*, but seemed to accept the common ground within the conversation built by out-group members' use of *they*.

Interestingly, *I* showed the least variability, both in baseline and alignment, across the groups. However, *I* is also the only one of these pronoun groups that does not refer to someone else, and thus should be least affected by group dynamics. In fact, we see Chung and Pennebaker (2007)'s general finding of solid *I*-alignment, even in cross-group communication.

Overall, we see effects both in the baseline and alignment values that are consistent with a strong group-identity construction process. Furthermore, we see strong negative alignment in cross-group communication on pronouns tied to group identity and grounding, showing that cross-group animosity can overrule the general pattern of positive alignment in certain dimensions. However, the overall alignment is still positive; even the rejection of certain aspects of the conversation do not lead to across-the-board divergence.

5.2 Rhetorical Categories

Despite our hypothesis that the rhetorical categories of words could indicate different groups' preferred style of argumentation, these categories showed limited variation compared to the pronouns. The baseline values only varied a small amount between groups, with Clinton supporters having slightly elevated baseline use of social and cognitive words, and slightly less positive emotion.

The alignment values were mostly small positive values, much as has been observed in stylistic alignment in previous work. However, cross-group Trump-Clinton conversations did have negative alignment on cognitive processes. This category spans markers of certainty, discrepancy, and inclusion, and has been argued to reflect argumentation framing that appeals to rationality. This may be a sign of rejecting or dismissing their interlocutors' argument framing. But overall, there is no strong evidence of differences in alignment in argumentative style in this data, and the bulk of the effect remains on group identification.

A possible reason for the lack of differences in argumentation style may be uncertainty about the setting of the cross-group communication. Elevated causation word usage has been argued to be employed by the minority position within a debate, to provide convincing evidence against the status quo (Pennebaker et al., 2003; Van Swol and Carlson, 2017). The datasets consist of conversations from the middle of the election campaign, when it was uncertain which group was in the majority or minority (as seen in the first TT conversation in Table 2). This uncertainty may have led both groups to adopt more similar argumentation styles than if they believed themselves to occupy different points in the power continuum.

6 Discussion

From our results, we see that social context affected pronoun use and alignment, which fits into the Communication Accommodation Theory account (Giles et al., 1991). Meanwhile, rhetorical word use and alignment was independent of social context between speakers, though it is unclear whether this reflects a perception of equal footing in their power dynamics or is driven primarily by automatic alignment influences rather than social factors (Pickering and Garrod, 2004). To expand the scope of this argument, we can further test if the negative alignment can be found in other LIWC categories as well, which have no clear group-dynamic predictions.

One thing to point out is that even though pronouns and some rhetorical words are categorized as function words, which have been hypothesized to reflect structural rather than semantic alignment (Chung and Pennebaker, 2007), these category words are still somewhat context- and content-oriented. That is, use and alignment of some function words is inevitable for speakers to stay within the topic of conversation or to mention the entity whose referential term is already set in the common ground. From Trump supporters' negative alignment on *they*, we could see that speakers were in fact able to actively reject the reference method by not using the content-oriented function words. In the future work, it will be meaningful to separate the alignment motivated by active acceptance and agreement from the alignment that must have occurred in order to stay within the conversation.

Testing our hypotheses in different settings can help to resolve this issue. One possibility is to separate the election debate into small sets of conversations with different topics, and then compare the alignment patterns between sets. Because of the lexical coherence that each topic of conversations have, we will be able to better separate the effect of context- and content-oriented words from the linguistic alignment result. As a result, we might be able to see negative alignment on rhetorical category between subset of conversations. We can also test our hypotheses with different languages. Investigating alignment in languages that do not use pronouns heavily for reference can be useful to see how the group dynamics are expressed through different word categories. Particles in some languages, such as Japanese and Korean, can mark specific argument roles, and this linguistic structure can allow us to detect syntactic alignment without looking much into the context- and content-oriented function words. Lastly, the SWAM model is an adaptation of the WHAM model, and while the basic patterns look similar to those found by WHAM, a more precise comparison of the models' estimates with a larger dataset is an important step to ensure that the SWAM estimates are accurate.

7 Conclusion

Pronoun usage and alignment reflect the group dynamics between Trump supporters and Clinton supporters, and observations of negative alignment are consistent with a battle over who defines the groups and common ground. However, the use and alignment of rhetorical words were not substantially affected by the group dynamics but rather reflected that there was an uncertainty about who belongs to the majority or minority group. In a political debate or conversation between opponents, speakers are likely to project their group identity with the usage of pronouns but are likely to maintain their rhetorical style as a way to maintain their group identity.

References

Penelope Brown and Stephen C. Levinson. 1987. *Politeness: Some universals in language usage*, volume 4. Cambridge university press.

Brant R. Burleson and Deborah A. Fennelly. 1981. The effects of persuasive appeal form and cognitive complexity on children's sharing behavior. *Child Study Journal*, 11:75–90.

Cindy Chung and James W Pennebaker. 2007. The psychological functions of function words. *Social communication*, 1:343–359.

Herbert H. Clark. 1996. *Using Language*. Cambridge University Press, Cambridge.

Cristian Danescu-Niculescu-Mizil, Michael Gamon, and Susan Dumais. 2011. Mark my words!: linguistic style accommodation in social media. In *Proceedings of the 20th international conference on World Wide Web*, pages 745–754.

Cristian Danescu-Niculescu-Mizil, Lillian Lee, Bo Pang, and Jon Kleinberg. 2012. Echoes of power: Language effects and power differences in social interaction. In *Proceedings of the 21st international conference on World Wide Web*, pages 699–708.

Gabriel Doyle and Michael C. Frank. 2016. Investigating the sources of linguistic alignment in conversation. In *Proceedings of the 54th Annual Meeting of the Association for Computational Linguistics (Volume 1: Long Papers)*, volume 1, pages 526–536.

Gabriel Doyle, Amir Goldberg, Sameer Srivastava, and Michael Frank. 2017. Alignment at work: Using language to distinguish the internalization and self-regulation components of cultural fit in organizations. In *Proceedings of the 55th Annual Meeting of the Association for Computational Linguistics (Volume 1: Long Papers)*, volume 1, pages 603–612.

Gabriel Doyle, Dan Yurovsky, and Michael C. Frank. 2016. A robust framework for estimating linguistic alignment in Twitter conversations. In *Proceedings of the 25th international conference on World Wide Web*, pages 637–648.

Nicholas D. Duran and Riccardo Fusaroli. 2017. Conversing with a devils advocate: Interpersonal coordination in deception and disagreement. *PloS one*, 12(6):e0178140.

Howard Giles, Nikolas Coupland, and Justine Coupland. 1991. Accommodation theory: Communication, context, and consequences. In Howard Giles, Justine Coupland, and Nikolas Coupland, editors, *Contexts of accommodation: Developments in applied sociolinguistics*, pages 1–68. Cambridge University Press, Cambridge.

Howard Giles, Donald M. Taylor, and Richard Bourhis. 1973. Towards a theory of interpersonal accommodation through language: Some canadian data. *Language in society*, 2(2):177–192.

Fangjian Guo, Charles Blundell, Hanna Wallach, and Katherine Heller. 2015. The Bayesian Echo Chamber: Modeling Social Influence via Linguistic Accommodation. In *Proceedings of the 18th International Conference on Artificial Intelligence and Statistics*, pages 315–323.

Molly E. Ireland, Richard B. Slatcher, Paul W. Eastwick, Lauren E. Scissors, Eli J. Finkel, and James W. Pennebaker. 2011. Language style matching predicts relationship initiation and stability. *Psychological Science*, 22:39–44.

Kate G. Niederhoffer and James W. Pennebaker. 2002. Linguistic style matching in social interaction. *Journal of Language and Social Psychology*, 21(4):337–360.

James W. Pennebaker, Roger J. Booth, and Martha E. Francis. 2007. Linguistic Inquiry and Word Count: LIWC. *Austin, TX: liwc.net*.

James W. Pennebaker, Matthias R. Mehl, and Kate G. Niederhoffer. 2003. Psychological aspects of natural language use: Our words, our selves. *Annual review of psychology*, 54(1):547–577.

Martin J. Pickering and Simon Garrod. 2004. Toward a mechanistic psychology of dialogue. *Behavioral and brain sciences*, 27(2):169–190.

Sara Rosenthal and Kathy McKeown. 2015. I couldnt agree more: The role of conversational structure in agreement and disagreement detection in online discussions. In *Proceedings of the 16th Annual Meeting of the Special Interest Group on Discourse and Dialogue*, pages 168–177.

H. Andrew Schwartz, Johannes C. Eichstaedt, Margaret L. Kern, Lukasz Dziurzynski, Stephanie M. Ramones, Megha Agrawal, Achal Shah, Michal Kosinski, David Stillwell, Martin E.P. Seligman, and Lyle H. Ungar. 2013. Personality, gender, and age in the language of social media: The open-vocabulary approach. *PloS one*, 8(9):e73791.

Lyn M. Van Swol and Cassandra L. Carlson. 2017. Language use and influence among minority, majority, and homogeneous group members. *Communication Research*, 44(4):512–529.

Combining Abstractness and Language-specific Theoretical Indicators for Detecting Non-Literal Usage of Estonian Particle Verbs

Eleri Aedmaa[1], Maximilian Köper[2] and Sabine Schulte im Walde[2]
[1] Institute of Estonian and General Linguistics, University of Tartu, Estonia
[2] Institut für Maschinelle Sprachverarbeitung, Universität Stuttgart, Germany
`eleri.aedmaa@ut.ee`
`{maximilian.koeper,schulte}@ims.uni-stuttgart.de`

Abstract

This paper presents two novel datasets and a random-forest classifier to automatically predict literal vs. non-literal language usage for a highly frequent type of multi-word expression in a low-resource language, i.e., Estonian. We demonstrate the value of language-specific indicators induced from theoretical linguistic research, which outperform a high majority baseline when combined with language-independent features of non-literal language (such as abstractness).

1 Introduction

Estonian particle verbs (PVs) are multi-word expressions combining an adverbial particle with a base verb (BV), cf. Erelt et al. (1993). They are challenging for automatic processing because their components do not always appear adjacent to each other, and the particles are homonymous with adpositions. In addition, as illustrated in examples (1a) vs. (1b), the same PV type can be used in literal vs. non-literal language.

> (1) a. Ta **astu-s**   kaks sammu **tagasi**.
>   he step-PST.3SG two step.PRT back
>   'He took two steps back.'
>
>   b. Ta **astu-s**   ameti-st **tagasi**.
>   he step-PST.3SG job-ELA back
>   'He resigned from his job.'

Given that the automatic detection of non-literal expressions (including metaphors and idioms) is critical for many NLP tasks, the last decade has seen an increase in research on distinguishing literal vs. non-literal meaning (Birke and Sarkar, 2006, 2007; Sporleder and Li, 2009; Turney et al., 2011; Shutova et al., 2013; Tsvetkov et al., 2014; Köper and Schulte im Walde, 2016).

Most research up to date has, however, focused on resource-rich languages (mainly English and German), and elaborated on general indicators – such as contextual abstractness – to identify non-literal language. As to our knowledge, only Tsvetkov et al. (2014) and Köper and Schulte im Walde (2016) explored language-specific features.

The aim of this work is to automatically predict literal vs. non-literal language usage for a very frequent type of multi-word expression in a low-resource language, i.e., Estonian. The predicate is the center of grammatical and usually semantic structure of the sentence, and it determines the meaning and the form of its arguments, cf. Erelt et al. (1993). Hence, the surrounding words (i.e., the context), their meanings and grammatical forms could help to decide whether the PV should be classified as compositional or non-compositional.

In addition to applying language-independent features of non-literal language, we demonstrate the value of indicators induced from theoretical linguistic research, that have so far not been explored in the context of compositionality. For this purpose, this paper introduces two novel datasets and a random-forest classifier with standard and language-specific features.

The remainder of this paper is structured as follows. We give a brief overview of previous studies on Estonian PVs in Section 2, and Section 3 introduces the target dataset. All features are described in Section 4. Section 5 lays out the experiments and evaluation of the model, and we conclude our work in Section 6.

2 Related Work

The compositionality of Estonian PVs has been under discussion in the theoretical literature for

9

Proceedings of NAACL-HLT 2018: Student Research Workshop, pages 9–16
New Orleans, Louisiana, June 2 - 4, 2018. ©2017 Association for Computational Linguistics

decades but still lacks a comprehensive study. Tragel and Veismann (2008) studied six verbal particles and their aspectual meanings, and described how horizontal and vertical dimensions are represented. Veismann and Sahkai (2016) investigated the prosody of Estonian PVs, finding PVs expressing perfectivity the most problematic to classify.

Recent computational studies on Estonian PVs involve their automatic acquisition (Kaalep and Muischnek, 2002; Uiboaed, 2010; Aedmaa, 2014), and predicting their degrees of compositionality (Aedmaa, 2017). Muischnek et al. (2013) investigated the role of Estonian PVs in computational syntax, focusing on Constraint Grammar. Most research on automatically detecting non-literal language has been done on English and German (as mentioned above), and elaborated on general indicators to identify non-literal language. Our work is the first attempt to automatically distinguish literal and non-literal usage of Estonian PVs, and to specify on theory- and language-specific features.

3 Target PV Dataset

For creating a dataset of literal and non-literal language usage for Estonian PVs, we selected 210 PVs across 34 particles: we started with a list of 1,676 PVs that occurred at least once in a 170-million token newspaper subcorpus of the Estonian Reference Corpus[1] (ERC) and removed PVs with a frequency ≤ 9. Then we sorted the PVs according to their frequency and selected PVs across different frequency ranges for the dataset. In addition, we included the 20 most frequent PVs. We plan to analyse the influence of frequency on the compositionality of PVs in future work, thus it was necessary to collect evaluations for PVs with different frequencies.

For each of the 210 target PVs, we then automatically extracted 16 sentences from the ERC. The sentences were manually double-checked to make sure that verb and adverb formed a PV and did not appear as independent word units in a clause. The choice of the numbers of PVs and sentences relied on the fact of limited time and other resources that allowed us to evaluate approximately 200 PVs and 2,000 sentences.

The resulting set of sentences was evaluated by three annotators with a linguistic background. They were asked to assess each sentence by answering the question: "What is the usage of the PV in the sentence on a 6-point scale ranging from clearly literal (0) to clearly non-literal (5) language usage?" In case of multiple PVs in the same sentence, the information of which PV to evaluate was provided for the annotators. Although we use binary division of PVs in this study, it was reasonable to collect evaluations on a larger than binary scale because of the following reasons: first, it is a well-known fact that multi-word expressions do not fall into the binary classes of compositional vs. non-compositional expressions (Bannard et al., 2003), and second, it was important to create a dataset that would be applicable to multiple tasks. Thus our dataset can be used to investigate the degrees of compositionality of PVs in the future.

The agreement among 3 annotators on all 6 categories is fair (Fleiss' $\kappa = 0.36$). A binary distinction based on the average sentence scores into literal (average ≤ 2.4) and non-literal (average ≥ 2.5) resulted in substantial agreement ($\kappa = 0.73$). Our experiments below use the binary-class setting, disregarding all cases of disagreement.

This final dataset[2] includes 1,490 sentences: 1,102 non-literal and 388 literal usages across 184 PVs with 120 different base verbs and 32 particle types. 63 PVs occur only in non-literal sentences, 15 only in literal sentences and 106 PVs in non-literal and literal sentences. From 120 verbs 50 appear only in non-literal sentences, 15 only in literal sentences, and 55 verbs in both literal and non-literal sentences. The distribution of (non-)literal sentences across particle types is shown in Figure 1. While many particles appear mostly in non-literal language (and *esile*, *alt*, *ühte*, *ära* are exclusively used in their non-literal meanings in our dataset), they all have literal correspondences. No particle types appear only in literal sentences.

4 Features

In this section we introduce standard, language-independent features (unigrams and abstractness) as well as language-specific features (case and animacy) that we will use to distinguish literal and non-literal language usage of Estonian PVs.

---

[1]www.cl.ut.ee/korpused/segakorpus/

[2]The dataset is accessible from https://github.com/eleriaedmaa/compositionality.

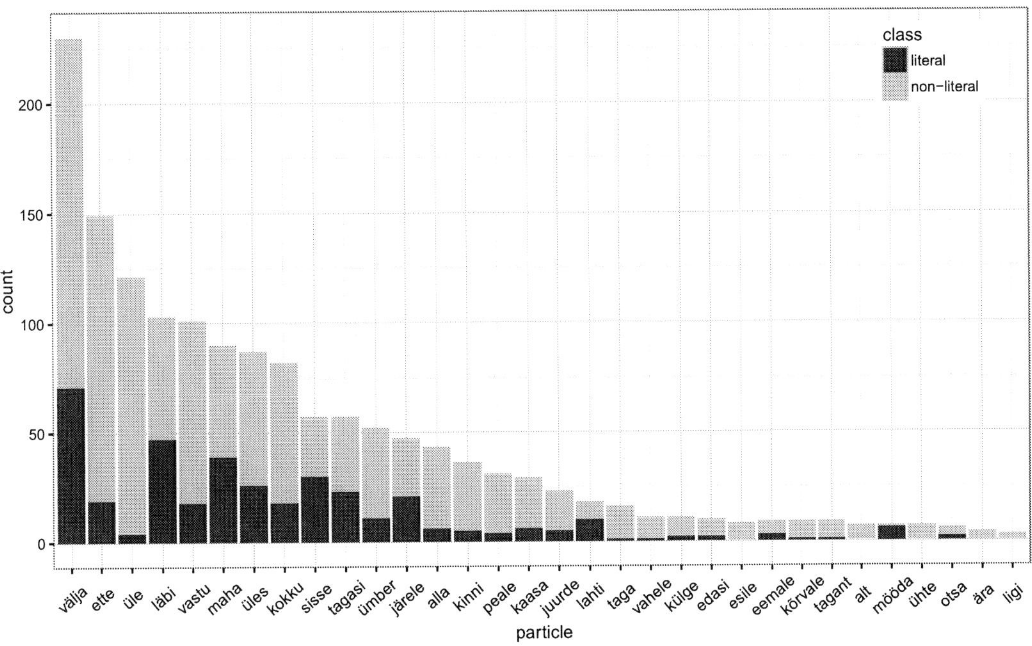

Figure 1: (Non-)literal language usage across particles.

Unigrams Our simplest language-independent features are unigrams, i.e., lemmas of content words that occur in the same sentences with our target PVs. More precisely, unigrams are the list of lemmas of all words that we induced from all our target sentences (there is at least one PV in each sentence), after excluding lemmas that occurred ≤ 5 times in total.

Abstractness Abstractness has previously been used in the automatic detection of non-literal language usage (Turney et al., 2011; Tsvetkov et al., 2014; Köper and Schulte im Walde, 2016), as abstract words tend to appear in non-literal sentences. Since there were no ratings for Estonian, we followed Köper and Schulte im Walde (2016) to automatically generate abstractness ratings for Estonian lemmas: we translated 24,915 English lemmas from Brysbaert et al. (2014) to Estonian relying on the English-Estonian Machine Translation dictionary[3]. We then lemmatized the 170-million token ERC subcorpus and created a vector space model. To learn word representations, we relied on the skip-gram model from Mikolov et al. (2013). Finally, we applied the algorithm from Turney et al. (2011) using the 29,915 translated ratings from Brysbaert et al. (2014) as seeds.

This algorithm relies on the hypothesis that the degree of abstractness of a word's context is predictive of whether the word is used in a metaphorical or literal sense. The algorithm learns to assign abstractness scores to every word representation in our vector space, resulting in a novel resource[4] of automatically created ratings for 243,675 Estonian lemmas.

Unfortunately we can not provide an evaluation for this dataset at the moment, because Estonian is lacking a suitable human-judgement-based gold standard. In addition, the creation would require extensive psycholinguistic research which falls far from the authors' specialization.

We adopted the following abstractness features from Turney et al. (2011) and Köper and Schulte im Walde (2016): average rating of all words in a sentence, average rating of all nouns in a sentence (including proper names), rating of the PV subject, and rating of the PV object.

The ratings of PV subject and object express the abstractness score of the head of the noun phrase. For example, the average score of the object (i.e., *oma koera*) in the sentence (2c) is the rating of the head of the noun phrase (i.e., *koer*), not the average of the ratings of the determiner and the head.

---

[3] http://www.eki.ee/dict/ies/

[4] The dataset is accessible from https://github.com/eleriaedmaa/compositionality.

We assume that the subjects and objects are more concrete in literal sentences. For example, the subject (*sõber*) and the object (*koer*) in the literal sentences (2a) and (2c) are more concrete than the subject (*surm*) and object (*viha*) in the non-literal sentences (2b) and (2d).

(2)　a.　**Sõber** jooks-i-s　mu-lle järele.
　　　　friend run-PST-3SG I-ALL　after
　　　　'A friend ran after me.'

　　b.　**Surm** jooks-i-s　ta-lle　järele.
　　　　death run-PST-3SG he-ALL after
　　　　'The death ran after him.'

　　c.　Mees suru-s　**koera**　maha.
　　　　man　push-PST.3SG **dog.GEN** down
　　　　'The man pushed the dog down.'

　　d.　Mees suru-s　**viha**　maha.
　　　　man　push-PST.3SG **anger.GEN** down
　　　　'The man suppressed his anger.'

Figure 2 illustrates the abstractness scores for literal vs. non-literal sentences. In general, literal sentences are clearly more concrete, especially when looking at nouns only, and even more so when looking at the nouns in specific subject and object functions.

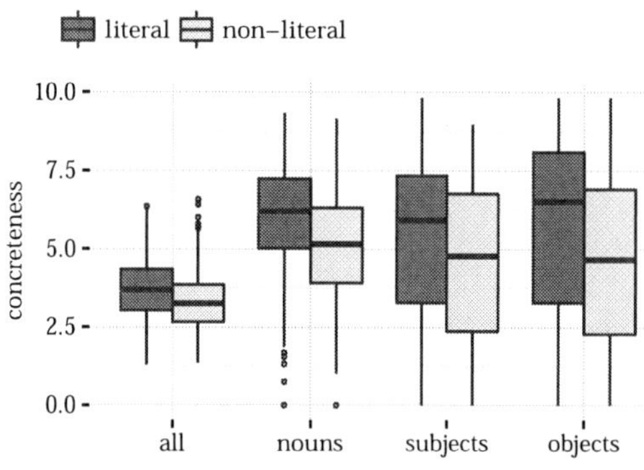

Figure 2: Abstractness scores across literal and non-literal sentences.

Subject and object case Estonian distinguishes between "total" subjects in the nominative case and "partial" subjects in the partitive case. Partial subjects are not in subject-predicate agreement (Erelt et al., 1993). For example, the subject *külaline* receives nominative case in sentence (3b) and partitive case in sentence (3a). We observed that subject case assignment often correlates with (non-)literal readings; in the examples, sentence (3a) is literal, and sentence (3b) is non-literal.

(3)　a.　**Külaline** tule-b　juurde.
　　　　guest.NOM come-3SG near
　　　　'The guest approaches.'

　　b.　**Külali-si** tule-b　juurde.
　　　　guest.PL.PRT come-3SG up
　　　　'The number of guests is increasing.'

Similarly, a "total" object in Estonian receives nominative or genitive case, and a "partial" object receives partitive case. For example, the object *supi* in sentence (4a) is assigned genitive case, and the object *mida* in sentence (4b) partitive case. In sentence (4a), the meaning of the PV *ette võtma* is literal; in sentence (4b) the meaning is non-literal.

(4)　a.　Tüdruk võt-tis　ette **supi.**
　　　　girl　take-PST.3SG front **soup.GEN**
　　　　'The girl took the soup in front of her.'

　　b.　**Mida**　koos　ette võt-ta?
　　　　what.SG.PRT together front take-INF
　　　　'What should we do together?'

Figure 3 illustrates that the distribution of subject and object cases across literal and non-literal sentences does not provide clear indicators. In addition, the correlation between subject/object case and (non-)literalness has not been examined thoroughly in theoretical linguistics. But based on corpus analyses as exemplified by the sentences (3b)–(4b), we hypothesize that the case distribution might provide useful indicators for (non-)literal language usage.

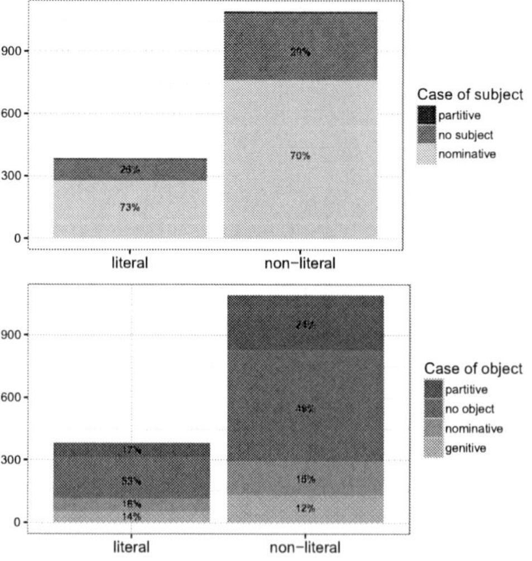

Figure 3: Distribution of subject/object case across literal and non-literal sentences.

Subject and object animacy   According to Estonian Grammar (Erelt et al., 1993) the meaning of the predicate might determine (among other features) the animacy of its arguments in a sentence. If the verb requires an animate subject, but the subject is inanimate, the meaning of the sentence is non-literal. For example, the PV in the sentences (5a) and (5b) is the same (*sisse kutsuma 'to invite in'*), but in the first sentence the subject *sõber* is animate and the sentence is literal, while the subject *maja* in sentence (5b) is inanimate and the sentence is non-literal. Similarly, the subject *naine* in sentence (5c) is animate and the sentence is literal, while the subject *välimus* in sentence (5d) is inanimate and the sentence is non-literal.

As before, the correlation between subject animacy and (non-)literalness has not been examined thoroughly in theoretical linguistics, but the animacy of the subject seems to correlate with the (non-)literalness of the sentences.

(5)   a.   **Sõber** kutsu-s   mu   sisse.
           friend invite-PST.3SG I.GEN in

           'A friend invited me in.'

      b.   **Maja** ei   kutsu   sisse.
           house NEG invite.CONNEG in

           'The house doesn't look inviting.'

      c.   **Naine** tõuka-s   mehe   eemale.
           woman push-PST.3SG man.GEN away

           'A woman pushed a man away.'

      d.   Poe   **välimus**   tõuka-s
           shop.GEN **appearance** push-PST.3SG
           mehe   eemale.
           man.GEN away

           'The appearance of the shop made the man go away.'

The impact of the object animacy on the meaning of the PVs is less intuitive, but still the object in sentence (6a) is inanimate and the meaning of the PV is literal, while the object in sentence (6b) is animate and the meaning of the PV is non-literal.

(6)   a.   Mees põleta-s   **kaitsme** läbi.
           man burn-PST.3SG fuse.GEN out

           'The man burned the fuse.'

      b.   Mees põleta-s   **enese**   läbi.
           man burn-PST.3SG himself.GEN out

           'The man had a burnout.'

There are no explicit connections between the subject animacy pointed out in the literature. Figure 4 shows the distribution of animacy across subjects and objects across the literal and non-literal usage. The differences in numbers are not remarkable, but based on the examples, we assume that the animacy of the subject might have an impact on the literal and non-literal usage of PVs. Thus, we include animacy into our feature space.

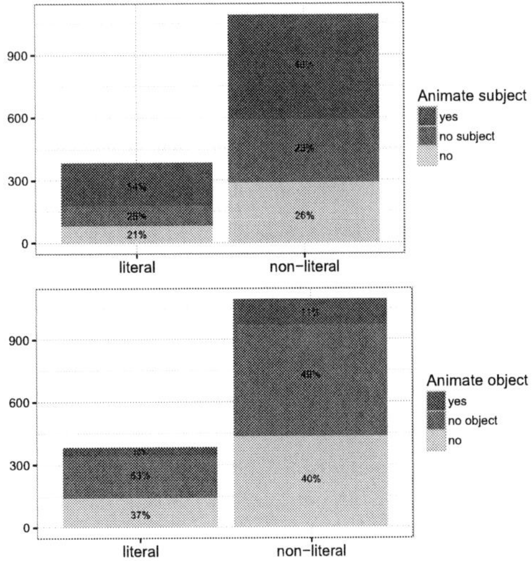

Figure 4: Distribution of subject/object animacy across literal and non-literal language.

Sentences (6a) and (6b) demonstrate that the abstractness/concreteness scores may already indicate the (non-)literal usage of the PV and the feature of animacy does not add any information: the concrete words are inanimate and they appear in the literal sentences, and the animate (and abstract) words in non-literal sentences. Still, as shown in sentences (5a)–(5d), the concrete subject of literal sentence can be also animate (i.e., *sõber*, *naine*), the concrete subject of non-literal sentence can be inanimate (i.e., *maja*), and the inanimate subject of non-literal sentence might be abstract (i.e., *välimus*). Thus, we argue that the abstractness ratings are not sufficient to express the animacy of the words and animacy can be useful as feature for the detection of (non-)literal usage of Estonian PV.

Case government   Case government is a phenomenon where the lexical meaning of the base verb influences the grammatical form of the argument, e.g., the predicate determines the case of the

13

argument (Erelt et al., 1993). Thus, argument case depends on the meaning of the PV. For example, in sentence (7a) the PV *läbi minema 'to go through'*[5] is literal and requires an argument that answers the question *from where?* Hence, the argument has to receive elative case. In sentence (7b) the PV provides a non-literal meaning (*'to succeed'*) and does not require any additional arguments. We hypothesize that the case of the argument is helpful to predict (non-)literal usage of PVs.

(7) a. Ta läks   **metsa-st**   läbi.
        she go.PST.3SG **forest-SG.EL** through
        'She went through the forest.'

     b. Mu   ettepanek läks   läbi.
        I.GEN proposal go.PST.3SG through
        'My proposal was successful.'

Note that the cases of the subject and object are individual features in our experiments, the feature of case government includes the cases of other types of arguments, i.e., adverbials and modifiers.

In addition, Figure 5 introduces the distribution of the argument case across the literal and non-literal sentences, and shows that not all cases (e.g., inessive, translative) appear in both types of sentences.

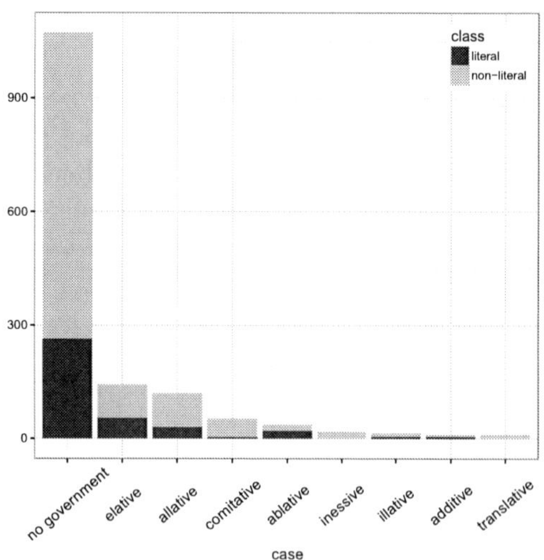

Figure 5: Distribution of argument case across literal and non-literal sentences.

Compared to all other features described in this section, animacy is the most problematic because the information is not obtained automatically. For the abstractness scores we use the previously described dataset, and the cases of subjects, objects and other arguments are accessible with the help of the morphological analyser[6] and the part-of-speech tagger[7]. At the moment, the animacy information about the subject and object are added manually by the authors.

5 Experiments and Results

The classification experiments to distinguish between literal and non-literal language usage of Estonian PVs rely on the sentence features defined above. They were carried out using a random forest classifier (Breiman, 2001) that constructs a number of randomized decision trees during the training phase and makes prediction by averaging the results. For our experiments, we used 100 random decision trees. The random forest classifier performs better in comparison of other classification methods that we have applied in the Weka toolkit (Witten et al., 2016). For the evaluation we perform 10-fold cross validation, hence we use the previously described data for training and testing.

The classification results across features and combinations of features are presented in Table 1. We report accuracy as well as F_1 for literal and non-literal sentences.

Table 1 shows that the best single feature types are the unigrams (acc: 82.3%) and the base verbs (81.2%). Combining the two, the accuracy reaches 84.2%. No other single feature type goes beyond the high majority baseline (74.0%), but the combinations in the Table 1 significantly outperform the baseline, according to χ^2 with p<0.01.

Adding the particle type to the base verb information (1–2) correctly classifies 85.2% of the sentences. Further adding unigrams (1–3), however, does not help. Regarding abstractness, adding the ratings for all but objects to the particle-verb information (1–2, 4–6) is best and reaches an accuracy of 86.3%. Subject case information, animacy and case government in combination with 1–2 reach similar values (85.3–86.3%). The overall best result (87.9%) is reached when combining particle and base verb information with all-noun and subject abstractness ratings, subject case, subject animacy, and case government.

---

[5]The verb *minema* 'to go' is irregular and the stem is not derivable from the infinitive.

[6]http://www.filosoft.ee/html_morf_et/
[7]http://kodu.ut.ee/~kaili/parser/

feature type	acc	F_1	
		n-lit	lit
majority baseline	74.0%	85.0	0.00
1 particle (p)	73.6%	84.4	13.6
2 base verb (v)	81.2%	87.9	58.0
3 unigrams, f>5 (uni)	82.3%	89.0	54.6
4 average rating of words (abs)	68.1%	79.8	24.5
5 average rating of nouns (abs)	68.5%	79.7	30.1
6 rating of the PV subject (abs)	72.3%	83.1	23.7
7 rating of the PV object (abs)	73.0%	83.5	25.2
8 subject case (case)	74.0%	85.0	0.00
9 object case (case)	74.0%	85.0	0.00
10 subject animacy (animacy)	74.0%	85.0	0.00
11 object animacy (animacy)	74.0%	85.0	0.00
12 case government (govern)	73.8%	84.6	10.1
p+v, 1–2	85.2%	90.3	68.7
v+uni, 2–3	84.2%	89.6	66.4
p+v+uni, 1–3	85.0%	90.1	68.5
p+v+abs, 1–2, 4–6	86.3%	90.9	72.3
p+v+abs, 1–2, 4–7	86.0%	90.7	71.3
p+v+abs, 1–2, 5–6	86.0%	90.7	71.9
p+v+case, 1–2, 8	85.3%	90.4	68.9
p+v+case, 1–2, 8–9	84.6%	89.7	69.3
p+v+animacy, 1–2, 10–11	86.2%	90.8	72.3
p+v+govern, 1–2, 12	86.2%	90.9	71.6
p+v+abs+lang, 1–2, 4–6, 10-12	87.3%	91.6	73.8
p+v+abs+lang, 1–2, 4–12	87.5%	91.8	73.8
p+v+abs+lang, 1–2, 5–6, 8, 10, 12	**87.9%**	**92.0**	**75.0**

Table 1: Overview of classification results.

While Table 1 only lists a selection of all possible combinations of features to present the most interesting cases, it illustrates that the combination of language-independent features and language-specific features is able to outperform the high majority baseline. Although the difference between the best combination without language-specific features (86.3%) and the best combination with language-specific features (87.9%) is not statistically significant, the best-performing combination provides F_1=92.0 for non-literal sentences and F_1=75.0 for literal sentences.

6   Conclusion

This paper introduced a new dataset with 1,490 sentences of literal and non-literal language usage for Estonian particle verbs, a new dataset of abstractness ratings for >240,000 Estonian lemmas across word classes, and a random-forest classifier that distinguishes between literal and non-literal sentences with an accuracy of 87.9%.

The most salient feature selection confirms our theory-based hypotheses that subject case, subject animacy and case government play a role in non-literal Estonian language usage. Combined with abstractness ratings as language-independent indicators of non-literal language as well as verb and particle information, the language-specific features significantly outperform a high majority baseline of 74.0%.

Acknowledgements

This research was supported by the University of Tartu ASTRA Project PER ASPERA, financed by the European Regional Development Fund (Eleri Aedmaa), and by the Collaborative Research Center SFB 732, financed by the German Research Foundation DFG (Maximilian Köper, Sabine Schulte im Walde).

References

Eleri Aedmaa. 2014. Statistical methods for Estonian particle verb extraction from text corpus. In *Proceedings of the ESSLLI 2014 Workshop: Computational, Cognitive, and Linguistic Approaches to the Analysis of Complex Words and Collocations*. Tübingen, Germany, pages 17–22.

Eleri Aedmaa. 2017. Exploring compositionality of Estonian particle verbs. In *Proceedings of the ESSLLI 2017 Student Session*. Toulouse, France, pages 197–208.

Colin Bannard, Timothy Baldwin, and Alex Lascarides. 2003. A statistical approach to the semantics of verb-particles. In *Proceedings of the ACL Workshop on Multiword Expressions: Analysis, Acquisition and Treatment*. Sapporo, Japan, pages 65–72.

Julia Birke and Anoop Sarkar. 2006. A clustering approach for the nearly unsupervised recognition of nonliteral language. In *Proceedings of the 11th Conference of the European Chapter of the ACL*. Trento, Italy, pages 329–336.

Julia Birke and Anoop Sarkar. 2007. Active learning for the identification of nonliteral language. In *Proceedings of the Workshop on Computational Approaches to Figurative Language*. Rochester, NY, pages 21–28.

Leo Breiman. 2001. Random forests. *Machine learning* 45(1):5–32.

Marc Brysbaert, Amy Beth Warriner, and Victor Kuperman. 2014. Concreteness ratings for 40 thousand generally known English word lemmas. *Behavior Research Methods* 64:904–911.

Tiiu Erelt, Ülle Viks, Mati Erelt, Reet Kasik, Helle Metslang, Henno Rajandi, Kristiina Ross, Henn Saari, Kaja Tael, and Silvi Vare. 1993. *Eesti keele grammatika II. Süntaks. Lisa: kiri [The Grammar of the Estonian Language II: Syntax]*. Tallinn: Eesti TA Keele ja Kirjanduse Instituut.

Heiki-Jaan Kaalep and Kadri Muischnek. 2002. Using the text corpus to create a comprehensive list of phrasal verbs. In *Proceedings of the 3rd International Conference on Language Resources and Evaluation*. Las Palmas de Gran Canaria, Spain, pages 101–105.

Maximilian Köper and Sabine Schulte im Walde. 2016. Automatically generated affective norms of abstractness, arousal, imageability and valence for 350 000 German lemmas. In *Proceedings of the 10th International Conference on Language Resources and Evaluation*. Portoroz, Slovenia, pages 2595–2598.

Maximilian Köper and Sabine Schulte im Walde. 2016. Distinguishing literal and non-literal usage of German particle verbs. In *Proceedings of the Conference of the North American Chapter of the Association for Computational Linguistics: Human Language Technologies*. San Diego, California, USA, pages 353–362.

Tomas Mikolov, Ilya Sutskever, Kai Chen, Greg S. Corrado, and Jeff Dean. 2013. Distributed representations of words and phrases and their compositionality. In *Advances in Neural Information Processing Systems 26*. Lake Tahoe, Nevada, USA, pages 3111–3119.

Kadri Muischnek, Kaili Müürisep, and Tiina Puolakainen. 2013. Estonian particle verbs and their syntactic analysis. In *Proceedings of Human Language Technologies as a Challenge for Computer Science and Linguistics: 6th Language & Technology Conference*. Poznan, Poland, pages 7–11.

Ekaterina Shutova, Simone Teufel, and Anna Korhonen. 2013. Statistical Metaphor Processing. *Computational Linguistics* 39(2):301–353.

Caroline Sporleder and Linlin Li. 2009. Unsupervised recognition of literal and non-literal use of idiomatic expressions. In *Proceedings of the 12th Conference of the European Chapter of the Association for Computational Linguistics*. Athens, Greece, pages 754–762.

Ilona Tragel and Ann Veismann. 2008. Kuidas horisontaalne ja vertikaalne liikumissuund eesti keeles aspektiks kehastuvad? [Embodiment of the horizontal and vertical dimensions in Estonian aspect]. *Keel ja Kirjandus* 7:515–530.

Yulia Tsvetkov, Leonid Boytsov, Anatole Gershman, Eric Nyberg, and Chris Dyer. 2014. Metaphor detection with cross-lingual model transfer. In *Proceedings of the 52nd Annual Meeting of the Association for Computational Linguistics*. Baltimore, Maryland, pages 248–258.

Peter Turney, Yair Neuman, Dan Assaf, and Yohai Cohen. 2011. Literal and metaphorical sense identification through concrete and abstract context. In *Proceedings of the Conference on Empirical Methods in Natural Language Processing*. Edinburgh, UK, pages 680–690.

Kristel Uiboaed. 2010. Statistilised meetodid murdekorpuse ühendverbide tuvastamisel [Statistical methods for phrasal verb detection in Estonian dialects]. *Eesti Rakenduslingvistika Ühingu aastaraamat* 6:307–326.

Ann Veismann and Heete Sahkai. 2016. Ühendverbidest läbi prosoodia prisma [Particle verbs and prosody]. *Eesti Rakenduslingvistika Ühingu aastaraamat* 12:269–285.

Ian H. Witten, Eibe Frank, Mark A. Hall, and Christopher J. Pal. 2016. *Data Mining: Practical Machine Learning Tools and Techniques*. Morgan Kaufmann.

Verb Alternations and Their Impact on Frame Induction

Esther Seyffarth

Dept. of Computational Linguistics

Heinrich Heine University

Düsseldorf, Germany

`Esther.Seyffarth@hhu.de`

Abstract

Frame induction is the automatic creation of frame-semantic resources similar to FrameNet or PropBank, which map lexical units of a language to frame representations of each lexical unit's semantics. For verbs, these representations usually include a specification of their argument slots and of the selectional restrictions that apply to each slot. Verbs that participate in diathesis alternations have different syntactic realizations whose semantics are closely related, but not identical. We discuss the influence that such alternations have on frame induction, compare several possible frame structures for verbs in the causative alternation, and propose a systematic analysis of alternating verbs that encodes their similarities as well as their differences.

1 Introduction

One of the aims of natural language processing is to access and process the meaning of texts automatically. For tasks like question answering, automatic summarization, or paraphrase detection, annotating the text with semantic representations is a useful first step. A good annotation represents the semantics of each element in the text as well as the relations that exist between the elements, such as the relations between a verb and its arguments and adjuncts.

Frame semantics, founded on work by Fillmore (1968), Minsky (1974), Barsalou (1992), and others, provides a powerful method for the creation of such representations. A frame-semantic representation of a concept expresses the attributes that contribute to its semantics as functional relations in a recursive attribute-value structure. Frame-semantic lexical resources, such as FrameNet (Ruppenhofer et al., 2006) or PropBank (Palmer et al., 2005), map lexical units of a language to frames, which are described in terms of the frame elements, or roles, that are central to the concept.

Since the manual compilation of such resources is time-consuming, costly, and error-prone, much can be gained from the use of semi-supervised or unsupervised methods. The process of creating a frame lexicon automatically is known as frame induction.

Unsupervised frame induction draws on observations about each lexical item's behavior in a corpus to create a frame lexicon. If two different lexical units can evoke the same frame, they share certain semantic properties, and the frame inducer has to determine the amount of semantic overlap between them based on observable and latent features of each of the lexical items. In this paper, we discuss some of the problems that occur in frame induction when lexical units have a relatively large semantic overlap, but are not close enough to each other to be treated as total synonyms.

While there are several types of frame-evoking predicates, we focus here on verbs and the frames they evoke. We assume that the meaning of a sentence can be expressed using the frame representation of the sentence's root verb. The semantic contribution of all other elements in the sentence is then specified with respect to their relation to the root verb. Therefore, it is crucial to assign the correct semantic frame to the root verb.

Diathesis alternations are a phenomenon that is observed when verbs can occur with more than one valency pattern. In some alternations, the different uses of the participating verbs introduce changes in the semantics as well (Levin, 1993). This is particularly relevant for alternations that change the *Aktionsart* of the verb, such as the causative-inchoative alternation (Levin, 1993, Chapter 1.1.2). Verbs in this alternation can be used either transitively or intransitively, where the transitive use adds a causative meaning to the sen-

17

Proceedings of NAACL-HLT 2018: Student Research Workshop, pages 17–24

New Orleans, Louisiana, June 2 - 4, 2018. ©2017 Association for Computational Linguistics

tence that is not present in the intransitive use, as in the sentences in (1).

(1)   a.   Mary opened the door.
        b.   The door opened.

In this paper, we argue that sentence pairs like this differ in their semantics to a degree that warrants their annotation with different frames, but in a way that still expresses their semantic relation to each other. We compare different possible frame representations for verbs in the causative alternation and propose some guidelines for the way a frame inducer should analyze alternating verbs.

2 The Causative Alternation

The causative alternation is characterized by a role switch (McCarthy, 2001) between transitive and intransitive uses of participating verbs, as shown in the sentences in (2). The role switch determines the position of the semantic THEME, the rent, as syntactic object (in (2-a)) or subject (in (2-b)). An AGENT is only present in the transitive sentence.

(2)   a.   They have increased my rent.
        b.   My rent has increased.

Both sentences describe a situation which results in the rent being higher than before.

Transitive uses of verbs in the causative alternation can be paraphrased as "cause to [verb]-intransitive" (see Levin, 1993, p. 27). For instance, sentence (2-a) can be paraphrased as "They have caused my rent to increase."

In some cases, this type of paraphrase is not completely synonymous with the causative use of the verb; for a discussion of such cases, see e.g. Dowty (1991, pp. 96-99) and Cruse (1972). These authors claim that a difference between scenarios of direct and indirect causation renders some paraphrases ungrammatical or different in meaning from the original sentences with causative verbs. However, for the purposes of this paper, we focus on the regular cases, where the causative use and the paraphrased form do express the same meaning.

Dowty (1991) decomposes causative verbs as [x CAUSE [BECOME y]], where an inchoative event [BECOME y] is embedded in a causative one. Thus, for verbs in the causative alternation, the transitive sentence has a more complex semantic structure. This is not the case for verbs outside the alternation: Sentences (3-a) and (3-b) below

have the same semantic complexity, and one does not describe something that causes the other.

(3)   a.   I'm eating an apple.
        b.   I'm eating.

If (3-a) is true, then (3-b) must necessarily also be true, but there is no causation relationship between the sentences. Instead, (3-b) is a less specific description of the same situation that is also described by (3-a).

Like Rappaport Hovav (2014), we assume that a causative sentence entails its inchoative counterpart. In both sentences in (2), the verb *increase* describes an event that affects the semantic THEME; if it is true that a CAUSE is responsible for the event that increases the rent, then a statement that does not contain a CAUSE, but otherwise describes the same event, is necessarily also true. In other words, it is impossible for (2-a) to be true without (2-b) also being true.

2.1 Possible Frame Representations

A frame representation of the sentences in (2) that focuses on their shared semantics is given in Figure 1. A similar structure could also be used to represent the sentences in (3).

$$\begin{bmatrix} increase \\ \text{CAUSE} \quad \text{they} / \emptyset \\ \text{THEME} \quad \text{my rent} \end{bmatrix}$$

Figure 1: Frame representation that is agnostic towards the question of causativity or inchoativity.

This analysis assigns an *increase* frame, independent of the syntactic realization and observed arguments. If a cause is given, it is included; otherwise, it is not, and the CAUSE slot is unfilled.

A disadvantage of this choice is that the structure does not differentiate between causative and inchoative uses of alternating verbs, except by the presence and absence of the CAUSE slot. As discussed in the previous section, this is acceptable for sentences like (3), but undesirable for sentences like (2).

The representation in Figure 1 is similar to the structure used in PropBank (see Palmer et al., 2005, p. 77). There, both uses of an alternating verb are associated with one shared frameset. The PropBank annotation makes no difference between the sentences in (2) and the sentences in (3).

The FrameNet frame hierarchy includes a mechanism to connect frames with an "is causative of" relation and its inverse, "is inchoative of" (Ruppenhofer et al., 2006, p. 85). Different frames for alternating verbs are stored in the database and connected by these relations. Figure 2 gives the FrameNet representations for the sentences in (2). For a discussion of these representations, see Ruppenhofer et al. (2006, p. 12 and pp. 15-16).

$$\begin{bmatrix} cause\_change\_position\_on\_a\_scale \\ \text{CAUSE} \qquad\qquad\qquad \text{they} \\ \text{ITEM} \qquad\qquad\qquad \text{my rent} \end{bmatrix}$$

$$\begin{bmatrix} change\_position\_on\_a\_scale \\ \text{ITEM} \qquad\qquad \text{my rent} \end{bmatrix}$$

Figure 2: FrameNet representations for the sentences in (2).

These frames show a clear conceptual separation between the causative meaning of *increase* and its inchoative counterpart. The two frames are linked by the relations mentioned above, and their names hint at the semantic connection that exists between them.

However, it is not obvious from the separate frames that the two sentences are connected by an entailment relationship. If a sentence like (2-a) is observed, the first representation will be chosen; if a sentence like (2-b) is observed, the second representation will be chosen. Without referring to the FrameNet frame hierarchy, it will not be possible to recognize that sentence (2-a) necessarily entails sentence (2-b).

A frame representation that encodes this relationship more visibly is presented in Figure 3. That representation is analogous to the decomposition for causative verbs given by Dowty (1991), which is [*x* CAUSE [BECOME *y*]]. The specific sentence (2-a) is represented as [[they do something] CAUSE [BECOME [my rent is higher]]].

Figure 3 represents the event as a *causation* frame. The EFFECT slot of that frame is linked to the content of the [BECOME *y*] part of the decomposition, which is an *inchoation* frame. The RESULT of the inchoation is the formula's *y*.

These representations are inspired by Osswald and Van Valin Jr (2014). They visibly express the relationship between the frames and are consistent with the decompositional event structures used by Rappaport Hovav and Levin (1998) in their dis-

cussion of alternating verbs. The frame in Figure 3 provides a slot for the result state of the *inchoation* frame, here expressed as a frame of the type *higher*. Osswald and Van Valin Jr (2014) suggest that the semantics of verbs that express a gradual change of state should be represented in terms of the initial and final state and a specification of the relation between them. Thus, the frame should state that the rent had an initial and final amount, and the meaning of "They have increased my rent" is that the states are connected by a GREATER_THAN relation.

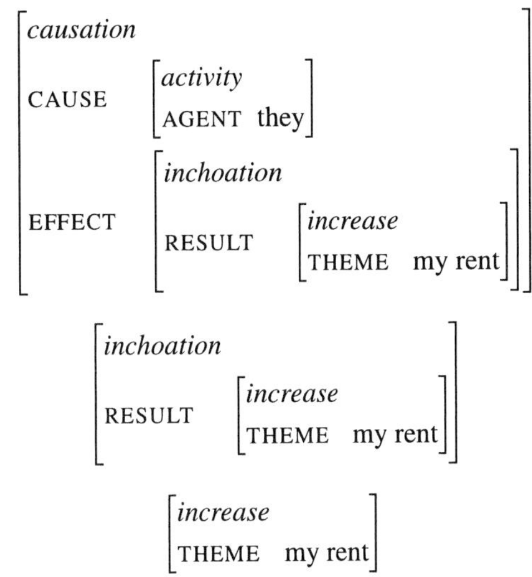

Figure 3: Decompositional frame representation of the sentences in (2), inspired by Osswald and Van Valin Jr (2014).

While the decompositional approach has advantages over the other representations shown above, it is difficult to use in a computational setting, where this level of detail in the expression of gradual changes is often neither attainable nor desirable. Additionally, only a subset of the alternating verbs specify a change of state that can be represented like this. Other verbs (*roll, fly, ...*) describe movement or induced action, and we aim at a representation that works universally for alternating verbs.

This is why we prefer the frame representations in Figure 4. They are related to the decompositional frames in Figure 3, but do not make use of the innermost embedding layer.

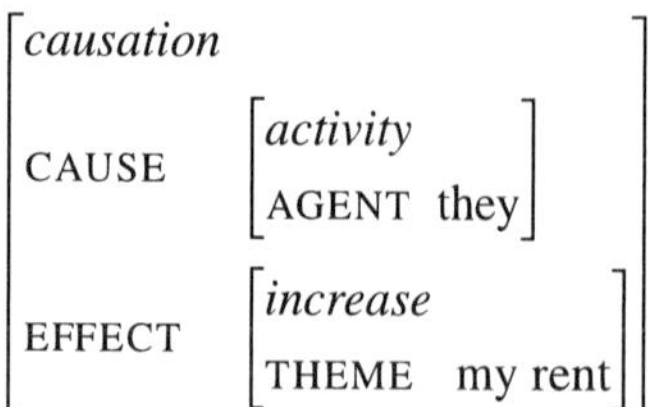

Figure 4: Frame representation for (2-a)

Compared to the frames in Figure 3, this structure is more compact. Like them, it acknowledges that the transitive use of *increase* adds not only an additional argument slot, but also a causative meaning that "wraps around" the *increase* frame.

This analysis is consistent with that of Rappaport Hovav (2014), who supports an analysis of alternating verbs that assumes they are lexically associated with their internal arguments only.

A question that is often discussed in research on diathesis alternations is that of underlying and derived forms; for an overview of perspectives on this question that are discussed in the literature, see e.g. Piñón (2001). The assumption is that knowledge of the derivation processes involved in diathesis alternations can inform the semantic analysis. Here, we do not claim that one use of alternating verbs is derived from the other. We do however note that inchoative sentences specify fewer participants of the event they describe, since they do not contain an argument slot for the entity that has causative control over the situation – unlike causative sentences, where these entities are part of the frame.

3 Frame Induction

Verbs that participate in diathesis alternations are likely to be observed in different syntactic configurations in a corpus. For a frame inducer, it is important to distinguish between these cases on the one hand, and homographs whose semantics are not (or less closely) related on the other hand. For instance, the system should recognize that the verb *run* in the sentences in (4) has two meanings that are less closely related than the transitive and intransitive meanings of *open* or *increase*.

(4)   a.   I ran ten miles this morning.
        b.   I started the program two days ago, but it's still running.

A frame induction system that uses the observed syntactic subjects and objects as indicators for the correct frame will initially treat both *run* and *increase* in the same way: It notices that the (syntactic) slot fillers in the observed sentences are not homogeneous enough to assign a single frame for both uses, and therefore assumes different frames. In the case of *run*, this is desirable, but in the case of verbs that participate in diathesis alternations, it results in an unnecessarily large number of frames in the lexicon, and the relationship between the semantics of transitive and intransitive uses of the verbs would not be represented.

The architecture we propose is one that combines existing probabilistic approaches to frame induction with an additional level of analysis that makes sure the learned frames are distinguished with regard to their participation in the alternation.

Thus, the system will be able to make an informed decision whether different uses of a verb are due to non-obligatory arguments, as in the sentences in (3); due to polysemy, as in the sentences in (4); or due to a diathesis alternation, as in the sentences in (2). In the first case, a single frame must be assigned to all uses of the verb, with optional arguments as observed in the data. In the second case, different semantic frames need to be assigned, because the meanings of the different uses of the verb do not have a large enough overlap to be subsumed into the same frame. Finally, if the frame inducer has correctly identified the verb as one which does participate in a diathesis alternation, the alternating frame structure of that alternation can be used to create frames for the particular verb in a way that relates the meanings of the different uses to each other.

In order to distinguish between alternating verbs and non-alternating verbs, the frame inducer can employ one of the methods for alternation identification that have been proposed in the literature. Early approaches to this relied on WordNet or similar resources to identify the slot overlap of different subcategorization frames (McCarthy and Korhonen, 1998; Schulte im Walde, 2000; McCarthy, 2001) or on the evaluation of latent semantic properties of the slot fillers, approximated using manually-defined rules (Stevenson and Merlo, 1999). More recently, distributional representations of slot fillers have been used to create clusters whose overlap can be used for the distinction (Baroni and Lenci, 2009; Sun and Korhonen, 2009; Sun et al., 2013). We propose that distributional methods be used by the frame inducer, in order to minimize the dependence on manually-created resources.

The frame inducer can store the different frames with cross-references between the alternating variants. This ensures that the core semantics that describes the event and its result state is stored in one place only – the inchoative frame –, while the lexicon entry for the causative frame can access the inchoative frame to build the causative semantics around it.

Frame induction is notoriously difficult to evaluate quantitatively. Since the structure of semantic frames depends on a number of factors, including the perspective on the event, the desired level of granularity of the description, and the application context in which the frame representation is to be used, there is no single, objectively correct frame structure for a given event. However, to get a general indicator for the performance of the system, one can evaluate the induced frames against resources like SemLink (Bonial et al., 2013) to calculate the amount of overlap between the induced frame hierarchy and manually-created hierarchies. Note that among other data sources, SemLink contains annotations from FrameNet, where causative and inchoative uses of alternating verbs are associated with different frames, but also annotations from PropBank, where no distinction is being made. We leave a detailed specification of an optimal evaluation setup to future work.

4 Discussion

The frame representation we propose has a number of advantages in the context of the semantic tasks mentioned in the introduction.

First, it expresses overtly the fact that the main difference between the semantics of the causative and inchoative use of each verb is the added causative meaning in the transitive form. This helps because inferences about the result state of the event should be consistent across both transitive and intransitive uses, and the structure we propose that embeds the inchoative frame into the causative one means that all relevant information about the result state can be derived from the embedded frame as needed.

A similar point applies to the question of entailment. As mentioned in Section 2, a transitive sentence with a verb in the causative alternation as the root entails the intransitive version of that sentence. With our frame structure, this entailment

is expressed in the frame already, since the truth of the embedded frame contributes directly to the truth of the whole frame.

We also look to frame-semantic parsing in choosing this frame structure. The paraphrase of sentence (2-a) as "They have caused my rent to increase" is an illustration of the benefit of our analysis: A frame-semantic annotation of the paraphrased sentence should include a structure that is like the one we propose for the causative use of *increase*.

Contrast this with the way a parser that relies on FrameNet frames (see Figure 2 above) would analyze the paraphrase: FrameNet will assign a *causation* frame to the verb *cause*, with the increasing of the rent being specified in the EFFECT slot of the *causation* frame. The resulting mismatch does not encode the fact that the paraphrase carries the same meaning as the causative use of the verb.

4.1 Productivity of the Causative Alternation

We view the causative alternation as an open class. Levin (1993) lists verbs that regularly participate in the alternation and verbs that cannot alternate, but we assume that there are also verbs that can be used in an alternating way to produce a novel causative construction. An example is given in (5).

(5)   The bad weather decided him to take the car.[1]

Sentences like this are indicative of a certain productivity of the causative alternation. When a verb that usually only occurs in intransitive forms is used transitively, we can assume that this change adds a causative dimension. Our frame structure allows us to embed any verb frame into a causative frame to create the frame in Figure 5 for sentence (5). Note that the role of AGENT is being filled by different entities in the subframes CAUSE and EFFECT. This is different from the frame given in Figure 4 because *decide* does not usually select a THEME.

---

[1]This sentence is a heavily adapted version of a passage from Chapter 4 of David Lodge's novel *The British Museum is Falling Down* (1965).

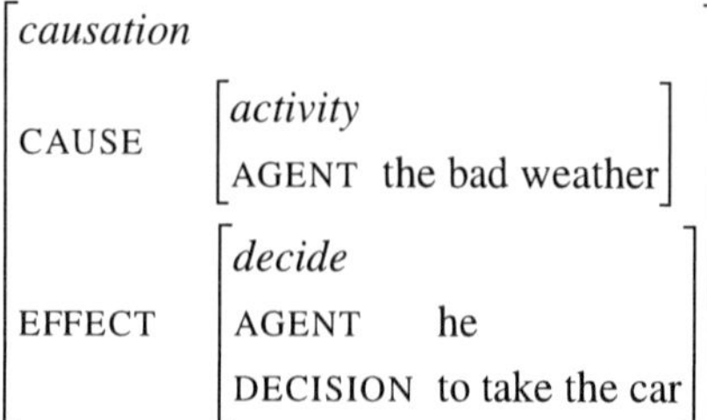

Figure 5: Frame representation for (5)

Separating the core semantics of each verb from the alternating mechanism results in a frame lexicon that is more flexible and therefore better equipped to deal with unseen constructions than the alternative analyses we have discussed.

4.2 Extending the Analysis to Other Alternations

So far, we have focussed on the causative alternation, but similar analyses are also conceivable for other alternations. In the conative alternation (Levin, 1993, p. 41), one of the syntactic environments in which the alternating verb can occur describes an attempted action and lacks entailment of success or completion of the action described. A representation that uses embedded frames, analogous to the ones described above, may look like the frame in Figure 6. The frame represents the semantics of the sentence in (6).

(6)   Mary cut at the rope.

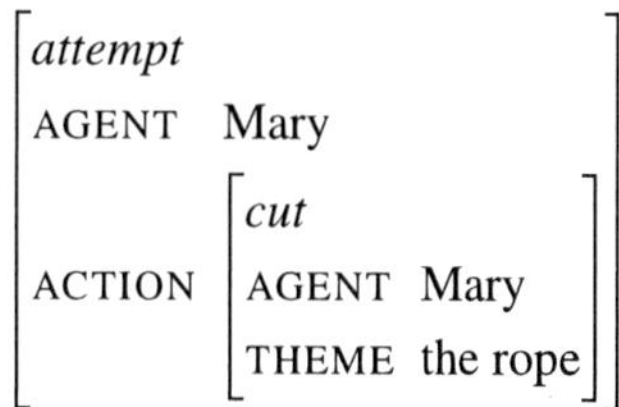

Figure 6: Frame representation for (6)

As in the causative alternation, a precondition for such an analysis is knowledge of the alternatability of a sentence's root verb and access to rules that control the creation of the embedding frames. Having access to rules that govern the creation of such complex frames allows the frame inducer to represent the conative meaning by combining the *attempt* part of the meaning with a reference to the *cut* frame stored in the lexicon.

5   Future Work

We will employ the strategies outlined here to develop a frame inducer that is sensitive to slight differences in semantics, such as the ones observed in diathesis alternations, and that is equipped to handle these differences in a systematic way.

The resulting system will be semi-supervised, since the productive rules for complex frames like the ones presented above can be created manually. The frame inducer then has the task of identifying verbs that participate in the alternations to which the pre-defined rules apply, and of storing the different uses of the alternating verbs in an appropriate way. Using cross-references to link a causative frame to the inchoative frame embedded in it will ensure that the lexicon can be kept to a small size while providing as much expressive power as necessary for the semantic distinctions at hand.

While we are optimistic about the system suggested here for the treatment of alternating verbs, we are aware that frame induction is not a trivial task. Particularly, we note that it is difficult, if not impossible, to argue that one specific frame representation of a concept is correct while another is incorrect. The way frames are being formed to represent semantics is highly subjective, and the decisions one makes always have to depend on the purpose for which the frame lexicon is being created.

However, we find it important to identify ways in which the induction of frames may be systematized. We are convinced that the idea of storing complex frames in the lexicon that embed semantically related frames is useful for the analysis of diathesis alternations as well as similar phenomena.

An important part of working on frame induction is the exploration of different ways to evaluate the induced frame hierarchy. In addition to the approach mentioned in Section 3, where the overlap of the new hierarchy and some manually-built resource is being determined, we are also interested in the possibility of extrinsic evaluation. For instance, a question-answering task may be set up and tested using the output of versions of the frame inducer with and without alternation-specific functions, in order to enable a comparison of each system's success in this type of application context.

6 Conclusion

Diathesis alternations pose a challenge to the creation of frame-semantic resources, because they license verb uses that are closely related, but not similar enough to be treated as synonyms. In this paper, we argued that alternating verbs should be represented with frames that highlight this relationship while also specifying the differences between the alternating verb uses.

Unlike the frames defined in PropBank and FrameNet for alternating verbs, our proposed analysis involves the embedding of one frame (the "core meaning" of the verb) into another (the causation frame that "wraps around" the core meaning in transitive uses). We find that this analysis is consistent with the appropriate analysis when parsing a sentence like (5), where a verb that may not be stored in the lexicon as having a causative property (here, the verb *decide*) is used exactly like verbs that participate in the alternation. We wish to minimize the difference between such analyses that are conducted at parsing time and the entries in the frame lexicon.

The successful induction of frames of the type described here depends on the successful identification of the alternation. If the frame inducer mistakes a verb that has several unrelated meanings for a verb that participates in the alternation, the system will create frames that are inappropriate for that verb. For instance, the sentences in (4) should not be analyzed with frames that embed one another, since the meanings of their root verbs are too dissimilar and there is no entailment relation between the different uses of *run*.

A frame induction system that follows the suggestions outlined in this paper will be able to represent the semantics of alternating verbs (and phenomena that exhibit similar behaviors) in a way that not only clarifies the semantic relations that exist between the different uses of the verbs, but is also consistent with annotations that are created in the context of frame-semantic parsing.

Acknowledgments

The work presented in this paper was financed by the Deutsche Forschungsgemeinschaft (DFG) within the CRC 991 "The Structure of Representations in Language, Cognition, and Science". I would like to thank Laura Kallmeyer and all reviewers of this work for their valuable comments and suggestions.

References

Marco Baroni and Alessandro Lenci. 2009. One Distributional Memory, Many Semantic Spaces. In *Proceedings of the Workshop on Geometrical Models of Natural Language Semantics*, pages 1–8, Athens, Greece. Association for Computational Linguistics.

Lawrence W. Barsalou. 1992. Frames, concepts, and conceptual fields. In A. Lehrer and E. Kittay, editors, *Frames, Fields, and Contrasts: New Essays in Semantic and Lexical Organization*, pages 21–74. Lawrence Erlbaum Associates, Hillsdale, N.J.

Claire Bonial, Kevin Stowe, and Martha Palmer. 2013. Renewing and Revising SemLink. In *Proceedings of the 2nd Workshop on Linked Data in Linguistics (LDL-2013): Representing and linking lexicons, terminologies and other language data*, pages 9–17. Association for Computational Linguistics.

Donald A. Cruse. 1972. A Note on English Causatives. *Linguistic Inquiry*, 3(4):520–528.

David R. Dowty. 1991. The semantics of aspectual classes of verbs in English. In *Word meaning and Montague grammar*, pages 37–132. Springer.

Charles J. Fillmore. 1968. The Case for Case. In E. Bach and R. T. Harms, editors, *Universals in Linguistic Theory*, pages 1–88. Holt, Rinehart and Winston.

Beth Levin. 1993. *English Verb Classes and Alternations: A Preliminary Investigation*. University of Chicago press.

Diana McCarthy. 2001. *Lexical Acquisition at the Syntax-Semantics Interface: Diathesis Alternations, Subcategorization Frames and Selectional Preferences*. Ph.D. thesis, University of Sussex, UK.

Diana McCarthy and Anna Korhonen. 1998. Detecting Verbal Participation in Diathesis Alternations. In *COLING 1998 Volume 2: The 17th International Conference on Computational Linguistics*.

Marvin Minsky. 1974. A Framework for Representing Knowledge. Technical report, Massachusetts Institute of Technology, Cambridge, MA, USA.

Rainer Osswald and Robert D. Van Valin Jr. 2014. FrameNet, Frame Structure, and the Syntax-Semantics Interface. In Thomas Gamerschlag, Doris Gerland, Rainer Osswald, and Wiebke Petersen, editors, *Frames and Concept Types*, pages 125–156. Springer.

Martha Palmer, Daniel Gildea, and Paul Kingsbury. 2005. The Proposition Bank: An Annotated Corpus of Semantic Roles. *Computational Linguistics*, 31(1):71–106.

Christopher Piñón. 2001. A Finer Look at the Causative-Inchoative Alternation. *Semantics and Linguistic Theory*, 11:346–364.

Malka Rappaport Hovav. 2014. Lexical content and context: The causative alternation in English revisited. *Lingua*, 141:8–29.

Malka Rappaport Hovav and Beth Levin. 1998. Building Verb Meanings. In *The projection of arguments: Lexical and compositional factors*, pages 97–134. University of Chicago Press.

Josef Ruppenhofer, Michael Ellsworth, Miriam R.L. Petruck, Christopher R. Johnson, and Jan Scheffczyk. 2006. *FrameNet II: Extended Theory and Practice*. International Computer Science Institute, Berkeley, California. Distributed with the FrameNet data.

Suzanne Stevenson and Paola Merlo. 1999. Automatic Verb Classification Using Distributions of Grammatical Features. In *Ninth Conference of the European Chapter of the Association for Computational Linguistics*, pages 45–52. Association for Computational Linguistics.

Lin Sun and Anna Korhonen. 2009. Improving Verb Clustering with Automatically Acquired Selectional Preferences. In *Proceedings of the 2009 Conference on Empirical Methods in Natural Language Processing*, pages 638–647. Association for Computational Linguistics.

Lin Sun, Diana McCarthy, and Anna Korhonen. 2013. Diathesis alternation approximation for verb clustering. In *Proceedings of the 51st Annual Meeting of the Association for Computational Linguistics (Volume 2: Short Papers)*, pages 736–741. Association for Computational Linguistics.

Sabine Schulte im Walde. 2000. Clustering Verbs Semantically According to their Alternation Behaviour. In *COLING 2000 Volume 2: The 18th International Conference on Computational Linguistics*, pages 747–753. Association for Computational Linguistics.

A Generalized Knowledge Hunting Framework for the Winograd Schema Challenge

Ali Emami[1], Adam Trischler[2], Kaheer Suleman[2], and Jackie Chi Kit Cheung[1]

[1]School of Computer Science, McGill University
[2]Maluuba Research, Montreal, Quebec
ali.emami@mail.mcgill.ca
{adam.trischler, kasulema}@microsoft.com
jcheung@cs.mcgill.ca

Abstract

The Winograd Schema Challenge is a popular alternative Turing test, comprising a binary-choice coreference-resolution task that requires significant common-sense and world knowledge to solve. In this paper, we propose a novel framework that successfully resolves many Winograd questions while imposing minimal restrictions on their form and difficulty. Our method works by (i) generating queries from a parsed representation of a Winograd question, (ii) acquiring relevant knowledge using Information Retrieval, and (iii) reasoning on the gathered knowledge. Our approach improves the F1 performance by 0.16 over previous works, without task-specific supervised training.

1 Introduction

The Winograd Schema Challenge (WSC) has emerged as a popular alternative to the Turing test as a means to measure progress towards human-like artificial intelligence (Levesque et al., 2011). WSC problems are short passages containing a target pronoun that must be correctly resolved to one of two possible antecedents. They come in pairs which differ slightly and result in different correct resolutions. As an example:

(1)   a.   Jim <u>yelled</u> at Kevin because *he* was so upset. (Answer: Jim)

       b.   Jim <u>comforted</u> Kevin because *he* was so upset. (Answer: Kevin)

WSC problem pairs ("twins," using the terminology of Hirst (1988)) are carefully controlled such that heuristics involving syntactic salience, the number and gender of the antecedent, or other simple syntactic and semantic cues are ineffective. This distinguishes the task from the standard coreference resolution problem. Performant systems must make common-sense inferences; i.e.,

that someone who yells is likely to be upset, and that someone who is upset tends to be comforted. Additional examples are shown in Table 1.

WSC problems are simple for people to solve but difficult for automatic systems because common-sense reasoning encompasses many types of reasoning (causal, spatio-temporal, etc.) and requires a wide breadth of knowledge. There have been efforts to encode such knowledge directly, using logical formalisms (Bailey et al., 2015) or by using deep learning models (Liu et al., 2016a); however, these approaches have so far solved only restricted subsets of WSC questions with high precision, and show limited ability to generalize to new instances. Other work aims to develop a repository of common-sense knowledge (e.g., Cyc (Lenat, 1995), ConceptNet (Liu and Singh, 2004)) using semi-automatic methods. These knowledge bases are necessarily incomplete and further processing is required to retrieve the entries relevant to a given WSC context. Even given the appropriate entries, further reasoning operations must usually be performed as in Liu et al. (2016b); Huang and Luo (2017).

In this work we propose a three-stage knowledge hunting method for solving the WSC. We hypothesize that on-the-fly, large-scale processing of textual data can complement knowledge engineering efforts to automate common-sense reasoning. In this view, information that appears in natural text can act as implicit or explicit evidence for the truth of candidate WSC resolutions.

There are several challenges inherent to such an approach. First, WSC instances are explicitly designed to be robust to the type of statistical correlations that underpin modern distributional lexical semantics. In the example above, *yelled at* and *comforted* are both similar to *upset*, so it is difficult to distinguish the two cases by lexical similarity. Also, common sense involves background

25

Proceedings of NAACL-HLT 2018: Student Research Workshop, pages 25–31
New Orleans, Louisiana, June 2 - 4, 2018. ©2017 Association for Computational Linguistics

1 a)	The man couldn't lift his son because he was so <u>weak</u>. (Answer: the man)
1 b)	The man couldn't lift his son because he was so <u>heavy</u>. (Answer: son)
2 a)	The older students were bullying the younger ones, so we <u>punished</u> them. (Answer: the older students)
2 a)	The older students were bullying the younger ones, so we <u>rescued</u> them. (Answer: the younger ones)
3 a)	Sam tried to paint a picture of shepherds with sheep, but they ended up looking more like <u>golfers</u>. (Answer: shepherds)
3 b)	Sam tried to paint a picture of shepherds with sheep, but they ended up looking more like <u>dogs</u>. (Answer: sheep)

Table 1: Examples of Winograd Questions.

knowledge that is, by definition, shared by most readers. Common sense is thus assumed knowledge that is rarely stated explicitly in naturally occurring text. As such, even modern NLP corpora composed of billions of word tokens, like Gigaword (Graff and Cieri, 2003) and Google News (*http://news.google.com*), are unlikely to offer good coverage – or if they do, instances of specific knowledge are likely to be diffuse and rare ("long tail").

Information Retrieval (IR) techniques can sidestep some of these issues by using the *entire* indexed Internet as an input corpus. In particular, our method of **knowledge hunting** aims to retrieve scenarios that are similar to a given WSC question but where the ambiguities built into the question are absent. For example, to solve (1a), the following search result contains the relevant knowledge without the matching ambiguity:

(2)   I got really upset with her and I started to yell at her because...

Here, the same entity *I* is the subject of both *upset* and *yell at*, which is strong evidence for resolving the original ambiguity. This information can be extracted from a syntactic parse of the passage using standard NLP tools.

Previous work on end-to-end knowledge-hunting mechanisms for the WSC includes a recent framework that compares query counts of evidence retrieved online for the competing antecedents (Sharma et al., 2015). That framework's coverage is restricted to a small subset of the Winograd instances based on knowledge constraints. In contrast, our approach covers a much larger subset of WSC passages and is impartial to knowledge constraints. Our framework adopts a novel representation schema that achieves significant coverage on Winograd instances, as well as an antecedent selection process that considers the evidence strength of the knowledge retrieved to make a more precise coreference decision.

Our method achieves a balanced F1 of 0.46 on the WSC, which significantly improves over the previous state-of-the-art of 0.3. We will also discuss the importance of F1 as a basis for comparing systems on the WSC, since it prevents overspecifying systems to perform well on certain WSC instances (boosting precision at the cost of recall).

2   Knowledge Hunting Framework

Our framework takes as input a Winograd sentence and processes it through three stages that culminate in the final coreference decision. First, it fits the sentence to a semantic representation schema and generates a set of queries that capture the predicates in the sentence's clauses. The query set is then sent to a search engine to retrieve text snippets that closely match the schema. Finally, returned snippets are resolved to their respective antecedents and the results are mapped to a best guess for the original Winograd question's resolution. We detail these stages below.

2.1   Semantic Representation Schema

The first step of our system is to perform a partial parse of each sentence into a shallow semantic representation; that is, a general skeleton of each of the important semantic components in the order that they appear.

In general, Winograd questions can be separated into a *context* clause, which introduces the two competing antecedents, and a *query* clause, which contains the target pronoun to be resolved. We use the following notation to define the components in our representation schema:

E_1, E_2	the candidate antecedents
$Pred_C$	the context predicate
$+$	discourse connective
P	the target pronoun
$Pred_Q$	the query predicate

E_1 and E_2 are noun phrases in the sentence. In the WSC, these two are specified and can be identified without ambiguity. $Pred_C$ is the context predicate composed of the verb phrase relating both antecedents to some event. The context contains E_1, E_2, and the context predicate $Pred_C$. The context and the query clauses are often connected by a discourse connective $+$. The query contains the target pronoun, P, which is also specified unambiguously. In addition, preceding or succeeding P is the query predicate, $Pred_Q$, a verb phrase involving the target pronoun. Table 2 shows sentence pairs in terms of each of these components.

2.2 Query Generation

In query generation, we aim to generate queries to send to a search engine in order to extract text snippets that resemble the original Winograd sentence. Queries are of the form:

$$+Term_C +Term_Q -\text{``Winograd''} -E_1$$

We assume here that the search queries are composed of two fundamental components, $Term_C$ and $Term_Q$, which are strings that represent the events occurring in the first (context) and second (query) clause of the sentence, respectively. In addition, by excluding search results that may contain *Winograd* or E_1, we ensure that we do not retrieve some rewording of the original Winograd sentence itself.

The task then is to construct the two query sets, C and Q, whose elements are possible entries for $Term_C$ and $Term_Q$, respectively. We achieve this by identifying the root verbs along with any modifying adjective in the context and query clauses, using Stanford CoreNLP's dependency parse of the sentence. We then add the root verbs and adjectives into the sets C and Q along with their broader verb phrases (again identified directly using the dependency tree). These extracted queries serve as event information that will be used in the subsequent modules. Bean and Riloff (2004) also learn extraction patterns to support coreference, but unlike our method, their method relies on a static domain and constructs an explicit probabilistic model of the narrative chains learned.

Augmenting the query set with WordNet We use WordNet (Kilgarriff, 2000) to construct an augmented query set that contains synonyms for the verbs or adjectives involved in a representation. In particular, we include the synonyms listed for the top synset of the same part of speech as the extracted verb or adjective.

Manual query construction To understand the impact of the query generation step, we also manually extracted representations for all Winograd questions. We limited the size of these sets to five to prevent a blowing-up of search space during knowledge extraction.

In Table 3 we show examples of generated queries for C and Q using the various techniques.

2.3 Extracting Knowledge from Search Results

From the search results, we obtain a set of text snippets that sufficiently resemble the original Winograd sentence, as follows. First, $Term_C$ and $Term_Q$ are restricted to occur in the same snippet, but are allowed to occur in any order. We filter the resulting sentences further to ensure that they contain at least two entities that corefer to one another. These sentences may be structured as follows:

$$
\begin{array}{lll}
E_1' \ Pred_C' \ E_2' & + & E_3' \ Pred_Q' \\
E_1' \ Pred_C' \ E_2' & + & Pred_Q' \ E_3' \\
E_1' \ Pred_C' & + & E_3' \ Pred_Q' \\
E_1' \ Pred_C' & + & Pred_Q' \ E_3'
\end{array}
$$

We call these *evidence sentences*. They exhibit a structure similar to the corresponding Winograd question, but with different entities and event order. In particular, $Pred_C'$ and $Pred_Q'$ (resulting from the queries $Term_C$ and $Term_Q$, resp.) should ideally be similar if not identical to $Pred_C$ and $Pred_Q$ from the original Winograd sentence. Note, however, that E_1', E_2', and E_3' may not all have the same semantic type, potentially simplifying their coreference resolution and implying the correct resolution of their Winograd counterpart.

A sentence for which E_3' refers to E_1' is subsequently called an *evidence-agent*, and one for which E_3' refers to E_2' an *evidence-patient*. The exception to this rule is when an event occurs in the passive voice (e.g., *was called*), which reverses the conventional order of the agent and patient: where in active voice, the agent precedes the predicate, in passive voice, it succeeds it. Another exception is in the case of *causative alternation*, where a verb can be used both transitively and intransitively. The latter case can also reverse the conventional order of the agent and patient (e.g., *he opened the door* versus *the door opened*).

As an example of the previously mentioned

Pair	$Pred_C$	E_1	E_2	$Pred_Q$	P	Alternating Word (POS)
1	couldn't lift	the man	his son	was so heavy	he	weak/heavy (adjective)
2	were bullying	the older students	the younger ones	punished	them	punished/rescued (verb)
3	tried to paint	shepherds	sheep	ended up .. like	they	golfers/dogs (noun)

Table 2: Winograd sentence pairs from Table 1.

Sentence: The trophy doesn't fit into the brown suitcase because it is too large.

Query Generation Method	C	Q
Automatic	{"doesn't fit into", "brown", "fit" }	{"large", "is too large"}
Automatic, with synonyms	{"doesn't fit into", "brown", "accommodate", "fit", "suit" }	{"large", "big", "is too large" }
Manual	{"doesn't fit into", "fit into","doesn't fit" }	{"is too large", "too large"}

Table 3: Query generation techniques on an example Winograd sentences, where C and Q represent the sets of queries that capture the context and query clauses of the sentence, respectively.

coreference simplification, a valid evidence sentence is: *He tried to call **her** but **she** wasn't available.* Here, the sentence can be resolved simply on the basis of the gender of the antecedents; E'_3 – in this case, the pronoun *she* – refers to the patient, E'_2. Accordingly, the sentence is considered an evidence-patient.

2.4 Antecedent Selection

We collect and reason about the set of sentences acquired through knowledge extraction using a selection process that a) resolves E'_3 in each of these sentences to either E'_1 or E'_2 (rendering them either evidence-agent or evidence-patient), by direct use of CoreNLP's coreference resolution module; and b) uses both the count and individual features of the evidence sentences to resolve a given Winograd sentence. For example, the more similar evidence-**agents** there are for the sentence *Paul tried to call George on the phone, but he wasn't successful*, the more likely it is that the process would guess *Paul*, the **agent**, to be the correct referent of the target pronoun.

To map each sentence to either an evidence-agent or evidence-patient, we developed a rule-based algorithm that uses the syntactic parse of an input sentence. This algorithm outputs an evidence label along with a list of features.

The features indicate: which two entities co-refer according to Stanford CoreNLP's resolver, and to which category of E'_1, E'_2, or E'_3 each belong; the token length of the sentence's search terms, $Term_C$ and $Term_Q$; the order of the sentence's search terms; whether the sentence is in ac-

tive or passive voice; and whether or not the verb is causative alternating. Some of these features are straightforward to extract (like token length and order, and coreferring entities given by CoreNLP), while others require various heuristics. To map each coreferring entity in the snippet to E'_1, E'_2, or E'_3 (corresponding loosely to context subject, context object, and query entity, respectively), we consider their position relative to the predicates in the original Winograd question. That is, E'_1 precedes $Term_C$, E'_2 succeeds $Term_C$, and E'_3 may precede or succeed $Term_Q$ depending on the Winograd question. To determine the voice, we use a list of auxiliary verbs and verb phrases (e.g., *was, had been, is, are being*) that switch the voice from active to passive (e.g., "they are being bullied" vs "they bullied") whenever one of these precedes $Term_C$ or $Term_Q$ (if they are verbs). Similarly, to identify causative alternation, we use a list of causative alternating verbs (e.g., *break, open, shut*) to identify the phenomenon whenever $Term_C$ or $Term_Q$ is used intransitively.

These features determine the evidence label, evidence-agent (EA) or evidence-patient (EP), according to the following rules:

$$Label(e) = \begin{cases} \text{EA}, & \text{if } E'_3 \text{ refers to } E'_1, \text{ active (1)} \\ \text{EA}, & \text{if } E'_3 \text{ refers to } E'_2, \text{ passive (2)} \\ \text{EP}, & \text{if } E'_3 \text{ refers to } E'_2, \text{ active (3)} \\ \text{EP}, & \text{if } E'_3 \text{ refers to } E'_1, \text{ passive (4)} \\ \text{EP}, & \text{if } E'_1 \text{ refers to } E'_3, \text{ causative (5)} \end{cases}$$

The exceptions, (2), (4), and (5), can be illustrated with the following examples:

- *The weight couldn't be lifted by me, because I was so weak.* Here, because of the passive voice, E'_2 plays the agent role, while syntactically being the object. Using rule (2), the sentence is correctly reversed to evidence-agent.

- *The weight couldn't be lifted by me, because it was so heavy.* For similar reasons, the sentence is correctly reversed to evidence-patient by rule (4).

- *The weight lifted. It was heavy.* This is reversed to evidence-patient, since 'lift' is a causative alternating verb by rule (5).

In addition to determining the evidence label, the features are also used in a heuristic that generates scores we call *evidence strengths* for each evidence sentence, as follows:

$$Strength(e) = LengthScore(e) + OrderScore(e)$$

$$LengthScore(e) = \begin{cases} 2, & \text{if } len(Term_Q) > 1 \\ 2, & \text{if } len(Term_C) > 1 \\ 1, & \text{otherwise} \end{cases}$$

$$OrderScore(e) = \begin{cases} 2, & \text{if } Term_C \prec Term_Q \\ 1, & \text{if } Term_Q \prec Term_C \end{cases}$$

The final stage of our framework runs the above processes on all snippets retrieved for a Winograd sentence. The sum of strengths for the evidence-agents are compared to that of the evidence-patients to make a resolution decision.

3 Experiments

We tested three versions of our framework (varying in the method of query generation: automatic *vs.* automatic with synonyms *vs.* manual) on the original 273 Winograd sentences (135 pairs and one triple). We compared these systems with previous work on the basis of Precision (P), Recall (R), and F1, where precision is the fraction of correctly answered instances among answered instances, recall is the fraction of correctly answered instances among all instances, and

$$F1 = 2 * P * R / (P + R).$$

We used Stanford CoreNLP's coreference resolver (Raghunathan et al., 2010) during query generation to identify the predicates from the syntactic parse, as well as during antecedent selection

to retrieve the coreference chain of a candidate evidence sentence. Python's Selenium package was used for web-scraping and Bing-USA and Google (top two pages per result) were the search engines (we unioned all results). The search results comprise a list of document snippets that contain the queries (for example, "yelled at" and "upset"). We then extract the sentence/s within each snippet that contain the query terms (with the added restriction that the terms should be within 70 characters of each other to ensure relevance). For example, for the queries "yelled at" and "upset", one snippet is: "Once the football players left the car, she testified that she yelled at the girl because she was upset with her actions from the night before."

In the next section we compare the performance of our framework with the most recent automatic system that tackles the original WSC (Sharma et al., 2015) (S2015). In addition to P/R/F1, we also compare systems' evidence coverage, by which we mean the number of Winograd questions for which evidence sentences are retrieved by the search engine. This should not be conflated with the *schemal* coverage of our system, by which we mean the number of Winograd questions that syntactically obey Class A (85% of the Winograd questions). Our system is designed specifically to resolve these Class A questions. We nevertheless test on the remaining 15% in our experiments.

Although other systems for the WSC exist outside of S2015, their results are not directly comparable to ours for one or more of the following reasons: a) they are directed towards solving the larger, easier dataset; b) they are not entirely automatic; or c) they are designed for a much smaller, author-selected subset of the WSC. We elaborate on this point in Section 5.

4 Results

Table 4 shows the precision, recall, and F1 of our framework's variants, automatically generated queries (AGQ), automatically generated queries with synonyms (AGQS), and manually generated queries (MGQ), and compares these to the systems of Sharma et al. (2015) (S2015) and Liu et al. (2016b) (L2016). The system developed by Liu et al. (2016b) uses elements extracted manually from the problem instances, so is most closely comparable to our MGQ method. Our best automated framework, AGQS, outperforms S2015 by 0.16 F1, achieving much higher recall (0.39 vs

	# Correct	P	R	F1
AGQ	73	0.53	0.27	0.36
AGQS	106	0.56	**0.39**	**0.46**
S2015	49	**0.92**	0.18	0.30
Systems with manual information:				
L2016	43	0.61	0.15	0.25
MGQ	118	0.60	0.43	0.50

Table 4: Coverage and performance on the Winograd Challenge (273 sentences). The best system on each measure is shown in bold.

0.18). Our results show that the framework using manually generated queries (MGQ) performs best, with an F1 of 0.50. We emphasize here that the promise of our approach lies mainly in its generality, shown in its improved coverage of the original problem set: it produces an answer for 70% of the instances. This coverage surpasses previous methods, which only admit specific instance types, by nearly 50%.

The random baseline on this task achieves a P/R/F1 of .5. We could artificially raise the F1 performance of all systems to be above .5 by randomly guessing an answer in cases where the system makes no decision. We chose not to do this so that automatic systems are compared transparently based on when they decide to make a prediction.

5 Related work

All the IR approaches to date that have tackled the Winograd Schema Problem have done so in one of two ways. On the one hand, some systems have been developed exclusively for Rahman and Ng's expanded Winograd corpus, achieving performance much higher than baseline. Bean and Riloff (2004) learn domain-specific narrative chains by bootstrapping from a small set of coreferent noun pairs. Conversely, other systems are directed towards the original, more difficult Winograd questions. These systems demonstrate higher-than-baseline performance but only on a small, author-selected sub-set, where the selection is based often on some knowledge-type constraints.

Systems directed exclusively towards the expanded Winograd corpus include Rahman and Ng's system itself (Rahman and Ng, 2012), reporting 73% accuracy on Winograd-like sentences, and Peng et al.'s system that improves accuracy to 76% (Peng et al., 2015). Another system uses

sentence alignment of web query snippets to resolve the Winograd-like instances, reporting 70% accuracy on a small subset of the test sentences in the expanded corpus (Kruengkrai et al., 2014). Unfortunately, the passages in the original WSC confound these systems by ensuring that the antecedents themselves do not reveal the coreference answer. Many sentences in the expanded corpus can be resolved using similarity/association between candidate antecedents and the query predicate. One such sentence is "Lions eat zebras because they are predators." Many of the above systems simply query "Lions are predators" versus "zebras are predators" to make a decision.

This kind of exploitation is often the top contributor to such systems' overall accuracy (Rahman and Ng, 2012), but fails to hold for the majority (if not all of) the original Winograd questions. In these questions one vital property is enforced: that the question should not be "Google-able." Our work seeks to alleviate this issue by generating search queries that are based exclusively on the predicates of the Winograd sentence, and not the antecedents, as well as considering the strength of the evidence sentences.

The systems directed towars the Original Winograd questions include Schüller (2014), who use principles from relevance theory to show correct disambiguation of 4 of the Winograd instances; Sharma et al. (2015)'s knowledge-hunting module aimed at a subset of 71 instances that exhibit *causal* relationships; Liu et al. (2016a)'s neural association model, aimed at a similar causal subset of 70 Winograd instances, and for which events were extracted manually; and finally, a recent system by Huang and Luo (2017) directed at 49 selected Winograd questions. While these approaches demonstrate that difficult coreference problems can be resolved when they adhere to certain knowledge or structural constraints, we believe that such systems will fail to generalize to the majority of other coreference problems. This important factor often goes unnoticed in the literature when systems are compared only in terms of precision; accordingly, we propose and utilize F1-driven comparison that does not enable boosting precision at the cost of recall.

6 Conclusion

We developed a knowledge-hunting framework to tackle the Winograd Schema Challenge. Our system involves a novel semantic representation schema and an antecedent selection process acting on web-search results. We evaluated the performance of our framework on the original problem set, demonstrating performance competitive with the state-of-the-art. Through analysis, we determined our query generation module to be a critical component of the framework.

Our query generation and antecedent selection processes could likely be enhanced by various Machine Learning approaches. This would require developing datasets that involve schema identification, query extraction, and knowledge acquisition for the purpose of training. As future work, we consider using the extensive set of sentences extracted by our knowledge hunting framework in order to develop a large-scale, Winograd-like corpus. In addition, we are currently working to develop deep neural network models that perform both knowledge acquisition and antecedent selection procedures in an end-to-end fashion.

References

Dan Bailey, Amelia Harrison, Yuliya Lierler, Vladimir Lifschitz, and Julian Michael. 2015. The winograd schema challenge and reasoning about correlation. In *In Working Notes of the Symposium on Logical Formalizations of Commonsense Reasoning*.

David Bean and Ellen Riloff. 2004. Unsupervised learning of contextual role knowledge for coreference resolution. In *Proceedings of the Human Language Technology Conference of the North American Chapter of the Association for Computational Linguistics: HLT-NAACL 2004*.

David Graff and C Cieri. 2003. English gigaword corpus. *Linguistic Data Consortium* .

Graeme Hirst. 1988. Semantic interpretation and ambiguity. *Artificial intelligence* 34(2):131–177.

Wenguan Huang and Xudong Luo. 2017. Commonsense reasoning in a deeper way: By discovering relations between predicates. In *ICAART (2)*. pages 407–414.

Adam Kilgarriff. 2000. Wordnet: An electronic lexical database.

Canasai Kruengkrai, Naoya Inoue, Jun Sugiura, and Kentaro Inui. 2014. An example-based approach to difficult pronoun resolution. In *PACLIC*. pages 358–367.

Douglas B Lenat. 1995. Cyc: A large-scale investment in knowledge infrastructure. *Communications of the ACM* 38(11):33–38.

Hector J Levesque, Ernest Davis, and Leora Morgenstern. 2011. The winograd schema challenge. In *AAAI Spring Symposium: Logical Formalizations of Commonsense Reasoning*. volume 46, page 47.

Hugo Liu and Push Singh. 2004. Conceptnet—a practical commonsense reasoning tool-kit. *BT technology journal* 22(4):211–226.

Quan Liu, Hui Jiang, Andrew Evdokimov, Zhen-Hua Ling, Xiaodan Zhu, Si Wei, and Yu Hu. 2016a. Probabilistic reasoning via deep learning: Neural association models. *arXiv preprint arXiv:1603.07704* .

Quan Liu, Hui Jiang, Zhen-Hua Ling, Xiaodan Zhu, Si Wei, and Yu Hu. 2016b. Combing context and commonsense knowledge through neural networks for solving winograd schema problems. *arXiv preprint arXiv:1611.04146* .

Haoruo Peng, Daniel Khashabi, and Dan Roth. 2015. Solving hard coreference problems. *Urbana* 51:61801.

Karthik Raghunathan, Heeyoung Lee, Sudarshan Rangarajan, Nathanael Chambers, Mihai Surdeanu, Dan Jurafsky, and Christopher Manning. 2010. A multipass sieve for coreference resolution. In *Proceedings of the 2010 Conference on Empirical Methods in Natural Language Processing*. Association for Computational Linguistics, pages 492–501.

Altaf Rahman and Vincent Ng. 2012. Resolving complex cases of definite pronouns: the winograd schema challenge. In *Proceedings of the 2012 Joint Conference on Empirical Methods in Natural Language Processing and Computational Natural Language Learning*. Association for Computational Linguistics, pages 777–789.

Peter Schüller. 2014. Tackling winograd schemas by formalizing relevance theory in knowledge graphs. In *Fourteenth International Conference on the Principles of Knowledge Representation and Reasoning*.

Arpit Sharma, Nguyen Ha Vo, Somak Aditya, and Chitta Baral. 2015. Towards addressing the winograd schema challenge-building and using a semantic parser and a knowledge hunting module. In *IJCAI*. pages 1319–1325.

Towards Qualitative Word Embeddings Evaluation: Measuring Neighbors Variation

Bénédicte Pierrejean and **Ludovic Tanguy**
CLLE: CNRS & Université de Toulouse
Toulouse, France
{benedicte.pierrejean,ludovic.tanguy}@univ-tlse2.fr

Abstract

We propose a method to study the variation lying between different word embeddings models trained with different parameters. We explore the variation between models trained with only one varying parameter by observing the distributional neighbors variation and show how changing only one parameter can have a massive impact on a given semantic space. We show that the variation is not affecting all words of the semantic space equally. Variation is influenced by parameters such as setting a parameter to its minimum or maximum value but it also depends on the corpus intrinsic features such as the frequency of a word. We identify semantic classes of words remaining stable across the models trained and specific words having high variation.

1 Introduction

Word embeddings are widely used nowadays in Distributional Semantics and for a variety of tasks in NLP. Embeddings can be evaluated using extrinsic evaluation methods, i.e. the trained embeddings are evaluated on a specific task such as part-of-speech tagging or named-entity recognition (Schnabel et al., 2015). Because this type of evaluation is expensive, time consuming and difficult to interpret, embeddings are often evaluated using intrinsic evaluation methods such as word similarity or analogy (Nayak et al., 2016). Such methods of evaluation are a good way to get a quick insight of the quality of a model. Many different techniques and parameters can be used to train embeddings and benchmarks are used to select and tune embeddings parameters.

Benchmarks used to evaluate embeddings only focus on a subset of the trained model by only evaluating selected pairs of words. Thus, they lack information about the overall structure of the semantic space and do not provide enough information to understand the impact of changing one parameter when training a model.

We want to know if some parameters have more influence than others on the global structure of embeddings models and get a better idea of what varies from one model to another. We specifically investigate the impact of the architecture, the corpus, the window size, the vectors dimensions and the context type when training embeddings. We analyze to what extent training models by changing only one of these parameters has an impact on the models created and if the different areas of the lexicon are impacted the same by this change.

To do so, we provide a qualitative methodology focusing on the global comparison of semantic spaces based on the overlap of the N nearest neighbors for a given word. The proposed method is not bound to the subjectivity of benchmarks and gives a global yet precise vision of the variation between different models by evaluating each word from the model. It provides a way to easily investigate selected areas, by observing the variation of a word or of selected subsets of words.

We compare 19 word embedding models to a default model. All models are trained using the well-known *word2vec*. Using the parameters of the default model, we train the other models by changing the value of only one parameter at a time. We first get some insights by performing a quantitative evaluation using benchmark test sets. We then proceed to a qualitative evaluation by observing the differences between the default model and every other model. This allows us to measure the impact of each parameter on the global variation as well as to detect phenomena that were not visible when evaluating only with benchmark test sets. We also identify some preliminary features for words remaining stable independently of the parameters used for training.

Proceedings of NAACL-HLT 2018: Student Research Workshop, pages 32–39
New Orleans, Louisiana, June 2 - 4, 2018. ©2017 Association for Computational Linguistics

2   Related Work

The problems raised for the evaluation of Distributional Semantic Models (henceforth DSMs) is not specific to word embeddings and have been given attention for a long time. Benchmarks only focus on a limited subset of the corpus. For example, WordSim-353 (Finkelstein et al., 2002) is testing the behaviour of only 353 pairs of words meaning we only get a partial representation of the model performance. To get a better idea of the semantic structure of DSMs and of the type of semantic relations they encode, some alternative datasets were designed specifically for the evaluation of DSMs (Baroni and Lenci, 2011; Santus et al., 2015). Although these datasets provide a deeper evaluation, they focus on specific aspects of the model and we still need a better way to understand the global impact of changing a parameter when training DSMs.

Some extensive studies have been made comparing a large number of configurations generated by systematic variation of several parameters. Lapesa and Evert (2014) evaluated 537600 models trained using combinations of different parameters. Other studies focused on a specific parameter when training embeddings such as the corpus size (Asr et al., 2016; Sahlgren and Lenci, 2016), the type of corpus used (Bernier-Colborne and Drouin, 2016; Chiu et al., 2016) or the type of contexts used (Levy and Goldberg, 2014; Melamud et al., 2016; Li et al., 2017). Results showed that choosing the right parameters when training DSMs improve the performance for both intrinsic and extrinsic evaluation tasks and can also influence the type of semantic information captured by the model. Levy et al. (2015) even found that tuning hyperparameters carefully could prove better in certain cases than adding more data when training a model.

Chiu et al. (2016) showed that the performance of DSMs is influenced by different factors including corpora, preprocessing performed on the corpora, architecture chosen and the choice of several hyperparameters. However they also noticed that the effects of some parameters are mixed and counterintuitive.

Hamilton et al. (2016) measured the variation between models by observing semantic change using diachronic corpora. Hellrich and Hahn (2016) also used diachronic corpora to assess the reliability of word embeddings neighborhoods. Antoniak and Mimno (2018) showed how the corpus influences the word embeddings generated.

We relate to these studies but rather than finding the best combination of parameters or focusing on a single parameter, we assess the individual impact of selected parameters when training word embeddings. We intent to investigate those effects by getting a global vision of the change from one model to another. Unlike benchmarks test sets, we will not focus on evaluating only selected word pairs from the different models but we will evaluate the variation for each word from one model to the other.

3   Measuring neighbors variation

To evaluate the different models trained, we focus on the study of neighbors variation between two models. This type of approach was proposed by Sahlgren (2006) who globally compared syntagmatic and paradigmatic word space models by measuring their overlap. We go further by applying this method to a new type of models and by observing variation for words individually. We also identify zones with different degrees of variation.

The nearest neighbors of a given target word are words having the closest cosine similarity score with the target word. To compute the variation between models, we propose to compute the degree of nearest neighbors variation between two models. For two models M_1 and M_2, we first get the common vocabulary. We then compute the variation var by getting the common neighbors amongst the n nearest neighbors for each word in the two models such as:

$$var^n_{M_1,M_2}(w) = 1 - \frac{|neighb^n_{M_1}(w) \cap neighb^n_{M_2}(w)|}{n}$$

The value of n is important. To choose the most representative value, we selected a number of candidate values (1, 5, 10, 15, 25, 50 and 100). We found that for most pairs of models compared with this method, 25 was the value for which the variation scores had the highest correlation scores compared with other values of n across the entire vocabulary. In this work all comparisons use this value. We computed the variation for open-class parts of speech (henceforth POS) only i.e. nouns, verbs, adjectives and adverbs.

Parameters	Default	Values tested
Architecture	SG	CBOW
Corpus	BNC	ACL
Window size	5	1 to 10
Vectors dim.	100	50, 200, 300, 400, 500, 600
Context type	window	deps, deps+

Table 1. Parameters values used to train embeddings that are compared.

4 Experiments

4.1 Experiment setup

In this work, we use a DEFAULT model as a basis of comparison. Starting from this model, we trained new models by changing only one parameter at a time among the following parameters: architecture, corpus, window size, vectors dimensions, context type. We thus trained 19 models which will all be compared to the DEFAULT model. Although we compare less models and less parameters than other studies conducted on the evaluation of hyperparameters, we provide both a global and precise evaluation by computing the variation for each word of the model rather than evaluating selected pairs of words.

4.1.1 Default model

We trained our DEFAULT model using the widely used tool *word2vec* (Mikolov et al., 2013) with the default parameters values on the BNC corpus[1]. The parameters used were the following:

- architecture: Skip-gram,
- algorithm: negative sampling,
- corpus: BNC (written part only, made of about 90 million words),
- window size: 5,
- vector size: 100,
- negative sampling rate: 5,
- subsampling: 1e-3,
- iterations: 5.

The min-count parameter was set to a value of 100.

4.1.2 Variant models

5 different parameters are evaluated in this work: architecture, corpus, window size, vectors dimensions and context type. Using the default configuration, we then trained one model per possible parameter value stated in Table 1, e.g. we changed

the value of the window size or the number of dimensions. We did not change more than one parameter when training the models since this work aims at evaluating the influence of a single parameter when training word embeddings. We chose the parameters to be investigated as well as their values based on selected studies that analyze the influence of parameters used when training DSMs (Baroni et al., 2014; Levy and Goldberg, 2014; Li et al., 2017; Melamud et al., 2016; Bernier-Colborne and Drouin, 2016; Sahlgren and Lenci, 2016; Chiu et al., 2016).

Models were trained on the BNC except for the ACL model which was trained on the ACL Anthology Reference corpus (Bird et al., 2008), a corpus made of about 100 million words. Both corpora were parsed using Talismane, a dependency parser developed by Urieli (2013). We trained models with dimensions ranging from 50 to 600 (DIM50 to DIM600 models). We used two different types of contexts: window-based and dependency-based contexts. For window-based models we used a window size from 1 to 10 (WIN1 to WIN10 models). For dependency-based models (DEPS and DEPS+) we used *word2vecf*, a tool developed by Levy and Goldberg (2014). This tool is an extension of *word2vec*'s Skip-gram. *Word2vecf* uses syntactic triples as contexts. We extracted the triples from the corpus using the scripts provided by Levy and Goldberg (2014)[2] and obtained triples such as *head modifier#reltype*. Prepositions were "collapsed" as described in Levy and Goldberg (2014). To investigate the influence of the triples used for training on the embeddings generated we decided to train with selected syntactic relations triples (DEPS+ model). We based our selection on Padó and Lapata (2007) work and chose to keep the following dependency relations: subject, noun modifier, object, adjectival modifier, coordination, apposition, prepositional modifier, predicate, verb complement. Prepositions were still collapsed *à la* Levy and Goldberg (2014) and the same was done for conjuctions.

4.2 Quantitative evaluation

To get an overview of the different models performance we first ran a partial quantitative evalu-

---

[1] http://www.natcorp.ox.ac.uk/

[2] https://bitbucket.org/yoavgo/word2vecf

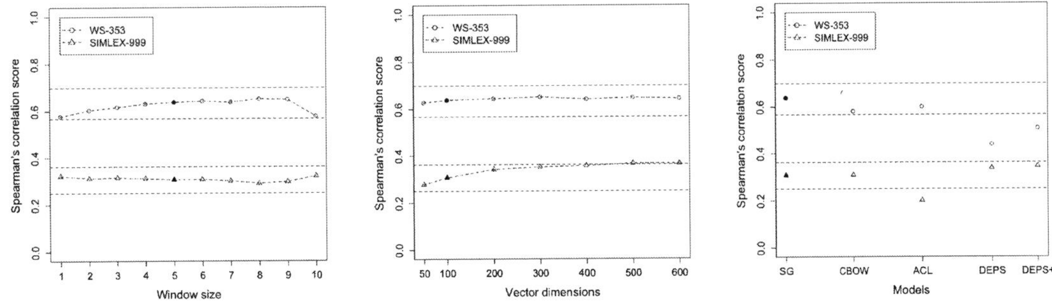

Figure 1. Evaluation results for all models on WordSim-353 and SimLex-999 with 95% confidence interval span computed from DEFAULT model (DEFAULT model is shown in bold).

ation. We used the toolkit[3] provided by Faruqui and Dyer (2014). This toolkit provides several benchmarks to test against the trained vectors. The evaluation is computed by ranking the different cosine scores obtained for each pair of the chosen dataset. The evaluation was run on WordSim-353 and Simlex-999 (Hill et al., 2015), two benchmarks commonly used for DSMs evaluation (e.g. see Levy and Goldberg (2014); Melamud et al. (2016)).

Figure 1 shows the performance of the different models on both test sets as well as the confidence interval for the DEFAULT model. We see that changing parameters creates differences in models performance and that this difference is generally not significant. Changing the architecture from Skip-gram to CBOW yields worse results for WordSim-353 than changing the corpus used for training. However, when testing on SimLex-999, performance is similar for the DEFAULT and CBOW models, while the ACL model performed worse. In a similar way, changing the training corpus gives better result on WordSim-353 than using a different type of contexts, as shown per the results of DEPS and DEPS+.

Performance is not consistent between the two benchmarks. DEPS and DEPS+ both yields the worst performance on WordSim-353 but at the same time their performance on SimLex-999 is better than most other models. The same is true for the WIN1 and WIN10 models. Increasing the vector dimensions gets slightly better performance, independently of the benchmark used. Increasing the window size gives better performance results for WordSim-353 but worse for SimLex-999. Dependency-based models performs the worst on

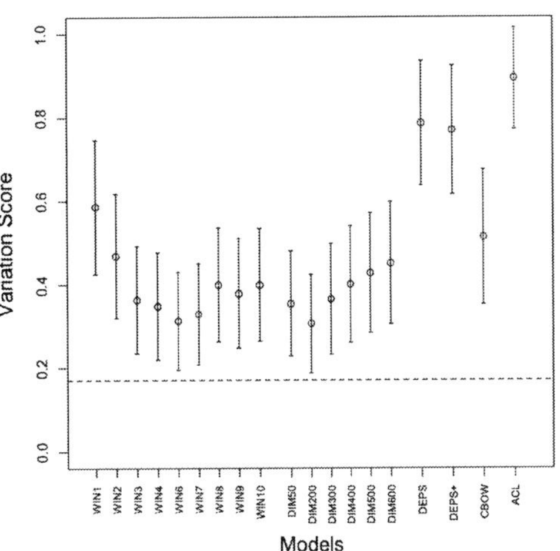

Figure 2. Mean variation value with standard deviation interval for all trained models compared to DEFAULT model. The dashed line corresponds to the mean variation value for the DEFAULT model trained 5 times with the exact same parameters.

WordSim-353.

This kind of evaluation is only performed on selected pairs of words and despite small differences in performance scores, larger differences may exist. In the next section we introduce a method that quantifies the variation between the different models trained by evaluating the distributional neighbors variation for every word in the corpus.

4.3 Qualitative evaluation

4.3.1 Exploring the variation

Figure 2 shows the mean variation score with the standard deviation span between the DEFAULT model and the 19 other models[4]. Since it is known

---

[3] https://github.com/mfaruqui/eval-word-vectors

[4] For models trained on the BNC, 27437 words were evaluated. When comparing DEFAULT to ACL the vocabulary size was smaller (10274) since the models were not trained on the same corpus.

there is inherent variation when training embeddings (Hellrich and Hahn, 2016), we measured the variation across 5 models using *word2vec* default settings. This variation is much lower than for the other models (0.17).

Training using the same parameters triggers variation with the DEFAULT model. Even for models varying the least, the variation is high with an average variation score of at least 0.3. This means that by changing only one parameter, among the 25 nearest neighbors of a given word about 1 neighbor out of 3 is different from one model to the other. Some variation scores are higher than 0.8 meaning that the two models compared are drastically different.

The ACL model is the one showing the highest variation. This is not surprising since it was trained on a specialized corpus. However, it is more surprising that DEPS and DEPS+ also display a very high variation. This could be explained by the fact that dependency-based and window-based models capture different type of semantic information (Levy and Goldberg, 2014).

Models showing the lowest variation are models with less drastic differences with the DEFAULT model, namely the vector size was changed from 100 to 200 or the window size from 5 to 6. A general tendency is that models trained with minimum and maximum values for a given parameter show more variation. Going back to the performance of the models (see Figure 1), we also notice that models having a performance score close to the DEFAULT model can still display a high variation. This is the case of the DIM600 model which had a performance score very close to the DEFAULT model on both benchmarks but still displays a variation higher than 0.4.

We observed that the variations between models do not follow the differences in performance on test sets shown in Figure 1. We measured the absence of correlation between the variation score and the performance scores on WordSim-353 ($\rho = -0.08$, $p = 0.78$) and Simlex-999 ($\rho = 0.25$, $p = 0.36$).

For every comparison shown in Figure 2, we can see a high standard deviation. This means that there are different behaviors across the lexicon and some words vary more than others. In the next section, we show how the frequency affects the variation across the different models.

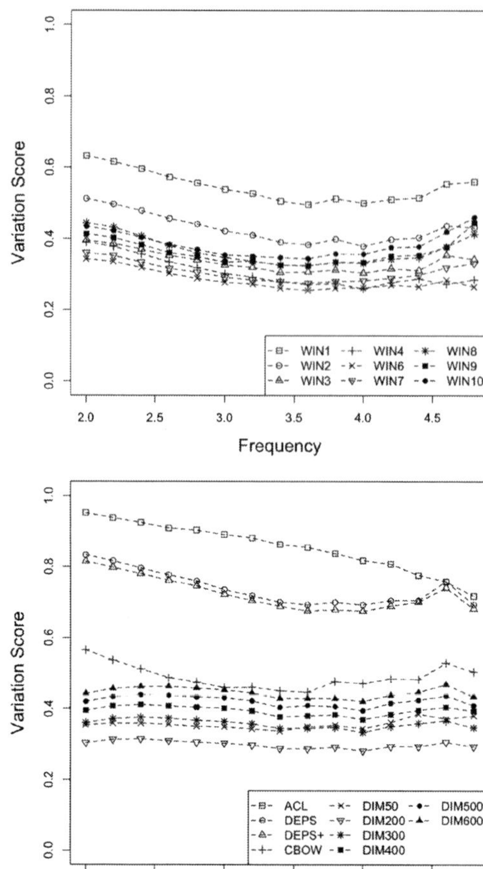

Figure 3. Effect of frequency on words variation.

4.3.2 Role of POS and frequency

To find some cues explaining the variation, we first investigated the interaction between the POS of a word and its variation score. However, we found for all models that the repartition of the variation was similar independently of the POS. This is surprising as we know embeddings perform differently across POS, especially when contexts vary.

We then investigated the role of the frequency in the variation. Figure 3 shows the average variation given the frequency of a word. For all window-based models, we observe a clear pattern: words in the mid-frequency range (1000 to 10000) display less variation than words in lower and higher frequency ranges. This is in line with Sahlgren and Lenci (2016) who showed that DSMs perform the best for medium to high-frequency ranges items. Models trained with different dimensions seem less affected by frequency. The variation is quite constant across all frequency ranges. CBOW, DEPS and DEPS+ follow the same pattern than

Model	Var.	Identified semantic classes
ACL	Low	numerals (*2nd, 14th, 10th...*)
		nationalities (*hungarian, french, danish, spanish...*)
		time nouns (*afternoon, week, evening...*)
	High	specialized lexicon (*embedded, differential, nominal, probabilistic, patch, spell, string, graph...*)
DIM200	Low	numerals (*40th, 15th...*)
		nationalities (*hungarian, dutch, french, spanish...*)
		family nouns (*grandparent, sister, son, father...*)
	High	generic adjectives (*all, near, very, real...*)
		polysemic nouns (*field, marker, turn, position...*)

Table 2. Words showing lowest and highest variation for ACL and DIM200 compared to DEFAULT.

the window models, with a variation less high for medium frequency words. ACL[5] display a very high variation for low frequency words but the variation decreases with frequency.

4.3.3 Getting a preview of the variation

The variation measure can also be used to examine more local differences. For example, for given pairs of models we can easily identify which words show the most extreme variation values. We did this for two of our models: ACL which shows the highest variation and DIM200 which shows the lowest variation. Table 2 shows a few of the most stable and unstable words. It appears that different semantic classes emerge in each case. It seems that these classes correspond to dense clusters, each word having all others as close neighbor. Some of these clusters remain the same across the two pairs of models (e.g. nationality adjectives) while other clusters are different. In the ACL model, we find a cluster of time nouns while in the DIM200 model we find family nouns. We see that words varying the most for the specialized corpus are words carrying a specific meaning (e.g. *nominal, graph*). We also find that words with a high variation score are highly polysemic or generic in the DIM200 model (e.g. *field, marker*). In the future we want to analyze the impact of the degree of polysemy on the variation score along with other characteristics of words.

5 Conclusion

This work compared 19 models trained using one different parameter to a default model. We measured the differences between these models with

benchmark test sets and a methodology which does not depend on the subjectivity and limited scope of benchmark test sets. Test sets show marginal differences while neighbors variation revealed that at least one third of the nearest 25 neighbors of a word are different from one model to the other. In addition it appears that the parameters have a different impact depending on the way differences are measured.

We saw that the variation is not affecting all words of the semantic space equally and we found features which help identify some areas of (in)stability in the semantic space. Words having a low and high frequency range have a tendency to display more variation. Words in the medium frequency range show more stability. We also found word features that could play a role in the variation (polysemy, genericity, semantic clusters etc.). These features can help understanding what really changes when tuning the parameters of word embeddings and give us more control over those effects.

In further work, we want to extend our analysis to more parameters. We especially want to see if the observations made in this study apply to models trained with specialized corpora or corpora of different sizes. We also want to distinguish features that will help classify words displaying more or less variation and qualify the variations themselves.

Acknowledgments

We would like to thank the Student Research Workshop for setting up the mentoring program that we benefited from. We especially thank our mentor, Shashi Narayan, for his very helpful comments. We are also thankful to the anonymous reviewers for their suggestions and comments.

---

[5]The variation for ACL was measured on a smaller vocabulary set. The frequency used in Figure 3 is the one from the BNC.

Experiments presented in this paper were carried out using the OSIRIM platform that is administered by IRIT and supported by CNRS, the Région Midi-Pyrénées, the French Government, and ERDF (see http://osirim.irit.fr/site/en).

References

Maria Antoniak and David Mimno. 2018. Evaluating the Stability of Embedding-based Word Similarities. *Transactions of the Association for Computational Linguistics*, 6:107–119.

Fatemeh Torabi Asr, Jon A. Willits, and Michael N. Jones. 2016. Comparing Predictive and Co-occurrence Based Models of Lexical Semantics Trained on Child-directed Speech. In *Proceedings of the 37th Meeting of the Cognitive Science Society*.

Marco Baroni, Georgiana Dinu, and German Kruszewski. 2014. Don't count, predict! A systematic comparison of context-counting vs. context-predicting semantic vectors. In *Proceedings of the 52nd Annual Meeting of the Association for Computational Linguistics*, pages 238–247, Baltimore, Maryland, USA.

Marco Baroni and Alessandro Lenci. 2011. How we BLESSed distributional semantic evaluation. In *Proceedings of the GEMS 2011 Workshop on Geometrical Models of Natural Language Semantics, EMNLP 2011*, pages 1–10, Edinburgh, Scotland, UK.

Gabriel Bernier-Colborne and Patrick Drouin. 2016. Evaluation of distributional semantic models: a holistic approach. In *Proceedings of the 5th International Workshop on Computational Terminology*, pages 52–61, Osaka, Japan.

Steven Bird, Robert Dale, Bonnie Dorr, Bryan Gibson, Mark Joseph, Min-Yen Kan, Dongwon Lee, Brett Powley, Dragomir Radev, and Yee Fan Tan. 2008. The ACL Anthology Reference Corpus: A Reference Dataset for Bibliographic Research in Computational Linguistics. In *Proceedings of Language Resources and Evaluation Conference (LREC 08)*, Marrakesh, Morrocco.

Billy Chiu, Gamal Crichton, Anna Korhonen, and Sampo Pyysalo. 2016. How to Train Good Word Embeddings for Biomedical NLP. In *Proceedings of the 15th Workshop on Biomedical Natural Language Processing*, pages 166–174, Berlin, Germany.

Manaal Faruqui and Chris Dyer. 2014. Community Evaluation and Exchange of Word Vectors at word-vectors.org. In *Proceedings of the 52nd Annual Meeting of the Association for Computational Linguistics: System Demonstrations*, pages 19–24, Baltimore, Maryland, USA.

Lev Finkelstein, Evgeniy Gabrilovich, Yossi Matias, Ehud Rivlin, Zach Solan, Gadi Wolfman, and Eytan Ruppin. 2002. Placing Search in Context: The Concept Revisited. In *ACM Transactions on Information Systems*, volume 20, page 116:131.

William L. Hamilton, Jure Leskovec, and Dan Jurafsky. 2016. Diachronic Word Embeddings Reveal Statistical Laws of Semantic Change. In *Proceedings of the 54th Annual Meeting of the Association for Computational Linguistics*, pages 1489–1501, Berlin, Germany.

Johannes Hellrich and Udo Hahn. 2016. Bad Company - Neighborhoods in Neural Embedding Spaces Considered Harmful. In *Proceedings of COLING 2016, the 26th International Conference on Computational Linguistics: Technical Papers*, pages 2785–2796, Osaka, Japan.

Felix Hill, Roi Reichart, and Anna Korhonen. 2015. SimLex-999: Evaluating Semantic Models with (Genuine) Similarity Estimation. *Computational Linguistics*, 41:665–695.

Gabriella Lapesa and Stefan Evert. 2014. A Large Scale Evaluation of Distributional Semantic Models: Parameters, Interactions and Model Selection. *Transactions of the Association for Computational Linguistics*, 2:531–545.

Omer Levy and Yoav Goldberg. 2014. Dependency-Based Word Embeddings. In *Proceedings of the 52nd Annual Meeting of the Association for Computational Linguistics*, pages 302–308, Baltimore, Maryland, USA.

Omer Levy, Yoav Goldberg, and Ido Dagan. 2015. Improving Distributional Similarity with Lessons Learned from Word Embeddings. *Transactions of the Association for Computational Linguistics*, 3:211–225.

Bofang Li, Tao Liu, Zhe Zhao, Buzhou Tang, Aleksandr Drozd, Anna Rogers, and Xiaoyong Du. 2017. Investigating Different Syntactic Context Types and Context Representations for Learning Word Embeddings. In *Proceedings of the 2017 Conference on Empirical Methods in Natural Language Processing*, pages 2411–2421.

Oren Melamud, David McClosky, Siddharth Patwardhan, and Mohit Bansal. 2016. The Role of Context Types and Dimensionality in Learning Word Embeddings. In *Proceedings of NAACL-HLT 2016*, San Diego, California.

Tomas Mikolov, Kai Chen, Greg Corrado, and Jeffrey Dean. 2013. Efficient Estimation of Word Representations in Vector Space. *CoRR*, abs/1301.3781.

Neha Nayak, Gabor Angeli, and Christopher D. Manning. 2016. Evaluating Word Embeddings Using a Representative Suite of Practical Tasks. In *Proceedings of the 1st Workshop on Evaluating Vector Space Representations for NLP*, pages 19–23, Berlin, Germany.

Sebastian Padó and Mirella Lapata. 2007. Dependency-Based Construction of Semantic Space Models. *Computational Linguistics*, 33(2):161–199.

Magnus Sahlgren. 2006. *The Word-Space Model*. Ph.D. thesis, Stockholm University, Sweden.

Magnus Sahlgren and Alessandro Lenci. 2016. The Effects of Data Size and Frequency Range on Distributional Semantic Models. In *Proceedings of the 2016 Conference on Empirical Methods in Natural Language Processing*, pages 975–980, Austin, Texas.

Enrico Santus, Frances Yung, Alessandro Lenci, and Chu-Ren Huang. 2015. EVALution1.0: an Evolving Semantic Dataset for Training and Evaluation of Distributional Semantic Models. In *Proceedings of the 4th Workshop on Linked Data in Linguistics (LDL-2015)*, pages 64–69, Beijing, China.

Tobias Schnabel, Igor Labutov, David Mimno, and Thorsten Joachims. 2015. Evaluation methods for unsupervised word embeddings. In *Proceedings of the 2015 Conference on Empirical Methods in Natural Language Processing*, pages 298–307.

Assaf Urieli. 2013. *Robust French syntax analysis: reconciling statistical methods and linguistic knowledge in the Talismane toolkit*. Ph.D. thesis, University of Toulouse, France.

A Deeper Look into Dependency-Based Word Embeddings

Sean MacAvaney
Information Retrieval Lab
Department of Computer Science
Georgetown University
Washington, DC, USA
`sean@ir.cs.georgetown.edu`

Amir Zeldes
Department of Linguistics
Georgetown University
Washington, DC, USA
`amir.zeldes@georgetown.edu`

Abstract

We investigate the effect of various dependency-based word embeddings on distinguishing between functional and domain similarity, word similarity rankings, and two downstream tasks in English. Variations include word embeddings trained using context windows from Stanford and Universal dependencies at several levels of enhancement (ranging from unlabeled, to Enhanced++ dependencies). Results are compared to basic linear contexts and evaluated on several datasets. We found that embeddings trained with Universal and Stanford dependency contexts excel at different tasks, and that enhanced dependencies often improve performance.

1 Introduction

For many natural language processing applications, it is important to understand word-level semantics. Recently, word embeddings trained with neural networks have gained popularity (Mikolov et al., 2013; Pennington et al., 2014), and have been successfully used for various tasks, such as machine translation (Zou et al., 2013) and information retrieval (Hui et al., 2017).

Word embeddings are usually trained using linear bag-of-words contexts, i.e. tokens positioned around a word are used to learn a dense representation of that word. Levy and Goldberg (2014) challenged the use of linear contexts, proposing instead to use contexts based on dependency parses. (This is akin to prior work that found that dependency contexts are useful for vector models (Pado and Lapata, 2007; Baroni and Lenci, 2010).) They found that embeddings trained this way are better at capturing semantic similarity, rather than relatedness. For instance, embeddings trained using linear contexts place *Hogwarts* (the fictional setting of the Harry Potter series) near *Dumbledore* (a character from the series), whereas embeddings trained with dependency contexts place *Hogwarts* near *Sunnydale* (fictional setting of the series Buffy the Vampire Slayer). The former is *relatedness*, whereas the latter is *similarity*.

Work since Levy and Goldberg (2014) examined the use of dependency contexts and sentence feature representations for sentence classification (Komninos and Manandhar, 2016). Li et al. (2017) filled in research gaps relating to model type (e.g., CBOW, Skip-Gram, GloVe) and dependency labeling. Interestingly, Abnar et al. (2018) recently found that dependency-based word embeddings excel at predicting brain activation patterns. The best model to date for distinguishing between similarity and relatedness combines word embeddings, WordNet, and dictionaries (Recski et al., 2016).

One limitation of existing work is that it has only explored one dependency scheme: the English-tailored Stanford Dependencies (De Marneffe and Manning, 2008b). We provide further analysis using the cross-lingual Universal Dependencies (Nivre et al., 2016). Although we do not compare cross-lingual embeddings in our study, we will address one important question for English: are Universal Dependencies, which are less tailored to English, actually better or worse than the English-specific labels and graphs? Furthermore, we investigate approaches to simplifying and extending dependencies, including Enhanced dependencies and Enhanced++ dependencies (Schuster and Manning, 2016), as well as two levels of relation simplification. We hypothesize that the cross-lingual generalizations from universal dependencies and the additional context from enhanced dependencies should improve the performance of word embeddings at distinguishing between functional and domain

40

Proceedings of NAACL-HLT 2018: Student Research Workshop, pages 40–45
New Orleans, Louisiana, June 2 - 4, 2018. ©2017 Association for Computational Linguistics

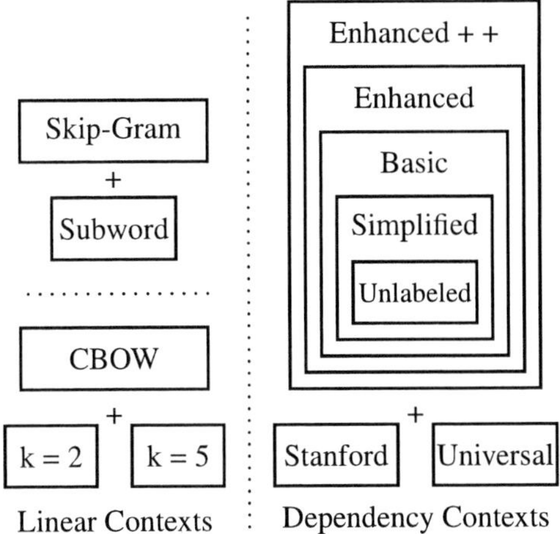

Figure 1: Visual relationship between types of embedding contexts. Each layer of enhancement adds more information to the dependency context (e.g., simplified adds dependency labels to the unlabeled context). We investigate CBOW using both a context window of $k = 2$ and $k = 5$, and we use the SkipGram model both with and without subword information.

Simp.	Basic
Stanford dependencies	
mod	poss, prt, predet, det, amod, tmod, npadvmod, possessive, advmod, quantmod, preconj, mark, vmod, nn, num, prep, appos, mwe, mod, number, neg, advcl, rcmod
arg	agent, iobj, dobj, acomp, pcomp, pobj, ccomp, arg, subj, csubj, obj, xcomp, nsubj
aux	aux, cop
sdep	xsubj, sdep
Universal dependencies	
core	iobj, dobj, ccomp, csubj, obj, xcomp, nsubj
ncore	discourse, cop, advmod, dislocated, vocative, aux, advcl, mark, obl, expl
nom	case, nmod, acl, neg, appos, det, amod, nummod
coord	cc, conj
special	goeswith, reparandum, orphan
loose	parataxis, list
mwe	compound, mwe, flat
other	punct, dep, root

Table 1: Simplified Stanford and Universal dependency labels. For simplified dependencies, basic labels are collapsed into the simplified label shown in this table. (Relations not found in this table were left as is.)

similarity. We also investigate how these differences impact word embedding performance at word similarity rankings and two downstream tasks: question-type classification and named entity recognition.

2 Method

In this work, we explore the effect of two dependency annotation schemes on the resulting embeddings. Each scheme is evaluated in five levels of enhancement. These embeddings are compared to embeddings trained with linear contexts using the continuous bag of words (CBOW) with a context window of $k = 2$ and $k = 5$, and Skip-Gram contexts with and without subword information. These configurations are summarized in Figure 1.

Two dependency annotation schemes for English are Stanford dependencies (De Marneffe and Manning, 2008b) and Universal dependencies (Nivre et al., 2016). Stanford dependencies are tailored to English text, including dependencies that are not necessarily relevant cross-lingually (e.g. a label *prt* for particles like *up* in *pick up*). Universal dependencies are more generalized and designed to work cross-lingually. Many structures are similar between the two schemes, but important differences exist. For instance, in Stanford dependencies, prepositions head their phrase and depend on the modified word (*in* is the

head of *in Kansas*), whereas in universal dependencies, prepositions depend on the prepositional object (*Kansas* dominates *in*). Intuitively, these differences should have a moderate effect on the resulting embeddings because different words will be in a given word's context.

We also investigate five levels of enhancement for each dependency scheme. *Basic* dependencies are the core dependency structure provided by the scheme. *Simplified* dependencies are more coarse basic dependencies, collapsing similar labels into rough classes. The categories are based off of the Stanford Typed Dependencies Manual (De Marneffe and Manning, 2008a) and the Universal Dependency Typology (De Marneffe et al., 2014), and are listed in Table 1. Note that the two dependency schemes organize the relations in different ways, and thus the two types of simplified dependencies represent slightly different structures. The *unlabeled* dependency context removes all labels, and just captures syntactically adjacent tokens.

Enhanced and *Enhanced++* dependencies (Schuster and Manning, 2016) address some practical dependency distance issues by extending basic dependency edges. Enhanced dependencies augment modifiers and conjuncts with their parents' labels, propagate governors and dependents for indirectly governed arguments, and add subjects to controlled verbs.

Enhanced++ dependencies allow for the deletion of edges to better capture English phenomena, including partitives and light noun constructions, multi-word prepositions, conjoined prepositions, and relative pronouns.

3 Experimental Setup

We use the Stanford CoreNLP parser[1] to parse basic, Enhanced, and Enhanced++ dependencies. We use the Stanford english_SD model to parse Stanford dependencies (trained on the Penn Treebank) and english_UD model to parse Universal dependencies (trained on the Universal Dependencies Corpus for English). We acknowledge that differences in both the size of the training data (Penn Treebank is larger than the Universal Dependency Corpus for English), and the accuracy of the parse can have an effect on our overall performance. We used our own converter to generate simple dependencies based on the rules shown in Table 1. We use the modified `word2vecf` software[2] Levy and Goldberg (2014) that works with arbitrary embedding contexts to train dependency-based word embeddings.

As baselines, we train the following linear-context embeddings using the original `word2vec` software:[3] CBOW with $k = 2$, CBOW with $k = 5$, and Skip-Gram. We also train enriched Skip-Gram embeddings including subword information (Bojanowski et al., 2016) using fastText.[4]

For all embeddings, we use a cleaned recent dump of English Wikipedia (November 2017, 4.3B tokens) as training data. We evaluate each on the following tasks:

Similarity over Relatedness Akin to the quantitative analysis done by Levy and Goldberg (2014), we test to see how well each approach ranks similar items above related items. Given pairs of similar and related words, we rank each word pair by the cosine similarity of the corresponding word embeddings, and report the area-under-curve (AUC) of the resulting precision-recall curve. We use the labeled WordSim-353 (Agirre et al., 2009; Finkelstein et al., 2001) and the Chiarello dataset (Chiarello et al., 1990) as a source of similar and related word pairs. For WordSim-353,

we only consider pairs with similarity/relatedness scores of at least 5/10, yielding 90 similar pairs and 147 related pairs. For Chiarello, we disregard pairs that are marked as both similar and related, yielding 48 similar pairs and 48 related pairs.

Ranked Similarity This evaluation uses a list of word pairs that are ranked by degree of functional similarity. For each word pair, we calculate the cosine similarity, and compare the ranking to that of the human-annotated list using the Spearman correlation. We use SimLex-999 (Hill et al., 2016) as a ranking of functional similarity. Since this dataset distinguishes between nouns, adjectives, and verbs, we report individual correlations in addition to the overall correlation.

Question-type Classification (QC) We use an existing QC implementation[5] that uses a bidirectional LSTM. We train the model with 20 epochs, and report the average accuracy over 10 runs for each set of embeddings. We train and evaluate using the TREC QC dataset (Li and Roth, 2002). We modified the approach to use fixed (non-trainable) embeddings, allowing us to compare the impact of each embedding type.

Named Entity Recognition (NER) We use the Dernoncourt et al. (2017) NER implementation[6] that uses a bidirectional LSTM. Training consists of a maximum of 100 epochs, with early stopping after 10 consecutive epochs with no improvement to validation performance. We evaluate NER using the F1 score on the CoNLL NER dataset (Tjong Kim Sang and De Meulder, 2003). Like the QC task, we use a non-trainable embedding layer.

4 Results

4.1 Similarity over Relatedness

The results for the WordSim-353 (WS353) and Chiarello datasets are given in Table 2a. For the WS353 evaluation, notice that the Enhanced dependencies for both Universal and Stanford dependencies outperform the others in each scheme. Even the poorest-performing level of enhancement (unlabeled), however, yields a considerable gain over the linear contexts. Both Skip-Gram variants yield the worst performance, indicating that they

---

[1] `stanfordnlp.github.io/CoreNLP/`
[2] `bitbucket.org/yoavgo/word2vecf`
[3] `code.google.com/p/word2vec/`
[4] `github.com/facebookresearch/fastText`
[5] `github.com/zhegan27/sentence_classification`
[6] `github.com/Franck-Dernoncourt/NeuroNER`

Embeddings	(a) Sim/rel (AUC)		(b) Ranked sim (Spearman)				(c) Downstream	
	WS353	Chiarello	Overall	Noun	Adj.	Verb	QC (Acc)	NER (F1)
Universal embeddings								
Unlabeled	0.786	0.711	0.370	0.408	0.484	0.252	0.915	0.877
Simplified	0.805	0.774	0.394	0.420	0.475	0.309	0.913	0.870
Basic	0.801	0.761	0.391	0.421	0.451	0.331	0.920	0.876
Enhanced	**0.823**	**0.792**	0.398	0.416	0.473	**0.350**	0.915	0.875
Enhanced++	0.820	0.791	0.396	0.416	0.461	0.348	0.917	0.882
Stanford embeddings								
Unlabeled	0.790	0.741	0.382	0.414	**0.507**	0.256	0.911	0.870
Simplified	0.793	0.748	0.393	0.416	0.501	0.297	**0.923**	0.873
Basic	0.808	0.769	**0.402**	**0.422**	0.494	0.341	0.910	0.865
Enhanced	0.817	0.755	0.399	0.420	0.482	0.338	0.911	0.871
Enhanced++	0.810	0.764	0.398	0.417	0.496	0.346	0.918	0.878
Baselines (linear contexts)								
CBOW, k=2	0.696	0.537	0.311	0.355	0.338	0.252	0.913	0.885
CBOW, k=5	0.701	0.524	0.309	0.353	0.358	0.258	0.899	0.893
Skip-Gram	0.617	0.543	0.264	0.304	0.368	0.135	0.898	0.881
SG + Subword	0.615	0.456	0.324	0.358	0.451	0.166	0.897	**0.887**

Table 2: Results of various dependency-based word embeddings, and baseline linear contexts at (a) similarity over relatedness, (b) ranked similarity, and (c) downstream tasks of question classification and named entity recognition.

capture relatedness better than similarity. For the Chiarello evaluation, the linear contexts perform even worse, while the Enhanced Universal embeddings again outperform the other approaches.

These results reinforce the Levy and Goldberg (2014) findings that dependency-based word embeddings do a better job at distinguishing similarity rather than relatedness because it holds for multiple dependency schemes and levels of enhancement. The Enhanced universal embeddings outperformed the other settings for both datasets. For Chiarello, the margin between the two is statistically significant, whereas for WS353 it is not. This might be due to the fact that the the Chiarello dataset consists of manually-selected pairs that exhibit similarity or relatedness, whereas the settings for WS353 allow for some marginally related or similar terms through (e.g., *size* is related to *prominence*, and *monk* is similar to *oracle*).

4.2 Ranked Similarity

Spearman correlation results for ranked similarity on the SimLex-999 dataset are reported in Table 2b. *Overall* results indicate the performance on the entire collection. In this environment, basic Stanford embeddings outperform all other embeddings explored. This is an interesting result because it shows that the additional dependency labels added for Enhanced embeddings (e.g. for conjunction) do not improve the ranking performance. This trend does not hold for Universal embeddings, with the enhanced versions outperforming the basic embeddings.

All dependency-based word embeddings significantly outperform the baseline methods (10 folds, paired t-test, $p < 0.05$). Furthermore, the unlabeled Universal embeddings performed significantly worse than the simplified Universal, and the simplified, basic, and Enhanced Stanford dependencies, indicating that dependency labels are important for ranking.

Table 2b also includes results for word pairs by part of speech individually. As the majority category, Noun-Noun scores ($n = 666$) mimic the behavior of the overall scores, with basic Stanford embeddings outperforming other approaches. Interestingly, Adjective-Adjective pairs ($n = 111$) performed best with unlabeled Stanford dependencies. Since unlabeled also performs best among universal embeddings, this indicates that dependency labels are not useful for adjective similarity, possibly because adjectives have comparatively few ambiguous functions. Verb-Verb pairs

Embeddings	QC (Acc)	NER (F1)
Universal embeddings		
Unbound	0.921 (+0.007)	0.887 (+0.000)
Simplified	0.929 (+0.016)	0.883 (+0.013)
Basic	0.920 (+0.000)	0.891 (+0.015)
Enhanced	0.923 (+0.008)	0.886 (+0.010)
Enhanced++	0.927 (+0.010)	0.890 (+0.008)
Stanford embeddings		
Unbound	0.926 (+0.015)	0.879 (+0.009)
Simplified	**0.933 (+0.010)**	0.877 (+0.004)
Basic	0.927 (+0.017)	0.885 (+0.020)
Enhanced	0.923 (+0.013)	0.885 (+0.014)
Enhanced++	0.929 (+0.011)	0.884 (+0.006)
Baselines (linear contexts)		
CBOW, k=2	0.921 (+0.008)	0.892 (+0.007)
CBOW, k=5	0.925 (+0.026)	0.892 (+0.001)
Skip-Gram	0.914 (+0.016)	0.887 (+0.006)
SG + Subword	0.919 (+0.022)	**0.896 (+0.009)**

Table 3: Performance results when embeddings are further trained for the particular task. The number in parentheses gives the performance improvement compared to when embeddings are not trainable (Table 2c).

($n = 222$) performed best with Enhanced universal embeddings. This indicates that the augmentation of governors, dependents, and subjects of controlled verbs is particularly useful given the universal dependency scheme, and less so for the English-specific Stanford dependency scheme. Both Stanford and universal unlabeled dependencies performed significantly worse compared to all basic, Enhanced, and Enhanced++ dependencies (5 folds, paired t-test, $p < 0.05$). This indicates that dependency labels are particularly important for verb similarity.

4.3 Downstream Tasks

We present results for question-type classification and named entity recognition in Table 2c. Neither task appears to greatly benefit from embeddings that favor similarity over relatedness or that can rank based on functional similarity effectively without the enhanced sentence feature representations explored by Komninos and Manandhar (2016). We compare the results using to the performance of models with embedding training enabled in Table 3. As expected, this improves the results because the training captures task-specific information in the embeddings. Generally, the worst-performing embeddings gained the most (e.g., CBOW $k = 5$ for QC, and basic Stanford for NER). However, the simplified Stanford embeddings and the embeddings with subword information still outperform the other approaches for QC and NER, respectively. This indicates that the initial state of the embeddings is still important to an extent, and cannot be learned fully for a given task.

5 Conclusion

In this work, we expanded previous work by Levy and Goldberg (2014) by looking into variations of dependency-based word embeddings. We investigated two dependency schemes: Stanford and Universal embeddings. Each scheme was explored at various levels of enhancement, ranging from unlabeled contexts to Enhanced++ dependencies. All variations yielded significant improvements over linear contexts in most circumstances. For certain subtasks (e.g. Verb-Verb similarity), enhanced dependencies improved results more strongly, supporting current trends in the universal dependency community to promote enhanced representations. Given the disparate results across POS tags, future work could also evaluate ways of using a hybrid approach with different contexts for different parts of speech, or using concatenated embeddings.

References

Samira Abnar, Rasyan Ahmed, Max Mijnheer, and Willem Zuidema. 2018. Experiential, distributional and dependency-based word embeddings have complementary roles in decoding brain activity. In *Proceedings of the 8th Workshop on Cognitive Modeling and Computational Linguistics (CMCL 2018)*. Salt Lake City, UT, pages 57–66.

Eneko Agirre, Enrique Alfonseca, Keith Hall, Jana Kravalova, Marius Pasca, and Aitor Soroa. 2009. A study on similarity and relatedness using distributional and wordnet-based approaches. In *Proceedings of HLT-NAACL 2009*. Boulder, CO, pages 19–27.

Marco Baroni and Alessandro Lenci. 2010. Distributional memory: A general framework for corpus-based semantics. *Comput. Linguist.* 36(4).

Piotr Bojanowski, Edouard Grave, Armand Joulin, and Tomas Mikolov. 2016. Enriching word vectors with subword information. *arXiv preprint arXiv:1607.04606* .

Christine Chiarello, Curt Burgess, Lorie Richards, and Alma Pollock. 1990. Semantic and associative priming in the cerebral hemispheres: Some words do, some words don't sometimes, some places. *Brain and language* 38(1):75–104.

Marie-Catherine De Marneffe, Timothy Dozat, Natalia Silveira, Katri Haverinen, Filip Ginter, Joakim Nivre, and Christopher D Manning. 2014. Universal Stanford dependencies: A cross-linguistic typology. In *Proceedings of LREC 2014*. Reykjavik, volume 14, pages 4585–4592.

Marie-Catherine De Marneffe and Christopher D Manning. 2008a. Stanford typed dependencies manual. Technical report, Stanford University.

Marie-Catherine De Marneffe and Christopher D Manning. 2008b. The Stanford typed dependencies representation. In *Coling 2008: proceedings of the workshop on cross-framework and cross-domain parser evaluation*. pages 1–8.

Franck Dernoncourt, Ji Young Lee, and Peter Szolovits. 2017. NeuroNER: an easy-to-use program for named-entity recognition based on neural networks. In *Proceedings of EMNLP 2017*. Copenhagen.

Lev Finkelstein, Evgeniy Gabrilovich, Yossi Matias, Ehud Rivlin, Zach Solan, Gadi Wolfman, and Eytan Ruppin. 2001. Placing search in context: The concept revisited. In *Proceedings of the 10th international conference on World Wide Web*. pages 406–414.

Felix Hill, Roi Reichart, and Anna Korhonen. 2016. Simlex-999: Evaluating semantic models with (genuine) similarity estimation. *Computational Linguistics* 41(4).

Kai Hui, Andrew Yates, Klaus Berberich, and Gerard de Melo. 2017. PACRR: A position-aware neural IR model for relevance matching. In *Proceedings of EMNLP 2017*. Copenhagen.

Alexandros Komninos and Suresh Manandhar. 2016. Dependency based embeddings for sentence classification tasks. In *Proceedings of HLT-NAACL*. San Diego, CA, pages 1490–1500.

Omer Levy and Yoav Goldberg. 2014. Dependency-based word embeddings. In *Proceedings of ACL 2014*. Baltimore, MD, pages 302–308.

Bofang Li, Tao Liu, Zhe Zhao, Buzhou Tang, Aleksandr Drozd, Anna Rogers, and Xiaoyong Du. 2017. Investigating different syntactic context types and context representations for learning word embeddings. In *Proceedings of EMNLP 2017*. Copenhagen, pages 2411–2421.

Xin Li and Dan Roth. 2002. Learning question classifiers. In *Proceedings of COLING 2002*. Taipei, pages 1–7.

Tomas Mikolov, Kai Chen, Greg Corrado, and Jeffrey Dean. 2013. Efficient estimation of word representations in vector space. *CoRR abs/1301.3781* .

Joakim Nivre, Marie-Catherine de Marneffe, Filip Ginter, Yoav Goldberg, Jan Hajic, Christopher D Manning, Ryan T McDonald, Slav Petrov, Sampo Pyysalo, Natalia Silveira, et al. 2016. Universal dependencies v1: A multilingual treebank collection. In *Proceedings of LREC 2016*. Portorož, Slovenia.

Sebastian Pado and Mirella Lapata. 2007. Dependency-based construction of semantic space models. *Computational Linguistics* .

Jeffrey Pennington, Richard Socher, and Christopher Manning. 2014. Glove: Global vectors for word representation. In *Proceedings of EMNLP 2014*. Doha, Qatar, pages 1532–1543.

Gábor Recski, Eszter Iklódi, Katalin Pajkossy, and Andras Kornai. 2016. Measuring semantic similarity of words using concept networks. In *Proceedings of the 1st Workshop on Representation Learning for NLP*. Berlin, Germany, pages 193–200.

Sebastian Schuster and Christopher D Manning. 2016. Enhanced English universal dependencies: An improved representation for natural language understanding tasks. In *Proceedings of LREC 2016*.

Erik F Tjong Kim Sang and Fien De Meulder. 2003. Introduction to the CoNLL-2003 shared task: Language-independent named entity recognition. In *Proceedings of HLT-NAACL 2003*. volume 4, pages 142–147.

Will Y Zou, Richard Socher, Daniel Cer, and Christopher D Manning. 2013. Bilingual word embeddings for phrase-based machine translation. In *Proceedings of EMNLP 2013*. Seattle, WA, pages 1393–1398.

Learning Word Embeddings for Data Sparse and Sentiment Rich Data Sets

Prathusha Kameswara Sarma
Electrical and Computer Engineering
UW - Madison

Abstract

This research proposal describes two algorithms that are aimed at learning word embeddings for data sparse and sentiment rich data sets. The goal is to use word embeddings adapted for domain specific data sets in downstream applications such as sentiment classification. The first approach learns word embeddings in a supervised fashion via SWESA (Supervised Word Embeddings for Sentiment Analysis), an algorithm for sentiment analysis on data sets that are of modest size. SWESA leverages document labels to jointly learn polarity-aware word embeddings and a classifier to classify unseen documents. In the second approach domain adapted (DA) word embeddings are learned by exploiting the specificity of domain specific data sets and the breadth of generic word embeddings. The new embeddings are formed by aligning corresponding word vectors using Canonical Correlation Analysis (CCA) or the related nonlinear Kernel CCA. Experimental results on binary sentiment classification tasks using both approaches for standard data sets are presented.

1 Introduction

Generic word embeddings such as Glove and word2vec (Pennington et al., 2014; Mikolov et al., 2013) which are pre-trained on large sets of raw text, in addition to having desirable structural properties have demonstrated remarkable success when used as features to a supervised learner in various applications such as the sentiment classification of text documents. There are, however, many applications with domain specific vocabularies and relatively small amounts of data. The performance of word embedding approaches in such applications is limited, since word embeddings pre-trained on generic corpora do not capture domain specific semantics/knowledge, while embeddings trained on small data sets are of low quality. Since word embeddings are used to initialize most algorithms for sentiment analysis etc, generic word embeddings further make for poor initialization of algorithms for tasks on domain specific data sets.

A concrete example of a small-sized domain specific corpus is the Substances User Disorders (SUDs) data set (Quanbeck et al., 2014; Litvin et al., 2013), which contains messages from discussion forums for people with substance addictions. These forums are part of mobile health intervention treatments that encourages participants to engage in sobriety-related discussions. The aim with digital intervention treatments is to analyze the daily content of participants' messages and predict relapse risk. This data is both domain specific and limited in size. Other examples include customer support tickets reporting issues with taxi-cab services, reviews of restaurants and movies, discussions by special interest groups, and political surveys. In general they are common in fields where words have different sentiments from what they would have elsewhere.

Such data sets present significant challenges for algorithms based on word embeddings. First, the data is on specific topics and has a very different distribution from generic corpora, so pre-trained generic word embeddings such as those trained on Common Crawl or Wikipedia are unlikely to yield accurate results in downstream tasks. When performing sentiment classification using pre-trained word embeddings, differences in domains of training and test data sets limit the applicability of the embedding algorithm. For example, in SUDs, dis-

Proceedings of NAACL-HLT 2018: Student Research Workshop, pages 46–53
New Orleans, Louisiana, June 2 - 4, 2018. ©2017 Association for Computational Linguistics

cussions are focused on topics related to recovery and addiction; the sentiment behind the word 'party' may be very different in a dating context than in a substance abuse context. Similarly seemingly neutral words such as 'holidays', 'alcohol' etc are indicative of stronger negative sentiment in these domains, while words like 'clean' are indicative of stronger positive sentiment. Thus domain specific vocabularies and word semantics may be a problem for pre-trained sentiment classification models (Blitzer et al., 2007).

Second, there is insufficient data to completely train a word embedding. The SUD data set consists of a few hundred people and only a fraction of these are active (Firth et al., 2017) and (Naslund et al., 2015). This results in a small data set of text messages available for analysis. Furthermore, the content is generated spontaneously on a day to day basis, and language use is informal and unstructured. Running the generic word embedding constructions algorithms on such a data set leads to very noisy outputs that are not suitable as input for downstream applications like sentiment classification. Fine-tuning the generic word embedding also leads to noisy outputs due to the highly nonconvex training objective and the small amount of the data.

This proposal briefly describes two possible solutions to address this problem. Section 3 describes a Canonical Correlation Analysis (CCA) based approach to obtain domain adapted word embeddings. Section 2 describes an biconvex optimization algorithm that jointly learns polarity aware word embeddings and a classifier. Section 4 discusses results from both approaches and outlines potential future work.

2 Supervised Word Embeddings for Sentiment Analysis on Small Sized Data Sets

Supervised Word Embedding for Sentiment Analysis (SWESA) algorithm is an iterative algorithm that minimizes a cost function for both a classifier and word embeddings under unit norm constraint on the word vectors. SWESA incorporates document label information while learning word embeddings from small sized data sets.

2.1 Mathematical model and optimization

Text documents d_i in this framework are represented as a weighted linear combination of words in a given vocabulary. Weights ϕ_i used are term frequencies. SWESA aims to find vector representations for words, and by extension of text documents such that applying a nonlinear transformation f to the product $(\theta^\top \mathbf{W} \phi)$ results in a binary label y indicating the polarity of the document. Mathematically we assume that,

$$\mathbb{P}[Y = 1 | d = \mathbf{W}\phi, \theta] = f(\theta^\top \mathbf{W} \phi) \quad (1)$$

for some function f The optimization problem in (1) can be solved as the following minimization problem,

$$J(\theta, \mathbf{W}) \stackrel{\text{def}}{=} \frac{-1}{N} \Big[\mathrm{C}_+ \sum_{y_i = +1} \log \mathbb{P}(Y = y_i | \mathbf{W}\phi_i, \theta) \\ + \mathrm{C}_- \sum_{y_i = -1} \log \mathbb{P}(Y = y_i | \mathbf{W}\phi_i, \theta) \Big] \\ + \lambda_\theta \| \theta \|_2^2.$$

This optimization problem can now be written as

$$\min_{\substack{\theta \in \mathbb{R}^k, \\ \mathbf{W} \in \mathbb{R}^{k \times V}}} J(\theta, \mathbf{W}) \quad (2)$$

$$\text{s.t. } \| \mathbf{w}_j \|_2 = 1 \ \forall j = 1, \dots V.$$

Class imbalance is accounted for by using misclassification costs $\mathrm{C}_-, \mathrm{C}_+$ as in (Lin et al., 2002). The unit norm constraint in the optimization problem shown in (2) is enforced on word embeddings to discourage degenerate solutions of $\mathbf{w}_j$. This optimization problem is bi-convex. Algorithm 1 shows the algorithm that we use to solve the optimization problem in (2). This algorithm is an alternating minimization procedure that initializes the word embedding matrix $\mathbf{W}$ with $\mathbf{W}_0$ and then alternates between minimizing the objective function w.r.t. the weight vector θ and the word embeddings $\mathbf{W}$.

The probability model used in this work is logistic regression. Under this assumption the minimization problem in Step 3 of Algorithm 1 is a standard logistic regression problem. In order to solve the optimization problem in line 4 of Algorithm 1 a projected stochastic gradient descent (SGD) with suffix averaging (Rakhlin et al., 2011). Algorithm 2 implements the SGD algorithm (with stochastic gradients instead of full gradients) for solving the optimization problem in step 4 of Algorithm 1. $\mathbf{W}_0$ is initialized via pre-trained word2vec embeddings and Latent Semantic Analysis (LSA) (Dumais, 2004) based word

Algorithm 1 Supervised Word Embeddings for Sentiment Analysis (SWESA)

Require: $\mathbf{W}_0$, Φ, C_+, C_-, λ_θ, $0 < k < V$, Labels: $\mathbf{y} = [y_1, \ldots, y_N]$, Iterations: $T > 0$,

1: Initialize $\mathbf{W} = \mathbf{W}_0$.
2: **for** $t = 1, \ldots, T$ **do**
3:    Solve $\theta_t \leftarrow \arg\min_\theta J(\theta, \mathbf{W}_{t-1})$.
4:    Solve $\mathbf{W}_t \leftarrow \arg\min_\mathbf{W} J(\theta_t, \mathbf{W})$.
5: **end for**
6: Return $\theta_T, \mathbf{W}_T$

Algorithm 2 Stochastic Gradient Descent for $\mathbf{W}$

Require: $\theta, \gamma, \mathbf{W}_0$, Labels: $\mathbf{y} = [y_1, \ldots, y_N]$, Iterations: N, step size: $\eta > 0$, and suffix parameter: $0 < \tau \le N$.

1: Randomly shuffle the dataset.
2: **for** $t = 1, \ldots, N$ **do**
3:    Set $C_t = C_+$ if $y_t = +1$, $C_t = C_-$ if $y_t = -1$.
4:    $\mathbf{W}_{t+1} = \mathbf{W}_t - \frac{\eta C_t}{1 + e^{y_i(\theta^\top \mathbf{W} \phi_i)}} \times (-y_i \, \theta \, \phi_i^\top)$
5:    $\mathbf{W}_{t+1,j} = \mathbf{W}_{t+1,j} / \|\mathbf{W}_{t+1,j}\|_2 \ \forall j = 1, 2, \ldots, V$
6:    $\eta \leftarrow \frac{\eta}{t}$
7: **end for**
8: Return $\mathbf{W} = \frac{1}{\tau} \sum_{t=N-\tau}^{N} \mathbf{W}_t$

embeddings obtained form a matrix of term frequencies from the given data. Dimension k of word vectors is determined empirically by selecting the dimension that provides the best performance across all pairs of training and test data sets.

2.2 Experiment evaluation and results

SWESA is evaluated against the following baselines and data sets,

Datasets: 3 balanced data sets (Kotzias et al., 2015) of 1000 reviews from Amazon, IMDB and Yelp with binary 'positive' and 'negative' sentiment labels are considered. One imbalanced data set with 2500 text messages obtained from a study involving subjects with alcohol addiction is considered. Only 8% of the messages are indicative of 'relapse risk' while the rest are 'benign'. Note that this imbalance influences the performance metrics and can be seen by comparing against the scores achieved by the balanced data sets. Additional information such as number of word tokens etc can

Data Set	Method	Avg Precision	Avg AUC
Yelp	SWESA (LSA)	78.09±2.84	86.06±2.4
	SWESA (word2vec)	**78.35±4.62**	**86.03±3.5**
	TS (LSA)	76.27±3.0	83.05±5.0
	TS (word2vec)	65.22±4.4	69.08±3.5
	NB	70.31±5.6	57.07±3.3
	RNTN (pre-trained)	83.31±1.1	-
	RNTN (re-trained)	51.15±4.3	-
Amazon	SWESA (LSA)	80.31±3.3	87.54±4.2
	SWESA (word2vec)	**80.36±2.8**	**87.19±3.3**
	TS (LSA)	77.32±4.6	85.00±6.2
	TS (word2vec)	71.09±6.2	77.09±5.3
	NB	72.54±6.4	61.16±4.5
	RNTN (pre-trained)	82.84±0.6	-
	RNTN (re-trained)	49.15±2.1	-
IMDB	SWESA (LSA)	76.40±5.2	81.08±7.6
	SWESA (word2vec)	**77.27±5.4**	**81.04±6.8**
	TS (LSA)	70.36±5.5	77.54±6.8
	TS (word2vec)	56.87±7.6	59.34±8.9
	NB	73.31±5.6	48.40±2.9
	RNTN (pre-trained)	80.88±0.7	-
	RNTN (re-trained)	53.95±1.9	-
A-CHESS	**SWESA (LSA)**	**35.80±2.5**	**83.80±3.1**
	SWESA (word2vec)	35.40±2.0	83.40±2.6
	TS (LSA)	32.20±3.2	**83.80±3.1**
	TS (word2vec)	23.60±2.4	68.00±1.2
	NB	30.30±3.8	45.23±3.3
	RNTN (pre-trained)	-	-
	RNTN (re-trained)	-	-

Table 1: This table shows results from a standard sentiment classification task on all four data sets. Results from SWESA are in boldface and results from pre-trained RNTN are in blue.

be found in the supplemental section.

- **Naive Bayes:** This is a standard baseline that is best suited for classification in small sized data sets.

- **Recursive Neural Tensor Network:** RNTN is a dependency parser based sentiment analysis algorithm. Both pre-trained RNTN and the RNTN algorithm retrained on the data sets considered here are used to obtain classification accuracy. Note that with the RNTN we do not get probabilities for classes hence we do not compute AUC.

- **Two-Step (TS):** In this set up, embeddings obtained via word2vec on the test data sets and LSA are used to obtain document representation via weighted averaging. Documents are then classified using a Logistic Regressor.

Hyperparameters: Parameters such as dimension of word embeddings, regularization on the logistic regressor etc are determined via 10-fold cross validation.

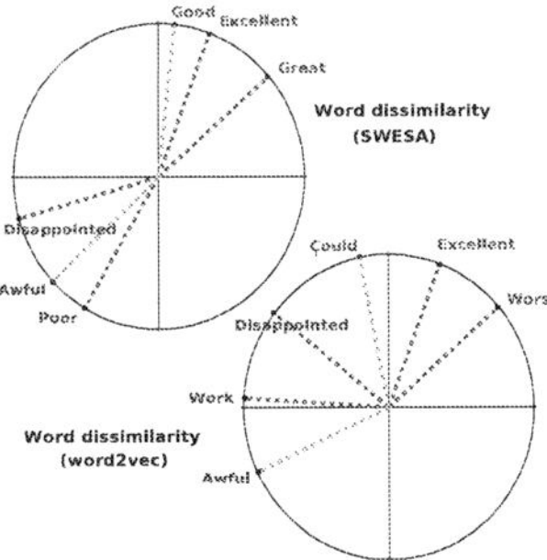

Figure 1: *This figure depicts word embeddings on a unit circle. Cosine angle between embeddings is used to show dissimilar word pairs learned via SWESA and word2vec.*

Results: Average Precision and AUC are reported in table 2. Note that, the word2vec embeddings used in TS are obtained by retraining the word2vec algorithm on the test data sets. To reinforce the point that retraining neural network based algorithms on sparse data sets depreciates their performance, results from pre-trained and retrained RNTN are presented to further support this fact. Since SWESA makes use of document labels when learning word embeddings, resulting word embeddings are polarity aware. Using cosine similarity, word antonym pairs are observed. Given words 'Good,' 'fair' and 'Awful,' the antonym pair 'Good/Awful' is determined via cosine similarity between $\mathbf{w}_{Good}$ and $\mathbf{w}_{Awful}$. Figure 1 shows a small sample of word embeddings learned on the Amazon data set by SWESA and word2vec. The cosine similarity (angle) between the most dissimilar words is calculated and words are depicted as points on the unit circle. These examples illustrate that SWESA captures sentiment polarity at word embedding level despite limited data.

3 Domain Adapted Word Embeddings for Improved Sentiment Classification

While SWESA learns embeddings from domain specific data alone, this approach proposes a method for obtaining high quality Domain Adapted (DA) embeddings by combining generic embeddings and Domain Specific (DS) embeddings via CCA/KCCA. Generic embeddings are trained on large corpora and do not capture domain specific semantics, while DS embeddings are obtained from the domain specific data set via algorithms such as Latent Semantic Analysis (LSA) or other embedding methods. Thus DA embeddings exploit the breath of generic embeddings and the specificity of DS embeddings. The two sets of embeddings are combined using a linear CCA (Hotelling, 1936) or a nonlinear kernel CCA (KCCA) (Hardoon et al., 2004). They are projected along the directions of maximum correlation, and a new (DA) embedding is formed by averaging the projections of the generic embeddings and DS embeddings. The DA embeddings are then evaluated in a sentiment classification setting. Empirically, it is shown that the combined DA embeddings improve substantially over the generic embeddings, DS embeddings and a concatenation-SVD (conc-SVD) based baseline.

3.1 Brief description of CCA/KCCA

Let $\mathbf{W}_{DS} \in \mathbb{R}^{|V_{DS}| \times d_1}$ be the matrix whose columns are the domain specific word embeddings (obtained by, e.g., running the LSA algorithm on the domain specific data set), where V_{DS} is its vocabulary and d_1 is the dimension of the embeddings. Similarly, let $\mathbf{W}_G \in \mathbb{R}^{|V_G| \times d_2}$ be the matrix of generic word embeddings (obtained by, e.g., running the GloVe algorithm on the Common Crawl data), where V_G is the vocabulary and d_2 is the dimension of the embeddings. Let $V_\cap = V_{DS} \cap V_G$. Let $\mathbf{w}_{i,DS}$ be the domain specific embedding of the word $i \in V_\cap$, and $\mathbf{w}_{i,G}$ be its generic embedding. For one dimensional CCA, let ϕ_{DS} and ϕ_G be the projection directions of $\mathbf{w}_{i,DS}$ and $\mathbf{w}_{i,G}$ respectively. Then the projected values are,

$$\bar{w}_{i,DS} = \mathbf{w}_{i,DS}\,\phi_{DS}$$
$$\bar{w}_{i,G} = \mathbf{w}_{i,G}\,\phi_G. \qquad (3)$$

CCA maximizes the correlation ρ between $\bar{w}_{i,DS}$ and $\bar{w}_{i,G}$ to obtain ϕ_{DS} and ϕ_G such that

$$\rho(\phi_{DS}, \phi_G) = \max_{\phi_{DS}, \phi_G} \frac{\mathbb{E}[\bar{w}_{i,DS}\bar{w}_{i,G}]}{\sqrt{\mathbb{E}[\bar{w}_{i,DS}^2]\mathbb{E}[\bar{w}_{i,G}^2]}} \qquad (4)$$

where the expectation is over all words $i \in V_\cap$.

The d-dimensional CCA with $d > 1$ can be defined recursively. Suppose the first $d - 1$ pairs of canonical variables are defined. Then the dth pair is defined by seeking vectors maximizing the same correlation function subject to the constraint that they be uncorrelated with the first $d - 1$ pairs. Equivalently, matrices of projection vectors $\boldsymbol{\Phi}_{DS} \in \mathbb{R}^{d_1 \times d}$ and $\boldsymbol{\Phi}_G \in \mathbb{R}^{d_2 \times d}$ are obtained for all vectors in $\mathbf{W}_{DS}$ and $\mathbf{W}_G$ where $d \leq$

Data Set		Embedding	Avg Precision	Avg F-score	Avg AUC
Yelp	$\mathbf{W}_{DA}$	KCCA(Glv, LSA)	85.36± 2.8	81.89±2.8	82.57±1.3
		CCA(Glv, LSA)	83.69± 4.7	79.48±2.4	80.33±2.9
		KCCA(w2v, LSA)	87.45± 1.2	83.36±1.2	84.10±0.9
		CCA(w2v, LSA)	84.52± 2.3	80.02±2.6	81.04±2.1
		KCCA(GlvCC, LSA)	**88.11± 3.0**	**85.35±2.7**	**85.80±2.4**
		CCA(GlvCC, LSA)	83.69± 3.5	78.99±4.2	80.03±3.7
		KCCA(w2v, DSw2v)	78.09± 1.7	76.04±1.7	76.66±1.5
		CCA(w2v, DSw2v)	86.22± 3.5	84.35±2.4	84.65±2.2
		concSVD(Glv, LSA)	80.14± 2.6	78.50±3.0	78.92±2.7
		concSVD(w2v, LSA)	85.11± 2.3	83.51±2.2	83.80±2.0
		concSVD(GlvCC, LSA)	84.20± 3.7	80.39±3.7	80.83±3.9
	$\mathbf{W}_G$	GloVe	77.13± 4.2	72.32±7.9	74.17±5.0
		GloVe-CC	82.10± 3.5	76.74±3.4	78.17±2.7
		word2vec	82.80± 3.5	78.28±3.5	79.35±3.1
	$\mathbf{W}_{DS}$	LSA	75.36± 5.4	71.17±4.3	72.57±4.3
		word2vec	73.08± 2.2	70.97±2.4	71.76±2.1
Amazon	$\mathbf{W}_{DA}$	KCCA(Glv, LSA)	86.30±1.9	83.00±2.9	83.39±3.2
		CCA(Glv, LSA)	84.68±2.4	82.27±2.2	82.78±1.7
		KCCA(w2v, LSA)	87.09±1.8	82.63±2.6	83.50±2.0
		CCA(w2v, LSA)	84.80±1.5	81.42±1.9	82.12±1.3
		KCCA(GlvCC, LSA)	**89.73±2.4**	85.47±2.4	85.56±2.6
		CCA(GlvCC, LSA)	85.67±2.3	83.83±2.3	84.21±2.1
		KCCA(w2v, DSw2v)	85.68±3.2	81.23±3.2	82.20±2.9
		CCA(w2v, DSw2v)	83.50±3.4	81.31±4.0	81.86±3.7
		concSVD(Glv, LSA)	82.36±2.0	81.30±3.5	81.51±2.5
		concSVD(w2v, LSA)	87.28±2.9	**86.17±2.5**	**86.42±2.0**
		concSVD(GlvCC, LSA)	84.93±1.6	77.81±2.3	79.52±1.7
	$\mathbf{W}_G$	GloVe	81.58±2.5	77.62±2.7	78.72±2.7
		GloVe-CC	79.91±2.7	81.63±2.8	81.46±2.6
		word2vec	84.55±1.9	80.52±2.5	81.45±2.0
	$\mathbf{W}_{DS}$	LSA	82.65±4.4	73.92±3.8	76.40±3.2
		word2vec	74.20±5.8	72.49±5.0	73.11±4.8
IMDB	DA	KCCA(Glv, LSA)	73.84±1.3	73.07±3.6	73.17±2.4
		CCA(Glv, LSA)	73.35±2.0	73.00±3.2	73.06±2.0
		KCCA(w2v, LSA)	**82.36±4.4**	**78.95±2.7**	**79.66±2.6**
		CCA(w2v, LSA)	80.66±4.5	75.95±4.5	77.23±3.8
		KCCA(GlvCC, LSA)	54.50±2.5	54.42±2.9	53.91±2.0
		CCA(GlvCC, LSA)	54.08±2.0	53.03±3.5	54.90±2.1
		KCCA(w2v, DSw2v)	60.65±3.5	58.95±3.2	58.95±3.7
		CCA(w2v, DSw2v)	58.47±2.7	57.62±3.0	58.03±3.9
		concSVD(Glv, LSA)	73.25±3.7	74.55±3.2	73.02±4.7
		concSVD(w2v, LSA)	53.87±2.2	51.77±5.8	53.54±1.9
		concSVD(GlvCC, LSA)	78.28±3.2	77.67±3.7	74.55±2.9
	$\mathbf{W}_G$	GloVe	64.44±2.6	65.18±3.5	64.62±2.6
		GloVe-CC	50.53±1.8	62.39±3.5	49.96±2.3
		word2vec	78.92±3.7	74.88±3.1	75.60±2.4
	$\mathbf{W}_{DS}$	LSA	67.92±1.7	69.79±5.3	69.71±3.8
		word2vec	56.87±3.6	56.04±3.1	59.53±8.9
A-CHESS	DA	KCCA(Glv, LSA)	32.07±1.3	39.32±2.5	**65.96±1.3**
		CCA(Glv, LSA)	32.70±1.5	35.48±4.2	62.15±2.9
		KCCA(w2v, LSA)	33.45±1.3	**39.81±1.0**	65.92±0.6
		CCA(w2v, LSA)	33.06±3.2	34.02±1.1	60.91±0.9
		KCCA(GlvCC, LSA)	**36.38±1.2**	34.71±4.8	**61.36±2.6**
		CCA(GlvCC, LSA)	32.11±2.9	36.85±4.4	62.99±3.1
		KCCA(w2v, DSw2v)	25.59±1.2	28.27±3.1	57.25±1.7
		CCA(w2v, DSw2v)	24.88±1.4	29.17±3.1	57.76±2.0
		concSVD(Glv, LSA)	27.27±2.9	34.45±3.0	61.59±2.3
		concSVD(w2v, LSA)	29.84±2.3	36.32±3.3	62.94±1.1
		concSVD(GlvCC, LSA)	28.09±1.9	35.06±1.4	62.13±2.6
	$\mathbf{W}_G$	GloVe	30.82±2.0	33.67±3.4	60.80±2.3
		GloVe-CC	38.13±0.8	27.45±3.1	57.49±1.2
		word2vec	32.67±2.9	31.72±1.6	59.64±0.5
	$\mathbf{W}_{DS}$	LSA	27.42±1.6	34.38±2.3	61.56±1.9
		word2vec	24.48±0.8	27.97±3.7	57.08±2.5

Table 2: This table shows results from the classification task using sentence embeddings obtained from weighted averaging of word embeddings. Metrics reported are average Precision, F-score and AUC and the corresponding standard deviations (STD). Best results are attained by KCCA (GlvCC, LSA) and are highlighted in boldface.

$\min \{d_1, d_2\}$. Embeddings obtained by $\bar{\mathbf{w}}_{i,DS} = \mathbf{w}_{i,DS}\,\mathbf{\Phi}_{DS}$ and $\bar{\mathbf{w}}_{i,G} = \mathbf{w}_{i,G}\,\mathbf{\Phi}_G$ are projections along the directions of maximum correlation.

The final domain adapted embedding for word i is given by $\hat{\mathbf{w}}_{i,DA} = \alpha\bar{\mathbf{w}}_{i,DS} + \beta\bar{\mathbf{w}}_{i,G}$, where the parameters α and β can be obtained by solving the

Data Set	Embedding	Avg Precision	Avg F-score	Avg AUC
Yelp	GlvCC	86.47±1.9	83.51±2.6	83.83±2.2
	KCCA(GlvCC, LSA)	**91.06±0.8**	**88.66±2.4**	**88.76±2.4**
	CCA(GlvCC, LSA)	86.26±1.4	82.61±1.1	83.99±0.8
	concSVD(GlvCC,LSA)	85.53±2.1	84.90±1.7	84.96±1.5
	RNTN	83.11±1.1	-	-
Amazon	GlvCC	87.93±2.7	82.41±3.3	83.24±2.8
	KCCA(GlvCC, LSA)	**90.56±2.1**	**86.52±2.0**	**86.74±1.9**
	CCA(GlvCC, LSA)	87.12±2.6	83.18±2.2	83.78±2.1
	concSVD(GlvCC, LSA)	85.73±1.9	85.19±2.4	85.17±2.6
	RNTN	82.84±0.6	-	-
IMDB	GlvCC	54.02±3.2	53.03±5.2	53.01±2.0
	KCCA(GlvCC, LSA)	59.76±7.3	**53.26±6.1**	56.46±3.4
	CCA(GlvCC, LSA)	53.62±1.6	50.62±5.1	**58.75±3.7**
	concSVD(GlvCC, LSA)	52.75±2.3	53.05±6.0	53.54±2.5
	RNTN	**80.88±0.7**	-	-
A-CHESS	GlvCC	52.21±5.1	**55.26±5.6**	**74.28±3.6**
	KCCA(GlvCC, LSA)	**55.37±5.5**	50.67±5.0	69.89±3.1
	CCA(GlvCC, LSA)	54.34±3.6	48.76±2.9	68.78±2.4
	concSVD(GlvCC, LSA)	40.41±4.2	44.75±5.2	68.13±3.8
	RNTN	-	-	-

Table 3: This table shows results obtained by using sentence embeddings from the InferSent encoder in the sentiment classification task. Metrics reported are average Precision, F-score and AUC along with the corresponding standard deviations (STD). Best results are obtained by KCCA (GlvCC, LSA) and are highlighted in boldface.

following optimization,

$$\min_{\alpha,\beta} \|\bar{\mathbf{w}}_{i,DS} - (\alpha\bar{\mathbf{w}}_{i,DS} + \beta\bar{\mathbf{w}}_{i,G})\|_2^2 +$$
$$\|\bar{\mathbf{w}}_{i,G} - (\alpha\bar{\mathbf{w}}_{i,DS} + \beta\bar{\mathbf{w}}_{i,G})\|_2^2. \quad (5)$$

Solving (5) gives a weighted combination with $\alpha = \beta = \frac{1}{2}$, i.e., the new vector is equal to the average of the two projections:

$$\hat{\mathbf{w}}_{i,DA} = \frac{1}{2}\bar{\mathbf{w}}_{i,DS} + \frac{1}{2}\bar{\mathbf{w}}_{i,G}. \quad (6)$$

Because of its linear structure, the CCA in (4) may not always capture the best relationships between the two matrices. To account for nonlinearities, a kernel function, which implicitly maps the data into a high dimensional feature space, can be applied. For example, given a vector $\mathbf{w} \in \mathbb{R}^d$, a kernel function K is written in the form of a feature map φ defined by $\varphi : \mathbf{w} = (\mathbf{w}_1, \ldots, \mathbf{w}_d) \mapsto \varphi(\mathbf{w}) = (\varphi_1(\mathbf{w}), \ldots, \varphi_m(\mathbf{w}))(d < m)$ such that given $\mathbf{w}_a$ and $\mathbf{w}_b$

$$K(\mathbf{w}_a, \mathbf{w}_b) = \langle \varphi(\mathbf{w}_a), \varphi(\mathbf{w}_b) \rangle.$$

In kernel CCA, data is first projected onto a high dimensional feature space before performing CCA. In this work the kernel function used is a Gaussian kernel, i.e.,

$$K(\mathbf{w}_a, \mathbf{w}_b) = \exp\left(-\frac{\|\mathbf{w}_a - \mathbf{w}_b\|^2}{2\sigma^2}\right).$$

The implementation of kernel CCA follows the standard algorithm described in several texts such as (Hardoon et al., 2004); see reference for details.

3.2 Experimental evaluation and results

DA embeddings are evaluated in binary sentiment classification tasks on four data sets described in Section 2.2. Document embeddings are obtained via i)a standard framework that expresses documents as weighted combination of their constituent word embeddings and ii) by initializing a state of the art sentence encoding algorithm InferSent (Conneau et al., 2017) with word embeddings to obtain sentence embeddings. Encoded sentences are then classified using a Logistic Regressor.

Word embeddings and baselines:

- **Generic word embeddings:** Generic word embeddings used are GloVe[1] from both Wikipedia and common crawl and the word2vec (Skip-gram) embeddings[2]. These generic embeddings will be denoted as Glv, GlvCC and w2v.

- **DS word embeddings:** DS embeddings are obtained via Latent Semantic Analysis (LSA) and via retraining word2vec on the test data sets using the implementation in gensim[3]. DS embeddings via LSA are denoted by LSA and DS embeddings via word2vec are denoted by DSw2v.

- **concatenation-SVD baseline:** Generic and DS embeddings are concatenated to form a single embeddings matrix. SVD is performed on this matrix and the resulting singular vectors are projected onto the d largest singular values to form resultant word embeddings. These meta-embeddings proposed by (Yin and Schütze, 2016) have demonstrated considerable success in intrinsic tasks such as similarities, analogies etc.

Details about dimensions of the word embeddings and kernel hyperparameter tuning are found in the supplemental material.

Note that InferSent is fine-tuned with a combination of GloVe common crawl embeddings and DA embeddings, and concSVD. Since the data sets at hand do not contain all the tokens required to retrain InferSent, we replace word tokens

that are common across our test data sets and InferSent training data with the DA embeddings and concSVD.

3.2.1 Discussion of results

From tables 2 and 3 we see that DA embeddings perform better than concSVD as well as the generic and DS word embeddings, when used in a standard classification task as well as when used to initialize a sentence encoding algorithm. As expected LSA DS embeddings provide better results than word2vec DS embeddings. Also since the A-CHESS dataset is imbalanced, we look at precision closely over the other metric since the positive class is in minority. These results are because i) CCA/KCCA provides an intuitively better technique to preserve information from both the generic and DS embeddings. On the other hand the concSVD based embeddings do not exploit information in both the generic and DS embeddings. ii) Furthermore, in their work (Yin and Schütze, 2016) propose to learn an 'ensemble' of meta-embeddings by learning weights to combine different generic word embeddings via a simple neural network. Via the simple optimization problem we propose in equation (5), we determine the proper weight for combination of DS and generic embeddings in the CCA/KCCA space. Thus, task specific DA embeddings formed by a proper weighted combination of DS and generic word embeddings are expected to do better than the concSVD and other embeddings and this is verified empirically. Also note that the LSA DS embeddings do better than the word2vec DS embeddings. This is expected due to the size of the test sets and the nature of the word2vec algorithm. We expect similar observations when using GloVe DS embeddings owing to the similarities between word2vec and GloVe.

4 Future work and Conclusions

From these initial preliminary results we can see that while SWESA learns embeddings from the domain specific data sets along, DA embeddings combine both generic and domain specific embeddings thereby achieving better performance metrics than SWESA or DS embeddings alone. However, SWESA imparts potentially desirable structural properties to its word embeddings. As a next step we would like to infer from both these approaches to learn better polarized and domain adapted word embeddings.

---

[1] https://nlp.stanford.edu/projects/glove/
[2] https://code.google.com/archive/p/word2vec/
[3] https://radimrehurek.com/gensim/

References

John Blitzer, Mark Dredze, Fernando Pereira, et al. 2007. Biographies, bollywood, boom-boxes and blenders: Domain adaptation for sentiment classification. In *ACL*. volume 7, pages 440–447.

Alexis Conneau, Douwe Kiela, Holger Schwenk, Loic Barrault, and Antoine Bordes. 2017. Supervised learning of universal sentence representations from natural language inference data. *arXiv preprint arXiv:1705.02364* .

Susan T Dumais. 2004. Latent semantic analysis. *Annual review of information science and technology* 38(1):188–230.

Joseph Firth, John Torous, Jennifer Nicholas, Rebekah Carney, Simon Rosenbaum, and Jerome Sarris. 2017. Can smartphone mental health interventions reduce symptoms of anxiety? a meta-analysis of randomized controlled trials. *Journal of Affective Disorders* .

David R Hardoon, Sandor Szedmak, and John Shawe-Taylor. 2004. Canonical correlation analysis: An overview with application to learning methods. *Neural computation* 16(12):2639–2664.

Harold Hotelling. 1936. Relations between two sets of variates. *Biometrika* 28(3/4):321–377.

Dimitrios Kotzias, Misha Denil, Nando De Freitas, and Padhraic Smyth. 2015. From group to individual labels using deep features. In *Proceedings of the 21th ACM SIGKDD International Conference on Knowledge Discovery and Data Mining*. ACM, pages 597–606.

Yi Lin, Yoonkyung Lee, and Grace Wahba. 2002. Support vector machines for classification in nonstandard situations. *Machine learning* 46(1-3):191–202.

Erika B Litvin, Ana M Abrantes, and Richard A Brown. 2013. Computer and mobile technology-based interventions for substance use disorders: An organizing framework. *Addictive behaviors* 38(3):1747–1756.

Tomas Mikolov, Ilya Sutskever, Kai Chen, Greg S Corrado, and Jeff Dean. 2013. Distributed representations of words and phrases and their compositionality. In *Advances in neural information processing systems*. pages 3111–3119.

John A Naslund, Lisa A Marsch, Gregory J McHugo, and Stephen J Bartels. 2015. Emerging mhealth and ehealth interventions for serious mental illness: a review of the literature. *Journal of mental health* 24(5):321–332.

Jeffrey Pennington, Richard Socher, and Christopher Manning. 2014. Glove: Global vectors for word representation. In *Proceedings of the 2014 conference on empirical methods in natural language processing (EMNLP)*. pages 1532–1543.

Andrew Quanbeck, Ming-Yuan Chih, Andrew Isham, Roberta Johnson, and David Gustafson. 2014. Mobile delivery of treatment for alcohol use disorders: A review of the literature. *Alcohol research: current reviews* 36(1):111.

Alexander Rakhlin, Ohad Shamir, and Karthik Sridharan. 2011. Making gradient descent optimal for strongly convex stochastic optimization. *arXiv preprint arXiv:1109.5647* .

Wenpeng Yin and Hinrich Schütze. 2016. Learning word meta-embeddings. In *Proceedings of the 54th Annual Meeting of the Association for Computational Linguistics (Volume 1: Long Papers)*. volume 1, pages 1351–1360.

A Supplemental Material

Dimensions of CCA and KCCA projections. Using both KCCA and CCA, generic embeddings and DS embeddings are projected onto their d largest correlated dimensions. By construction, $d \leq \min(d_1, d_2)$. The best d for each data set is obtained via 10 fold cross validation on the sentiment classification task. Table 2 provides dimensions of all word embeddings considered. Note that for LSA and DA, average word embedding dimension across all four data sets are reported. Generic word embeddings such as GloVe and word2vec are of fixed dimensions across all four data sets.

Kernel parameter estimation. Parameter σ of the Gaussian kernel used in KCCA is obtained empirically from the data. The median (μ) of pairwise distances between data points mapped by the kernel function is used to determine σ. Typically $\sigma = \mu$ or $\sigma = 2\mu$. In this section both values are considered for σ and results with the best performing σ are reported.

Word tokens and word embeddings dimensions:

Table 4 provide the number of unique word tokens in all four data sets used in SWESA as well as in learning DA embeddings.

Data Set	Word Tokens
Yelp	2049
Amazon	1865
IMDB	3075
A-CHESS	3400

Table 4: This table presents the unique tokens present in each of the four data sets considered in the experiments.

Table 5 presents the dimensions of DS and generic word embeddings used to obtain DA embeddings.

Word embedding	Dimension
GloVe	100
word2vec	300
LSA	70
CCA-DA	68
KCCA-DA	68
GloVe common crawl	300
AdaptGloVe	300

Table 5: This table presents the average dimensions of LSA, generic and DA word embeddings.

Igbo Diacritic Restoration using Embedding Models

Ignatius Ezeani   **Mark Hepple**   **Ikechukwu Onyenwe**   **Chioma Enemuo**
Department of Computer Science,
The University of Sheffield, United Kingdom.
`https://www.sheffield.ac.uk/dcs`
`{ignatius.ezeani, m.r.hepple, i.onyenwe, clenemuo1}@sheffield.ac.uk`

Abstract

Igbo is a low-resource language spoken by approximately 30 million people world-wide. It is the native language of the Igbo people of south-eastern Nigeria. In Igbo language, diacritics - orthographic and tonal - play a huge role in the distinction of the meaning and pronunciation of words. Omitting diacritics in texts often leads to lexical ambiguity. Diacritic restoration is a pre-processing task that replaces missing diacritics on words from which they have been removed. In this work, we applied embedding models to the diacritic restoration task and compared their performances to those of n-gram models. Although word embedding models have been successfully applied to various NLP tasks, it has not been used, to our knowledge, for diacritic restoration. Two classes of word embeddings models were used: those projected from the English embedding space; and those trained with Igbo bible corpus ($\approx$ 1m). Our best result, 82.49%, is an improvement on the baseline n-gram models.

1 Introduction

Lexical disambiguation is at the heart of a variety of NLP tasks and systems, ranging from grammar and spelling checkers to machine translation systems. In Igbo language, diacritics - orthographic and tonal - play a huge role in the distinction of the meaning and pronunciation of words (Ezeani et al., 2017, 2016). Therefore, effective restoration of diacritics not only improves the quality of corpora for training NLP systems but often improves the performance of existing ones (De Pauw et al., 2007; Mihalcea, 2002).

1.1 Diacritic Ambiguities in Igbo

There is a wide range of ambiguity classes in Igbo (Thecla-Obiora, 2012). In this paper, we focus on

diacritic ambiguities. Besides orthographic diacritics (i.e. dots below and above), tone marks also impose the actual pronunciation and meaning on different words with the same latinized spelling. Table 1 shows Igbo diacritic complexity which impacts on word meanings and pronunciations[1].

Char	Ortho	Tonal
a	–	à,á, ā
e	–	è,é, ē
i	ị	ì, í, ī̄, ị̀, ị́, ị̄
o	ọ	ò, ó, ō, ọ̀, ọ́, ọ̄
u	ụ	ù, ú, ū, ụ̀, ụ́, ụ̄
m	–	m̀,ḿ, m̄
n	ṅ	ǹ,ń, n̄

Table 1: Igbo diacritic complexity

An example of lexical ambiguity caused by the absence of tonal diacritics is the word *akwa* which could mean **ákwá** (cry), **àkwà** (bed/bridge), **ákwà** (cloth) and **àkwá** (egg). Another example of ambiguity due to lack of orthographic diacritics is the word *ugbo* which could mean **ụ́gbọ́** (craft:car|boat|plane); **úgbō** (farm).

1.2 Proposed Approach

As shown in section 2, previous approaches to diacritic restoration techniques depend mostly on existing human annotated resources (e.g. POS-tagged corpora, lexicon, morphological information). In this work, embedding models were used to restore diacritics in Igbo. For our experiments, models are created by training or projection. The evaluation method is a simple accuracy measure i.e. the average percentage of correctly restored instances over all instance keys. An accuracy of

---

[1]In Igbo, *m* and *n* are *nasal consonants* which are in some cases treated as tone marked vowels.

Proceedings of NAACL-HLT 2018: Student Research Workshop, pages 54–60
New Orleans, Louisiana, June 2 - 4, 2018. ©2017 Association for Computational Linguistics

82.49% is achieved with the **IgboBible** model using **Tweak3** confirming our hypothesis that the semantic relationships captured in embedding models could be exploited in the restoration of diacritics.

2   Related Works

Some of the key studies in diacritic restoration involve word-, grapheme-, and tag-based techniques (Francom and Hulden, 2013). Some examples of word-based approaches are the works of Yarowsky (Yarowsky, 1994., 1999) which combined decision list with morphological and collocational information.

Grapheme-based models tend to support low resource languages better by using character collocations. Mihalcea *et al* (2002) proposed an approach that used character based instances with classification algorithms for Romanian. This later inspired the works of Wagacha *et al* (2006), De Pauw *et al* (2011) and Scannell (2011) on a variety of relatively low resourced languages. However, it is a common position that the word-based approach is superior to character-based approach for well resourced languages.

POS-tags and language models have also been applied by Simard (1998) to well resourced languages (French and Spanish) which generally involved *pre-processing*, *candidate generation* and *disambiguation*. Hybrid techniques are common with this task e.g. Yarowsky (1999) used decision list, Bayesian classification and Viterbi decoding while Crandall (2005) applied Bayesian- and HMM-based methods. Tufiş and Chiţu (1999) used a hybrid approach that backs off to character-based method when dealing with "unknown words".

Electronic dictionaries, where available, often augment the *substitution schemes* used (Šantić et al., 2009). On Maori, Cocks and Keegan (2011) used naïve Bayes algorithms with word *n*-grams to improve on the character based approach by Scannell (2011).

For Igbo, however, one major challenge to applying most of the techniques mentioned above that depend on annotated datasets is the lack of these datasets for Igbo e.g tagged corpora, morphologically segmented corpora or dictionaries. This work aims at using a resource-light approach that is based on a more generalisable state-of-the-art representation model like word-embeddings which could be tested on other tasks.

2.1   Igbo Diacritic Restoration

Igbo was among the languages in a previous work (Scannell, 2011) with 89.5% accuracy on web-crawled Igbo data (31k tokens with a vocabulary size of 4.3k). Their *lexicon lookup* methods, *LL* and *LL2* used the most frequent word and a bigram model to determine the right replacement. However, their training corpus was too little to be representative and there was no language speaker in their team to validate their results.

Ezeani *et al* (2016) implemented a more complex set of n–gram models with similar techniques on a larger corpus and reported better results but their evaluation method assumed a closed-world by training and testing on the same dataset. Better results were achieved with the approach reported in (Ezeani et al., 2017) but it used a non-standard data representation model which assigns a sequence of real values to the words in the vocabulary. This method is not only inefficient but does not capture any relationship that may exist between words in the vocabulary.

Also, for Igbo, diacritic restoration does not always eliminate the need for sense disambiguation. For example, the restored word *àkwà* could be referring to either *bed* or *bridge*. Ezeani *et al* (2017) had earlier shown that with proper diacritics on ambiguous wordkeys[2](e.g. *akwa*), a translation system like *Google Translate* may perform better at translating Igbo sentences to other languages. This strategy, therefore, could be more easily extended to sense disambiguation in future.

Statement	*Google Translate*	Comment
O ji *egbe* ya gbuo *egbe*	He used his **gun** to kill *gun*	wrong
O ji **égbè** ya gbuo **égbé**	He used his **gun** to kill **kite**	correct
Akwa ya di n'elu *akwa* ya	It was on the **bed** in his room	fair
Ákwà ya di n'elu **àkwà** ya	his **clothes** on his **bed**	correct
Oke riri *oke* ya	Her addiction	confused
Òké riri **òkè** ya	**Mouse** ate his **share**	correct
O jiri *ugbo* ya bia	He came with his *farm*	wrong
O jiri **ụgbọ** ya bia	He came with his **car**	correct

Table 2: Disambiguation challenge for *Google Translate*

---

[2]A *wordkey* is a "latinized" form of a word i.e. a word stripped of its diacritics if it has any. Wordkeys could have multiple diacritic variants, one of which could be the same as the wordkey itself.

3 Embedding Projection

Embedding models are very generalisable and therefore will be a good resource for Igbo which has limited resources. We intend to use both trained and projected embeddings for the task. The intuition for embedding projection, illustrated in Figure 1, is hinged on the concept of the universality of meaning and representation.

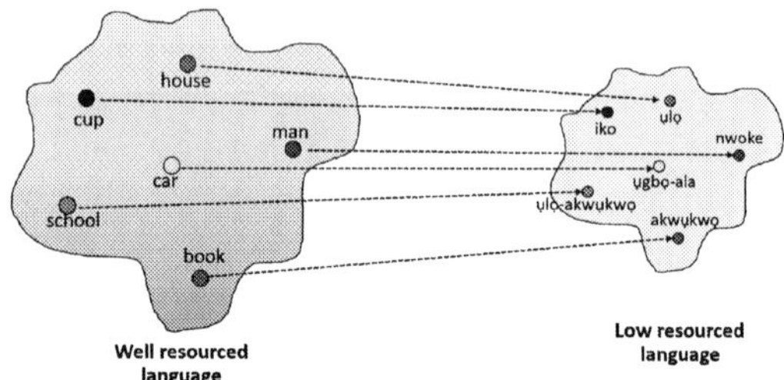

Figure 1: Embedding Projection

We adopt an alignment-based projection method similar to the one described in (Guo et al., 2015). It uses an Igbo-English alignment dictionary $A^{I|E}$ with a function $f(w_i^I)$ that maps each Igbo word w_i^I to all its co-aligned English words $w_{i,j}^E$ and their counts $c_{i,j}$ as defined in Equation 1. $|V^I|$ is the vocabulary size of Igbo and n is the number of co-aligned English words.

$$A^{I|E} = \{w_i^I, f(w_i^I)\}; i = 1..|V^I|$$
$$f(w_i^I) = \{w_{i,j}^E, c_{i,j}\}; j = 1..n \tag{1}$$

The projection is formalised as assigning the weighted average of the embeddings of the co-aligned English words $w_{i,j}^E$ to the Igbo word embeddings $\mathbf{vec}(w_i^I)$ (Guo et al., 2015):

$$\mathbf{vec}(w_i^I) \leftarrow \frac{1}{C} \sum_{w_{i,j}^E), c_{i,j} \in f(w_i^I)} vec(w_{i,j}^E) \cdot c_{i,j} \tag{2}$$

where $C \leftarrow \sum_{c_{i,j} \in f(w_i^I)} c_{i,j}$

4 Experimental Setup

4.1 Experimental Data

We used the English-Igbo parallel bible corpora, available from the *Jehova Witness* website[3], for

[3] jw.org

our experiments. The basic statistics are presented in Table 3[4].

Item	Igbo	English
Lines	32416	32416
Words+puncs	1,070,708	1,048,268
Words only	902,429	881,771
Unique words	16,084	15,000
Diacritized words	595,221	–
Unique diacritized words	8,750	–
All wordkeys	15,476	–
Unique wordkeys	14,926	–
Ambiguous wordkeys:	550	
– 2 variants	516	–
– 3 variants	19	–
– 4 variants	9	–
– 5 variants	3	–
– 6 variants	3	–

Table 3: Corpus statistics

Table 3 shows that both the total corpus words and its word types constitute over 50% diacritic words i.e. words with at least one diacritic character. Over 97% of the ambiguous wordkeys have 2 or 3 variants.

4.2 Experimental Datasets

We chose 29 wordkeys which have several variants occurring in our corpus, the wordkey itself occurring too[5]. For each wordkey, we keep a list of sentences (excluding punctuations and numbers), each with a blank (see Table 5) to be filled with the correct variant of the wordkey.

4.3 Experimental Procedure

The experimental pipeline, as illustrated in Figure 2, follows three fundamental stages:

4.3.1 Creating embedding model

Four embedding models, two trained and two projected, were created for Igbo in the first stage of the pipeline:

Trained: The first model, **IgboBible**, is produced from the data described in Table 3 using the Gensim *word2vec* Python libraries (Řehůřek and Sojka, 2010). Default

[4] In these counts, the case of words is preserved e.g. *Ọtụtụ* and *otụtụ* have different counts

[5] Highly dominant variants or very rarely occurring wordkeys were generally excluded from the datasets.

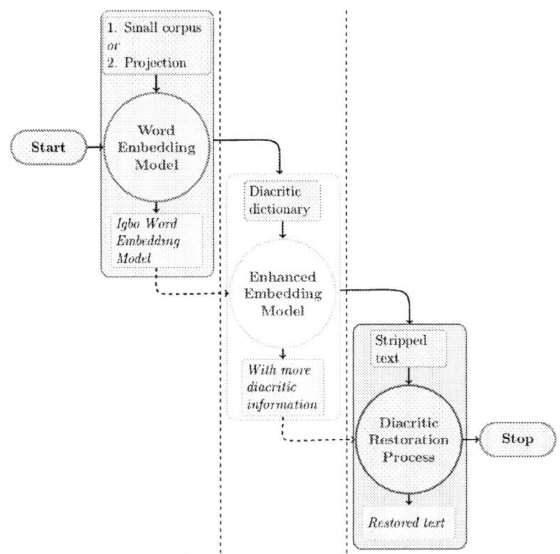

Figure 2: Pipeline for Igbo Diacritic Restoration using Word Embedding

configurations were used apart from optimizing $dimension(default = 100)$ and $window\_size(default = 5)$ parameters to 140 and 2 respectively on the **Basic** restoration method described in section 4.3.3.

We also used **IgboWiki**, a pre-trained Igbo model from *fastText Wiki word vectors*[6] project (Bojanowski et al., 2016).

Projected Using the projection method defined above, we created the **IgboGNews** model from the pre-trained *Google News*[7]*word2vec* model while the **IgboEnBbl** is projected from a model we trained on the English bible.

Table 4 shows the vocabulary sizes ($\#|V|^L$) for embedding models of each language L, as well as the dimensions (**#vecs**) of each of the models used in our experiments. While the pre-trained models and their projections have vector sizes of 300, our trained **IgboBible** performed best with vector size of 140 and so we trained the **IgboEnBbl** with the same dimension.

Model	$\#|V|^I$	#vecs	$\#|V|^E$	#data
IgboBible	4968	140	–	902.5k
IgboWiki	3111	300	–	(unknown)
IgboGNews	3046	300	3m	100bn
IgboEnBbl	4057	140	6.3k	881.8k

Table 4: Igbo and English models: vocabulary, vector and training data sizes

IgboGNews has a lot of *holes* i.e. 1101 out of 4057, (24.92%) entries in the alignment dictionary words were not represented in the Google News embedding model. A quick look at the list revealed that they are mostly bible names that do not exist in the Google News model and so have no vectors for their Igbo equivalents e.g. *kọṛịnt, nimshaị, manase, peletaịt, gọg, pileg, abịshag, arọna, frankịnsens.*

The projection process removes[8] these words thereby stripping the model of a quarter of its vocabulary with any linguistic information from them.

4.3.2 Deriving *diacritic* embedding models

In both training and projection of the embedding model, vectors are assigned to each word in the dictionary, and that includes each diacritic variant of a wordkey. The **Basic** restoration process (*section* 4.3.3) uses this initial embedding model *as-is*. The models are then refined by "tweaking" the variant vectors to get new ones that correlate more with context embeddings.

For example, let mcw_v contain the top n of the most co-occurring words of a certain variant, v and their counts, c. The following three *tweaking* methods are applied:

- **Tweak1**: adds to each diacritic variant vector the weighted average of the vectors of its most co-occurring words (see Equation (3)). At restoration time, *all* the words in the sentence are used to build the context vector.

- **Tweak2**: updates each variant vector as in *Tweak1* but its restoration process uses *only* the vectors of co-occurring words with each of the contesting variants excluding common words.

- **Tweak3**: is similar to the previous methods but *replaces* (not *updates*) each of the variant

---

[6]Pre-trained on 294 different languages of Wikipedia
[7]https://code.google.com/archive/p/word2vec/

[8]Other variants of this process assign zero vectors to these words or remove the same words from the other models.

Variant	*Left context*	*Placeholder*	*Right context*	Meaning
àkwá	ka okwa nke kpokotara	----	o na-eyighi eyi otu	egg
ákwà	a kpara akpa mee	----	ngebichi nke onye na-ekwe	cloth
ákwá	ozugbo m nuru mkpu	----	ha na ihe ndi a	cry

Table 5: Instances of the wordkey *akwa* in context

vectors (see Equation (4)).

$$\mathbf{diac_{vec}} \leftarrow diac_{vec} + \frac{1}{|mcw_v|} \sum_{w \in mcw_v} w_{vec} * w_c \tag{3}$$

$$\mathbf{diac_{vec}} \leftarrow \frac{1}{|mcw_v|} \sum_{w \in mcw_v} w_{vec} * w_c \tag{4}$$

where w_c is the 'weight' of w i.e. the probability distribution of the count of w in mcw_v.

4.3.3 Diacritic restoration process

Algorithm 1 sketches the steps followed to apply the diacritic embedding vectors to the diacritic restoration task. This algorithm is based on the assumption that combining the vectors of words in context is likely to yield a vector that is more similar to the correct diacritic variant. In this process, a set of candidate vectors, $D^{wk} = \{d_1, ..., d_n\}$ for each wordkey, wk, are extracted from the embedding model. C is defined as the list of the context words of a sentence containing a placeholder (examples are shown in Table 5) to be filled and vec_C is the context vector of C (Equation (5)).

Algorithm 1 Diacritic Restoration Process

Require: Embedding & instances with blanks
Ensure: Blanks filled with variants
1: *load embeddings and instances*
2: **for** *each instance* **do**
3:    *Get candidate vectors:* D^{wk}
4:    $\mathbf{vec_C} \leftarrow \frac{1}{|C|} \sum_{w \in C} embed[w]$ (5)
5:    $\mathbf{diac_{best}} \leftarrow \underset{d_i \in D^{wk}}{\mathbf{argmax}}\ sim(\mathbf{vec_C}, d_i)$ (6)
6: **end for**

---

5 Evaluation Strategies

A major subtask of this project is building the dataset for training the embedding and other language models. For all of the 29 wordkeys[9] used in the project, we extracted 38,911 instances each with the correct variant and no diacritics on all words in context. The dataset was used to optimise the parameters in the training of the **Basic** embedding model. Simple unigram and bigram methods were were used as the baseline for the restoration task. 10-fold cross-validation was applied in the evaluation of each of the models.

6 Results and Discussion

Our results (Table 6) indicate that with respect to the *n*-gram models, the embedding based diacritic restoration techniques perform comparatively well. Though the projected models (**IgboGNews** and **IgboEnBbl**) appear to have struggled a bit compared to the **IgboBible**, one can infer that having been trained originally with the same dataset and language of the task may have given the latter some advantage. It also captures all the necessary linguistic information for Igbo better than the projected models.

Again, **IgboEnBbl** did better than **IgboGNews** possibly because it was trained on a corpus that directly aligns with the Igbo data used in the experiment. The pre-trained **IgboWiki** model was abysmally poor possibly because, out of the 3111 entries in its vocabulary, 1,930 (62.04%) were English words while only 345 (11.09%) were found in our Igbo dictionary[10] used. It is not clear yet why all the results are the same across the methods. The best restoration technique across the models is the *Tweak3* which suggests that very frequent common words may have introduced some noise in the training process.

---

[9]The average number of instances is 1341 with the minimum and maximum numbers being 38 and 14,157 respectively.

[10]We note however that our Igbo dictionary was built from only the Igbo bible data and therefore is by no means complete. Igbo words and misspellings in **IgboWiki** that are not found in **IgboBible** vocabulary were simply dropped

Baselines: *n*-gram models		
	Unigram	*Bigram*
	72.25%	80.84%

Embedding models

	Trained		Projected	
	IgboBible	**IgboWiki**	**IgboGNews**	**IgboEnBbl**
Basic	69.28	18.94	57.57	64.72
Tweak1	74.11	18.94	61.10	69.88
Tweak2	78.75	18.94	67.28	74.84
Tweak3	**82.49**	18.94	**72.98**	**76.34**

Table 6: Accuracy Scores for the Baselines, *Trained* and *Projected* embedding models [Bolds indicate best tweaking method].

7   Conclusion and Future Research Direction

This work contributes to the IgboNLP[11] (Onyenwe et al., 2018) project with the ultimately goal to build a framework that can adapt, in an effective and efficient way, existing NLP tools to support the development of Igbo. This paper addresses the issue of building and projecting embedding models for Igbo as well as applying the models to diacritic restoration.

We have shown that word embeddings can be used to restore diacritics. However, there is still room for further exploration of the techniques presented here. For instance, we can investigate how generalizable the models produced are with regards to other tasks e.g. sense disambiguation, word similarity and analogy tasks. On the restoration task, the design here appear to be more simplistic than in real life as one may want to restore an entire sentence, and by extension a document, and not just fill a blank. Also, with Igbo being a morphologically rich language, the impact of character and sub-word embeddings as compared to word embeddings could be investigated.

References

Piotr Bojanowski, Edouard Grave, Armand Joulin, and Tomas Mikolov. 2016. Enriching word vectors with subword information. *CoRR*, abs/1607.04606.

John Cocks and Te-Taka Keegan. 2011. A Word-based Approach for Diacritic Restoration in Māori. In *Proceedings of the Australasian Language Technology Association Workshop 2011*, pages 126–130, Canberra, Australia. Url = http://www.aclweb.org/anthology/U/U11/U11-2016.

David Crandall. 2005. Automatic Accent Restoration in Spanish text. [Online; accessed 7-January-2016].

Guy De Pauw, Gilles-Maurice De Schryver, L. Pretorius, and L. Levin. 2011. Introduction to the Special Issue on African Language Technology. *Language Resources and Evaluation*, 45:263–269.

Guy De Pauw, Peter W Wagacha, and Gilles-Maurice De Schryver. 2007. Automatic Diacritic Restoration for Resource-Scarce Language. In *International Conference on Text, Speech and Dialogue*, pages 170–179. Springer.

Ignatius Ezeani, Mark Hepple, and Ikechukwu Onyenwe. 2016. Automatic Restoration of Diacritics for Igbo Language. In *Text, Speech, and Dialogue: 19th International Conference, TSD 2016, Brno , Czech Republic, September 12-16, 2016, Proceedings*, pages 198–205, Cham. Springer International Publishing.

Ignatius Ezeani, Mark Hepple, and Ikechukwu Onyenwe. 2017. Lexical Disambiguation of Igbo using Diacritic Restoration. *SENSE 2017*, page 53.

Jerid Francom and Mans Hulden. 2013. Diacritic error detection and restoration via part-of-speech tags. *Proceedings of the 6th Language and Technology Conference*.

Jiang Guo, Wanxiang Che, David Yarowsky, Haifeng Wang, and Ting Liu. 2015. Cross-lingual dependency parsing based on distributed representations. In *Proceedings of the 53rd Annual Meeting of the Association for Computational Linguistics and the 7th International Joint Conference on Natural Language Processing (Volume 1: Long Papers)*, volume 1, pages 1234–1244.

Rada Mihalcea. 2002. Diacritics restoration: Learning from letters versus learning from words. In *Proceedings of the Third International Conference on Computational Linguistics and Intelligent Text Processing*, CICLing '02, pages 339–348, London, UK, UK. Springer-Verlag.

[11]See `igbonlp.org`

Ikechukwu E Onyenwe, Mark Hepple, Uchechukwu Chinedu, and Ignatius Ezeani. 2018. A Basic Language Resource Kit Implementation for the Igbonlp Project. *ACM Trans. Asian Low-Resour. Lang. Inf. Process.*, 17(2):10:1–10:23.

Radim Řehůřek and Petr Sojka. 2010. Software Framework for Topic Modelling with Large Corpora. In *Proceedings of the LREC 2010 Workshop on New Challenges for NLP Frameworks*, pages 45–50, Valletta, Malta. ELRA. `http://is.muni.cz/publication/884893/en`.

Kevin P. Scannell. 2011. Statistical unicodification of african languages. *Language Resource Evaluation*, 45(3):375–386.

Michel Simard. 1998. Automatic Insertion of Accents in French texts. *Proceedings of the Third Conference on Empirical Methods in Natural Language Processing*, pages 27–35.

Udemmadu Thecla-Obiora. 2012. The issue of ambiguity in the igbo language. *AFRREV LALIGENS: An International Journal of Language, Literature and Gender Studies*, 1(1):109–123.

Dan Tufiş and Adrian Chiţu. 1999. Automatic Diacritics Insertion in Romanian Texts. *Proceedings of the International Conference on Computational Lexicography*, pages 185–194.

Nikola Šantić, Jan Šnajder, and Bojana Dalbelo Bašić. 2009. Automatic Diacritics Restoration in Croatian Texts. In *The Future of Information Sciences, Digital Resources and Knowledge Sharing*, pages 126–130. Dept of Info Sci, Faculty of Humanities and Social Sciences, University of Zagreb , 2009. ISBN: 978-953-175-355-5.

Peter W. Wagacha, Guy De Pauw, and Pauline W. Githinji. 2006. A Grapheme-based Approach to Accent Restoration in Gĩkũyũ. In *In Proceedings of the fifth international conference on language resources and evaluation.*

David Yarowsky. 1994. A Comparison of Corpus-based Techniques for Restoring Accents in Spanish and French Text. In *Proceedings, 2nd Annual Workshop on Very Large Corpora*, pages 19–32, Kyoto.

David Yarowsky. 1999. Corpus-based techniques for restoring accents in spanish and french text. In *Natural Language Processing Using Very Large Corpora*, pages 99–120. Kluwer Academic Publishers.

Using Classifier Features to Determine Language Transfer on Morphemes

Alexandra Lavrentovich
Department of Linguistics, University of Florida
Gainesville, FL 32601 USA
`alavrent@ufl.edu`

Abstract

The aim of this thesis is to perform a Native Language Identification (NLI) task where we identify an English learner's native language background based only on the learner's English writing samples. We focus on the use of English grammatical morphemes across four proficiency levels. The outcome of the computational task is connected to a position in second language acquisition research that holds all learners acquire English grammatical morphemes in the same order, regardless of native language background. We use the NLI task as a tool to uncover cross-linguistic influence on the developmental trajectory of morphemes. We perform a cross-corpus evaluation across proficiency levels to increase the reliability and validity of the linguistic features that predict the native language background. We include native English data to determine the different morpheme patterns used by native versus non-native English speakers. Furthermore, we conduct a human NLI task to determine the type and magnitude of language transfer cues used by human judges versus the classifier.

1 Introduction

Native Language Identification (NLI) is a text classification task that determines the native language background (L1) of a writer based solely on the writer's second language (L2) production. Within computational linguistics, there is a flurry of activity as researchers test the best classifier models with a wide range of linguistic and stylistic features to reach the highest classification accuracy scores. NLI is pursued in a variety of written genres such as argumentative essays (Crossley and McNamara, 2012), online journal entries (Brooke and Hirst, 2012), scientific articles (Stehwien and Padó, 2015) as well as transcribed spoken language (Zampieri et al., 2017), and even eye fixation data while reading (Berzak et al., 2017). Although the majority of NLI studies have used English as the L2, recent work expands the NLI task to other L2 languages including Arabic, Chinese, and Spanish (Malmasi, 2016).

These forays illustrate that computational methods are robust for identifying the first language background of the language learner. This task has interesting implications for exploring how the L1 permeates into the L2. Specifically, by selecting and analyzing the most informative linguistic features that predict the L1 background, we can generate testable hypotheses about language transfer that would be of value to second language acquisition (SLA) researchers and practitioners. One such application would be to determine if grammatical morphemes are susceptible to cross-linguistic influence (CLI) throughout development, which have previously been described to be learned in the same order, regardless of the L1.

The thesis consists of four main studies. First, we conduct the NLI task and feature analysis for ten L1 backgrounds across four proficiency levels to determine the nature and extent of CLI on the developmental trajectory of morpheme production. Second, we include native English data in a second iteration of the NLI task to determine the linguistic patterns that vary between native and non-native English writers. Third, we conduct a cross-corpus evaluation across proficiency levels to determine which features are more reliable and corpus-independent. Fourth, we conduct a human NLI task to determine the linguistic cues used by humans versus machines in detecting a writer's L1. Taking these studies together, the thesis uses NLI to support and inform topics in SLA, and conversely, we connect principles in SLA to NLI by expanding and building new NLI models.

61

Proceedings of NAACL-HLT 2018: Student Research Workshop, pages 61–66
New Orleans, Louisiana, June 2 - 4, 2018. ©2017 Association for Computational Linguistics

Stage	Morpheme
1	Progressive *-ing*
	Plural *-s*
	Copula *be*
2	Auxiliary *be*
	Articles *a/an/the*
3	Irregular past
4	Regular past *-ed*
	Third person singular *-s*
	Possessive *'s*

Table 1: Natural order of English L2 morpheme acquisition.

2 Background

We take the NLI task as a starting point for investigating CLI on the developmental trajectory of English grammatical morphemes. In particular, we determine the patterns of overuse, underuse, and erroneous use of morphemes by learners from ten L1 backgrounds across four proficiency levels. We focus on morphemes in particular in order to connect to SLA research that suggests English learners acquire English grammatical morphemes in a universal order, regardless of the learner's L1 background (Dulay and Burt, 1974; Larsen-Freeman, 1975). Krashen (1985) advocated for a shared order composed of four acquisition stages, illustrated in Table 1.

More recently, studies have identified multiple determinants predicting the shared order of accurate morpheme use among learners with different L1s (Goldschneider and DeKeyser, 2001; Luk and Shirai, 2009). For example, Murakami and Alexopoulou (2016) found the presence or absence of articles and the plural *-s* in a learner's L1 correlated with the learner's accurate use of the equivalent L2 English morpheme. This thesis complements the previous morpheme order studies by expanding the range of languages, the number of morphemes, and the span of proficiency levels considered. This expansion is enabled by the NLI task which can canvas large data sets, and represent thousands of learners from numerous L1 backgrounds. Our findings will demonstrate the extent of CLI on morphemes produced by learners with different language backgrounds. The findings will have repercussions on how we understand the interaction of two languages in a language learner's productions. Furthermore, we contribute to the NLI task by focusing on mor-

phosyntactic linguistic features which have not been investigated as the sole predictors in previous work.

3 Methodology

3.1 Corpus

We collect data from the EF Cambridge Open Language Database (EFCamDat), a longitudinal corpus consisting of 1.8 million English learner texts submitted by 174,000 students enrolled in a virtual learning environment (Huang et al., 2017). The corpus spans sixteen proficiency levels aligned with standards such as the Common European Framework of Reference for languages. The texts include metadata on the learner's proficiency level and nationality acts as a proxy to native language background. The texts are annotated with part of speech (POS) tags using the Penn Treebank Tagset, grammatical relationships using SyntaxNet, and some texts in the corpus (66%) include error annotations provided by teachers using predetermined error markup tags (Huang et al., 2017).

In addition to the English L2 subcorpus, we collect a corpus of English L1 writing samples. We crowdsource written responses through social media and undergraduate linguistics courses from self-described English monolingual speakers. Participants are asked to submit a paragraph addressing a prompt that mimics the EFCamDat tasks in the online English school. We collect enough responses to form an English L1 class that is similar in size and length to the English L2 subcorpus, which is described next.

3.2 Target Learner Groups

We create a subcorpus representing learners from ten L1 backgrounds: Arabic, Chinese, French, German, Japanese, Korean, Portuguese, Russian, Spanish, Turkish. We select these ten L1 backgrounds for three main reasons. First, typologically similar languages such as Spanish and Portuguese are included because more overt transfer effects occur in production when structural and functional cross-linguistic similarity is high (Ringbom, 2007). Thus we expect similar transfer effects that could make classification difficult between similar languages. Second, languages different from English in respect to orthography (e.g., Arabic) or word order (e.g., Korean and Russian) are included to detect if negative transfer, or erroneous use, occurs. Third, the ten selected groups are represented in the TOEFL11 corpus which will be used for a cross-corpus evaluation.

The individual learner texts from each language background will be grouped by proficiency level. Since not all learners progress through all sixteen instructional units and some proficiency levels are overrepresented, the proficiency levels will be merged into four groups covering Levels 1-3, 4-7, 8-11, 12-16. Previous research shows clustering these proficiency levels has been useful for identifying the native language of learners (Jiang et al., 2014). We ensure text size is homogeneous by merging texts into 1,000 word tokens and compiling texts into equally-sized sets for each language background at each proficiency level. The texts retain information on individual identification numbers and writing topics.

3.3 Target Morphemes and Feature Set

The target morphemes include nine morphemes that frequently appear in the morpheme order studies: articles *a/an/the*, auxiliary *be*, copula *be*, plural *-s*, possessive *'s*, progressive *-ing*, irregular past, regular past tense *-ed*, and third person singular *-s*. We include short plural *-s* (e.g., *boot/boots*) and long plural *-es* (e.g., *hoof/hooves*) and exclude irregular plurals (e.g., *foot/feet*). The copula and auxiliary will include the first, second, and third person present and progressive forms, respectively. We make a distinction between the definite (*the*) and indefinite (*a/an*) articles because previous research suggests learners acquire definite and indefinite articles at different rates depending on their L1 background (Crosthwaite, 2016; Díez-Bedmar and Papp, 2008). The irregular and regular past tense forms will be limited to lexical verbs (e.g., *went, walked*) and will exclude modals (e.g., *would*) and passive voice (e.g., *stolen*). The third person singular form *-s* will include the allomorphs *-s* and *-es* (e.g., *she waits and watches*). The possessive *'s* will include forms attached to a noun phrase (e.g., *cat's tail* or *cats' tails*).

We use features that capture morphemes and morphosyntactic relationships. The feature set includes function words, lexical n-grams, POS n-grams, dependency features, and error corrections. Function words include topic-independent grammatical lexical items, and will capture definite/indefinite articles and auxiliary verbs. We use lexical words to capture regular and irregular past tense verbs. To avoid some topic bias, we remove proper nouns from the texts. We use POS 1-3grams and dependency features to capture morphosyntactic relationships such as possession, progressive *-ing*, plural *-s*, and third person singular *-s*. Error corrections provided by the EFCamDat metadata capture morpheme errors such as article misuse and incorrect plurals. We evaluate the predictive power of the features through a step-wise procedure.

4 Native Language Identification Task

We use a Support Vector Machine (SVM) classifier to evaluate the data, and obtain the following metrics: precision, recall, accuracy, and the F-measure. We use a one-vs-all approach, and evaluate each feature type using 10-fold cross-validation. The linear SVM classifier is selected given its sustained success in NLI work, as seen in the recent 2017 NLI shared task (Malmasi et al., 2017).

To evaluate feature information as it relates to morpheme acquisition, we compare the overuse, underuse, and erroneous use of the linguistic features within the ten L1 groups and native English group. Following a methodology proposed by (Malmasi and Dras, 2014), we use SVM weights to identify the most predictive features that are unique to each L1 class. We compare if the same best-performing features appear for each proficiency band. If the features are different in each proficiency band, then we suspect these may be proficiency related effects and we follow with post hoc analysis.

Post hoc analysis is conducted to compare the morphemes appearing more or less regularly given a specific L1 background, and across proficiency levels. This method allows us to piece together a diachronic view of morpheme use. We determine if the linguistic features show evidence of language transfer based on statistical evidence of between-group differences and within-group similarities. We expect to see differential use of morphemes between L1 groups that may or may not have equivalent morphemes between the L1 and L2. For example, Russian L1 learners may underuse English articles because they are absent in the L1. On the other hand, Spanish L1 learners may overuse articles because Spanish articles follow a different semantic scheme, thus English articles may be oversupplied to inappropriate contexts.

We also determine how well the classifier performs with native English data to each L1 for each proficiency level. We expect the classifier will show more confusion for typologically similar languages to English, especially at higher proficiency levels where written productions may contain fewer L1 idiosyncrasies.

5 Cross-Corpus Evaluation

In this section, we address the following questions: (1) How well do the most discriminatory linguistic features used in the EFCamDat corpus perform on an independent corpus? (2) Which features are corpus-specific? (3) Which features best predict the L1 class when trained on the EFCamDat and tested on an independent corpus, and vice versa. The classifier trained on the EFCamDat subcorpus will be used in a cross-corpus evaluation to increase the reliability of the linguistic predictors as evidence for language transfer.

We train on the EFCamDat subcorpus and test on an independent corpus, the TOEFL11, and vice versa. The TOEFL11 corpus consists of 12,100 English essays written during high-stakes college entrance exams from learners across eleven L1 backgrounds (Arabic, Chinese, French, German, Hindi, Italian, Japanese, Korean, Spanish, Telugu, and Turkish) and distributed across eight prompts and three essay score levels (low/medium/high). The TOEFL11 corpus was designed with a native language identification task in mind and used in the first NLI shared task (Blanchard et al., 2013).

We match a subset of the learner groups from the TOEFL11 data with classes in the EFCamDat, use comparable text lengths for each language background, and match the proficiency levels between the two corpora. Success is measured by NLI accuracy that is higher than a chance baseline when the SVM is trained with the EFCamDat and tested on the TOEFL11, and vice versa. Most importantly, the corpus comparison determines which specific features serve as the strongest determiners of L1 background across proficiency levels, despite genre differences between the two corpora.

A cross-corpus methodology has the advantage of providing robust results that bolster the argument for CLI in the course of L2 morpheme development. The features that successfully distinguish between L1 groups will be analyzed to inform SLA research as to how certain morphemes may be more susceptible to language transfer than others, and how different L1 groups may follow unique trajectories of morpheme acquisition. Previous research has found some corpus-independent L1 transfer features that generalize across the different task requirements represented in the EFCamDat and TOEFL11 corpora (Malmasi and Dras, 2015). However, it is unknown if this generalizability will hold between proficiency bands. Thus, we test the classifier on different proficiency levels across EFCamDat and TOEFL11 to determine the features that are corpus-independent across proficiency levels. These findings will then be connected to formulating hypotheses on language transfer during the developmental trajectory of morpheme acquisition.

6 Human Cross-Validation

In this section, we address the following questions: (1) How does the performance of the classifier compare to humans performing the same task? (2) What linguistic predictors do humans use in classifying texts? To address these questions, we recruit native and non-native English speakers with a background in language instruction and/or self-reported linguistic training to perform a simplified online NLI task. We follow a similar procedure from Malmasi et al. (2015). The raters deal with five L1 classes representing the most disparate L1s from the EfCamDat subcorpus in order to facilitate classification. We split the texts into equal distributions of low and high proficiency essays for each L1 group. Raters perform the NLI task on roughly 50 essays and indicate the linguistic features that led to their decision and their confidence in that decision. We determine accuracy scores for the L1 groups across proficiency levels, and if the raters use morphemes and morphosyntactic relationships as indicators of the L1. The results of the study will indicate the qualitative and quantitative differences in detecting cross-linguistic influence based on human evaluations versus computational measures.

7 Conclusion

This thesis expands on NLI methodology and connects computational linguistics with SLA research. In terms of methodology, we investigate NLI using only grammatical morphemes, which have not been singled out in previous NLI research. English is considered a morphologically weak language with comparatively few requirements for agreement and declensions. Achieving an accuracy score higher than chance indicates that morphemes, however ubiquitous in writing, can reveal a significant distribution that correctly identifies a writer's L1 background. The thesis may provide motivation to perform NLI on morphologically rich languages such as Slavic or Bantu, to identify if a classifier can use a wider set of morphemes as the sole feature. Furthermore, we expand the methodology to cross-corpus evaluations on four proficiency levels. This line of research shows how robust a model may be for lower to higher proficiency English learners.

In terms of combining computational linguistics with SLA, we use the NLI task as a tool for uncovering cross-linguistic influence that may otherwise go unseen by a human researcher. We test if that is indeed the case in the human cross-validation study. The NLI task increases the number and type of comparisons we can make between languages, which can lead to new insights in the underuse, overuse, and erroneous use of morphemes. We determine how learner groups develop the capacity to use morphemes through development. The automatic detection of transfer is especially valuable for higher proficiency learners, where transfer is harder to discern because the effects may not be obviously visible as errors (Ringbom, 2007). The ability to detect subtle CLI effects holds the potential to generate new hypotheses about where and why language transfer occurs, so that understanding can be transferred to L2 education. This thesis accounts for these transfer effects and provides testable hypotheses.

Acknowledgements

I am grateful to Dr. Stefanie Wulff for constant support and helpful discussions, and thank the anonymous reviewers for comments and suggestions on improving the thesis proposal.

References

Yevgeni Berzak, Chie Nakamura, Suzanne Flynn, and Boris Katz. 2017. Predicting native language from gaze. *arXiv preprint arXiv:1704.07398*.

Daniel Blanchard, Joel Tetreault, Derrick Higgins, Aoife Cahill, and Martin Chodorow. 2013. Toefl11: A corpus of non-native english. *ETS Research Report Series*, 2013(2).

Julian Brooke and Graeme Hirst. 2012. Robust, lexicalized native language identification. *Proceedings of COLING 2012*, pages 391–408.

Scott Crossley and Danielle McNamara. 2012. Detecting the first language of second language writers using automated indices of cohesion, lexical sophistication, syntactic complexity and conceptual knowledge. *Approaching language transfer through text classification: Explorations in the detection-based approach*, pages 106–126.

Peter Crosthwaite. 2016. L2 english article use by l1 speakers of article-less languages. *International Journal of Learner Corpus Research*, 2(1):68–100.

María Belén Díez-Bedmar and Szilvia Papp. 2008. The use of the english article system by chinese and spanish learners. *Language and Computers Studies in Practical Linguistics*, 66:147.

Heidi Dulay and Marina Burt. 1974. Natural sequences in child second language acquisition. *Language Learning*, 24(1):37–53.

Jennifer M Goldschneider and Robert M DeKeyser. 2001. Explaining the natural order of l2 morpheme acquisition in english: A meta-analysis of multiple determinants. *Language Learning*, 51(1):1–50.

Yan Huang, Akira Murakami, Theodora Alexopoulou, and Anna Korhonen. 2017. Dependency parsing of learner english.

Xiao Jiang, Yufan Guo, Jeroen Geertzen, Dora Alexopoulou, Lin Sun, and Anna Korhonen. 2014. Native language identification using large, longitudinal data. In *Proceedings of the 9th International Conference on Language Resources and Evaluation*, pages 3309–3312.

Stephen Krashen. 1985. *The input hypothesis: Issues and implications*. Addison-Wesley Longman Ltd.

Diane Larsen-Freeman. 1975. The acquisition of grammatical morphemes by adult esl students. *TESOL Quarterly*, pages 409–419.

Zoe Pei-sui Luk and Yasuhiro Shirai. 2009. Is the acquisition order of grammatical morphemes impervious to l1 knowledge? evidence from the acquisition of plural -s, articles, and possessive 's. *Language Learning*, 59(4):721–754.

Shervin Malmasi. 2016. *Native language identification: explorations and applications*. Ph.D. thesis, Macquarie University.

Shervin Malmasi and Mark Dras. 2014. Language transfer hypotheses with linear svm weights. In *Proceedings of the 2014 Conference on Empirical Methods in Natural Language Processing*, pages 1385–1390.

Shervin Malmasi and Mark Dras. 2015. Large-scale native language identification with cross-corpus evaluation. In *Proceedings of the 2015 Conference of the North American Chapter of the Association for Computational Linguistics: Human Language Technologies*, pages 1403–1409.

Shervin Malmasi, Keelan Evanini, Aoife Cahill, Joel Tetreault, Robert Pugh, Christopher Hamill, Diane Napolitano, and Yao Qian. 2017. A Report on the 2017 Native Language Identification Shared Task. In *Proceedings of the 12th Workshop on Building Educational Applications Using NLP*, Copenhagen, Denmark. Association for Computational Linguistics.

Shervin Malmasi, Joel Tetreault, and Mark Dras. 2015. Oracle and human baselines for native language identification. In *Proceedings of the 10th Workshop on Innovative Use of NLP for Building Educational Applications*, pages 172–178.

Akira Murakami and Theodora Alexopoulou. 2016. L1 influence on the acquisition order of english grammatical morphemes: A learner corpus study. *Studies in Second Language Acquisition*, 38(3):365–401.

Håkan Ringbom. 2007. *Cross-linguistic similarity in foreign language learning*. Multilingual Matters.

Sabrina Stehwien and Sebastian Padó. 2015. Native language identification across text types: how special are scientists? *Italian Journal of Computational Linguistics*, 1(1).

Marcos Zampieri, Alina Maria Ciobanu, and Liviu P Dinu. 2017. Native language identification on text and speech. *arXiv preprint arXiv:1707.07182*.

End-to-End Learning of Task-Oriented Dialogs

Bing Liu, Ian Lane
Carnegie Mellon University
5000 Forbes Avenue, Pittsburgh, PA 15213, USA
`liubing@cmu.edu, lane@cmu.edu`

Abstract

In this thesis proposal, we address the limitations of conventional pipeline design of task-oriented dialog systems and propose end-to-end learning solutions. We design neural network based dialog system that is able to robustly track dialog state, interface with knowledge bases, and incorporate structured query results into system responses to successfully complete task-oriented dialog. In learning such neural network based dialog systems, we propose hybrid offline training and online interactive learning methods. We introduce a multi-task learning method in pre-training the dialog agent in a supervised manner using task-oriented dialog corpora. The supervised training agent can further be improved via interacting with users and learning online from user demonstration and feedback with imitation and reinforcement learning. In addressing the sample efficiency issue with online policy learning, we further propose a method by combining the learning-from-user and learning-from-simulation approaches to improve the online interactive learning efficiency.

1 Introduction

Dialog systems, also known as conversational agents or chatbots, are playing an increasingly important role in today's business and social life. People communicate with a dialog system in natural language form, via either textual or auditory input, for entertainment and for completing daily tasks. Dialog systems can be generally divided into chit-chat systems and task-oriented dialog systems based on the nature of conversation. Comparing to chit-chat systems that are designed to engage users and provide mental support, task-oriented dialog systems are designed to assist user to complete a particular task by understanding requests from users and providing relevant information. Such systems usually involve retrieving information from external resources and reasoning over multiple dialog turns. This thesis work focuses on task-oriented dialog systems.

Conventional task-oriented dialog systems have a complex pipeline (Raux et al., 2005; Young et al., 2013) consisting of independently developed and modularly connected components for spoken language understanding (SLU) (Sarikaya et al., 2014; Mesnil et al., 2015; Chen et al., 2016), dialog state tracking (DST) (Henderson et al., 2014; Mrkšić et al., 2016; Lee and Stent, 2016), and dialog policy learning (Gasic and Young, 2014; Su et al., 2016). Such pipeline system design has a number of limitations. Firstly, credit assignment in such pipeline systems can be challenging, as errors made in upper stream modules may propagate and be amplified in downstream components. Moreover, each component in the pipeline is ideally re-trained as preceding components are updated, so that we have inputs similar to the training examples at run-time. This domino effect causes several issues in practice.

We address the limitations of pipeline dialog systems and propose end-to-end learning solutions. The proposed model is capable of robustly tracking dialog state, interfacing with knowledge bases, and incorporating structured query results into system responses to successfully complete task-oriented dialog. With each functioning unit being modeled by a neural network and connected via differentiable operations, the entire system can be optimized end-to-end.

In learning such neural network based dialog model, we propose hybrid offline training and online interactive learning methods. We first let the agent to learn from human-human conversations with offline supervised training. We then improve the agent further by letting it to interact with users and learn from user demonstrations and feedback with imitation and reinforcement learning. In ad-

Proceedings of NAACL-HLT 2018: Student Research Workshop, pages 67–73
New Orleans, Louisiana, June 2 - 4, 2018. ©2017 Association for Computational Linguistics

dressing the sample efficiency issue with online policy learning via interacting with real users, we further propose a learning method by combining learning-from-user and learning-from-simulation approaches. We conduct empirical study with both automatic system evaluation and human user evaluation. Experimental results show that our proposed model can robustly track dialog state and produce reasonable system responses. Our proposed learning methods also lead to promising improvement on dialog task success rate and human user ratings.

2 Related Work

2.1 Task-Oriented Dialog Systems

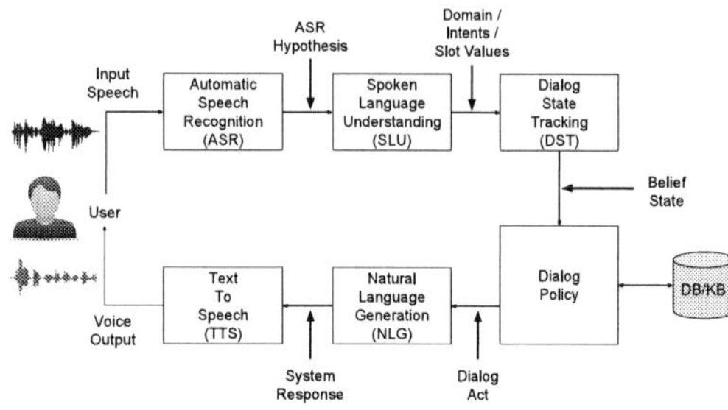

Figure 1: Pipeline architecture for spoken dialog systems

Figure 1 shows a typical pipeline architecture of task-oriented spoken dialog system. Transcriptions of user's speech are firstly passed to the SLU module, where the user's intention and other key information are extracted. This information is then formatted as the input to DST, which maintains the current state of the dialog. Outputs of DST are passed to the dialog policy module, which produces a dialog act based on the facts or entities retrieved from external resources (such as a database or a knowledge base). The dialog act emitted by the dialog policy module serves as the input to the NLG, through which a natural language format system response is generated. In this thesis work, we propose end-to-end solutions that focus on three core components of task-oriented dialog system: SLU, DST, and dialog policy.

2.2 End-to-End Dialog Models

Conventional task-oriented dialog systems use a pipeline design by connecting the above core system components together. Such pipeline system design makes it hard to track source of errors and align system optimization targets. To ameliorate these limitations, researchers have recently started exploring end-to-end solutions for task-oriented dialogs. Wen et al. (Wen et al., 2017) proposed an end-to-end trainable neural dialog model with modularly connected system components for SLU, DST, and dialog policy. Although these system components are end-to-end connected, they are trained separately. It is not clear whether common features and representations for different tasks can be effectively shared during the dialog model training. Moreover, the system is trained with supervised learning on fixed dialog corpora, and thus may not generalize well to unseen dialog states when interacting with users.

Bordes and Weston (Bordes and Weston, 2017) proposed a task-oriented dialog model from a machine reading and reasoning approach. They used an RNN to encode the dialog state and applied end-to-end memory networks to learn it. In the same line of research, people explored using query-regression networks (Seo et al., 2016), gated memory networks (Liu and Perez, 2017), and copy-augmented networks (Eric and Manning, 2017) to learn the dialog state RNN. Similar to (Wen et al., 2017), these systems are trained on fixed sets of simulated and human-machine dialog corpora, and thus are not capable to learn interactively from users. The knowledge base information is pulled offline based on existing dialog corpus. It is unknown whether the reasoning capability achieved in offline model training can generalize well to online user interactions.

Williams et al. (Williams et al., 2017) proposed a hybrid code network for task-oriented dialog that can be trained with supervised and reinforcement learning (RL). Li et al. (Li et al., 2017) and Dhingra et al. (Dhingra et al., 2017) also proposed end-to-end task-oriented dialog models that can be trained with hybrid supervised learning and RL. These systems apply RL directly on supervised pre-training models, without discussing the potential issue with dialog state distribution mismatch between supervised training and interactive learning. Moreover, current end-to-end dialog models are mostly trained and evaluated against user simulators. Ideally, RL based dialog learning should be performed with human users by collecting real user feedback. In interactive learning with human users, online learning efficiency becomes a critical factor. This sample efficiency issue with online policy learning is not addressed in these works.

3 End-to-End Dialog Learning

3.1 Proposed Dialog Learning Framework

Task-oriented dialog system assists human user to complete tasks by conducting multi-turn conversations. From a learning point of view, the dialog agent learns to act by interacting with users and trying to maximize long-term success or an expected reward. Ideally, the dialog agent should not only be able to passively receive signals from the environment (i.e. the user) and learn to act on it, but also to be able to understand the dynamics of the environment and predict the changes of the environment state. This is also how we human beings learn from the world. We design our dialog learning system following the same philosophy.

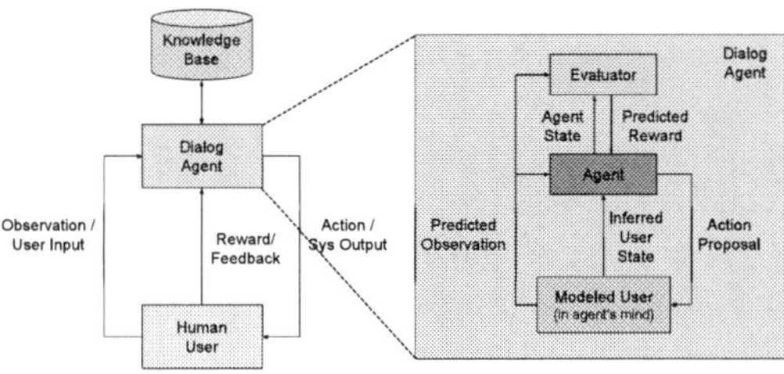

Figure 2: Proposed task-oriented dialog learning framework

Figure 2 shows our proposed learning framework for task-oriented dialog. The dialog agent interacts with user in natural language format and improves itself with the received user feedback. The dialog agent also learns to interface with external resources, such as a knowledge base or a database, so as to be able to provide responses to user that are based on the facts in the real world. Inside the dialog agent, the agent learns to model the user dynamics by predicting their behaviors in conversations. Such modeled user or simulated user in the agent's mind can help the agent to simulate dialogs that mimic the conversations between the agent and a real user. By "imagining" such conversations and learning from it, the agent can potentially learn more effectively and reduce the number of learning cycles with real users.

3.2 End-to-End System Architecture

Figure 3 shows the architecture of our proposed end-to-end task-oriented dialog system (Liu et al., 2017). We use a hierarchical LSTM to model a dialog with multiple turns. The lower level LSTM, which we refer to as the utterance-level LSTM, is used to encode the user utterance. The higher-level LSTM, which we refer to as the dialog-level LSTM, is used to model a dialog over a sequence of turns. User input to the system in natural language format is encoded in a continuous vector form via the utterance-level LSTM. The LSTM outputs can be fed to SLU decoders such as an intent classifier and a slot filler. We may use such SLU module outputs as input to the state tracker. Alternatively, we may directly use the continuous representation of user's utterance without passing it through a semantic decoder. The encoded user utterance, together with the encoding of the previous system turn, is connected to the dialog-level LSTM. State of this dialog-level LSTM maintains a continuous representation of the dialog state. Based on this state, the belief tracker generates a probability distribution over candidate values for each of the tracked goal slots. A query command can then be formulated with the belief tracking outputs and sent to a database to retrieve requested information. Finally, the system produces an action by combining information from the dialog state, the belief tracking outputs, and the encoding of the query results. This system dialog action, together with the belief tracking output and the query results, is used to generate the final natural language system response via a natural language generator. All system components are connected via differentiable operations, and the entire system (SLU, DST, and policy) can thus be optimized end-to-end.

4 Learning from Dialog Corpora

In this section, we describe our proposed corpus-based supervised training methods for task-oriented dialog. We first explain our supervised learning models for SLU, and then explain how these models are extended for dialog modeling.

4.1 SLU and Utterance Modeling

We first describe our proposed utterance representation learning method by jointly optimizing the two core SLU tasks, intent detection and slot filling. Intent detection and slot filling are usually handled separately by different models, without effectively utilizing features and representations that can be shared between the two tasks. We propose to jointly optimize the two SLU tasks with recurrent neural networks. A bidirectional LSTM reader is used to encode the user utterance. LSTM

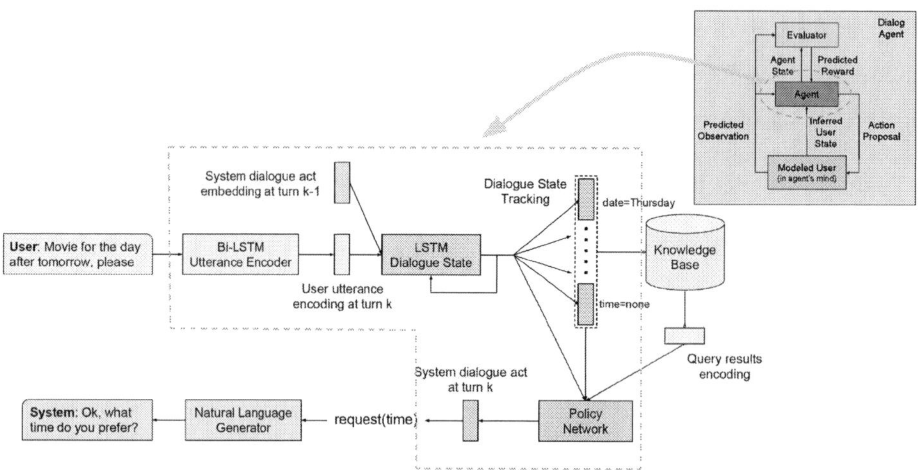

Figure 3: End-to-end task-oriented dialog system architecture

state output at each time step is used for slot label prediction for each word in the utterance. A weighted average of these LSTM state outputs is further used as the representation of the utterance for user intent prediction. The model objective function is a linear interpolation of the cross-entropy losses for intent and slot label predictions. Experiment results (Liu and Lane, 2016a,b) on ATIS SLU corpus show that the proposed joint training model achieves state-of-the-art intent detection accuracy and slot filling F1 scores. The joint training model also outperforms the independent training models on both tasks.

4.2 Dialog Modeling with Hierarchical LSTM

The above described SLU models operate on utterance or turn level. In dialog learning, we expect the system to be able to reason over the dialog context, which covers information over a sequence of past dialog turns. We extend the LSTM based SLU models by adding a higher level LSTM on top to model dialog context over multiple turns (Liu and Lane, 2017a). The lower level LSTM uses the same bidirectional LSTM design as in section 4.1 to encode natural language utterance. These encoded utterance representation at each turn serve as the input to the upper level LSTM that models dialog context. Based on the dialog state encoded in the dialog-level LSTM, the model produces a probability distribution over candidate values for each of the tracked goal slots. This serves the functionality of a dialog state tracker. Furthermore, the model predicts the system dialog act or

a delexicalised system response based on the current dialog state. This can be seen as learning a supervised dialog policy by following the expert actions via behavior cloning.

In supervised model training, we optimize the parameter set θ to minimize the cross-entropy losses for dialog state tracking and system action prediction:

$$\min_\theta \sum_{k=1}^{K} -\Big[\sum_{m=1}^{M} \lambda_{l^m} \log P(l_k^{m*}|\mathbf{U}_{\leq k}, \mathbf{A}_{<k}, \mathbf{E}_{<k}; \theta) + \lambda_a \log P(a_k^*|\mathbf{U}_{\leq k}, \mathbf{A}_{<k}, \mathbf{E}_{\leq k}; \theta) \Big]$$

$$(1)$$

where λs are the linear interpolation weights for the cost of each system output. l_k^{m*} and a_k^* are the ground truth labels for goal slots and system action at the kth turn. In the evaluation (Liu and Lane, 2017b) on DSTC2 dialog datset, the proposed model achieves near state-of-the-art performance in dialog goal tracking accuracy. Moreover, the proposed model demonstrates promising results in producing appropriate system responses, outperforming prior end-to-end neural network models using per-response accuracy evaluation metric.

5 Learning from Human Demonstration

The supervised training dialog model described in section 4 performs well in offline evaluation setting on fixed dialog corpora. The same model performance may not generalize well to unseen dialog states when the system interacts with users. We propose interactive dialog learning methods with imitation learning to address this issue.

5.1 Imitation Learning with Human Teaching

Supervised learning succeeds when training and test data distributions match. During dialog interaction with users, any mistake made by the system or any deviation in the user's behavior may lead it to a different state distribution that the supervised training agent has seen in the training corpus. The supervised training agent thus may fail due to the compounding errors and dialog state distribution mismatch between offline training and user interaction. To address this issue, we propose a dialog imitation learning method and let the dialog agent to learn interactively from user teaching. After obtaining a supervised training model, we deploy the agent to let it interact with users using its learned dialog policy. The agent may make errors during user interactions. We then ask expert users to correct the agent's mistakes and demonstrate the right actions for the agent to take (Ross et al., 2011). In this manner, we collect additional dialog samples that are guided by the agent's own policy. Learning on these samples directly addresses the limitation of the currently learned model. With experiments (Liu et al., 2018) in a movie booking domain, we show that the agent can efficiently learn from the expert demonstrations and improve dialog task success rate with the proposed imitation dialog learning method.

5.2 Dialog Reward Learning with Adversarial Training

Supervised learning models that imitate expert behavior in conducting task-oriented dialogs usually require a large amount of training samples to succeed due to the compounding errors from covariate shift as discussed in 5.1. A potential resolution to this problem is to infer a dialog reward function from expert demonstrations and use it to guide dialog policy learning. Task-oriented dialog systems are mainly designed to maximize overall user satisfaction, which can be seen as a reward, in assisting users with tasks. As claimed by Ng et al. (Ng et al., 2000), reward function as opposed to policy can usually provide the most succinct and robust definition of a task.

We propose a generative adversarial training method in recovering the dialog reward function in the expert's mind. The generator is the learned dialog agent, who interacts with users to generate dialog samples. The discriminator is a neu-

ral network model whose job is to distinguish between the agent's behavior and an expert's behavior. Specifically, we present two dialog samples, one from the human agent and one from the machine agent, to the discriminator. We let the discriminator to maximize the likelihood of the sample from the human agent and minimize that from the machine agent. The likelihood of the sample generated by the machine agent can be used as the reward to the agent. Gradient of the discriminator in optimization can be written as:

$$\nabla_{\theta_D} \left[\mathbb{E}_{d \sim \theta_{demo}} \left[log(D(d)) \right] + \mathbb{E}_{d \sim \theta_G} \left[log(1 - D(d)) \right] \right] \tag{2}$$

where θ_G is the learned policy of the machine agent and θ_{demo} is the human agent policy. θ_D is the parameters of the discriminator model.

6 Learning from Human Feedback

In this section, we describe our proposed methods in learning task-oriented dialog model interactively from human feedback with reinforcement learning (RL).

6.1 End-to-End Dialog Learning with RL

After the supervised and imitation training stage, we propose to further optimize the dialog model with RL by letting the agent to interact with users and collecting simple form of user feedback. The feedback is only collected at the end of a dialog. A positive reward is assigned for success tasks, and a zero reward is assigned for failure tasks. A small step penalty is applied to each dialog turn to encourage the agent to complete the task in fewer steps. We propose to use policy gradient based methods for dialog policy learning. With likelihood ratio gradient estimator, the gradient of the objective function can be derived as:

$$\begin{aligned} \nabla_\theta J_k(\theta) &= \nabla_\theta \mathbb{E}_\theta \left[R_k \right] \\ &= \mathbb{E}_{\theta_a} \left[\nabla_\theta \log \pi_\theta(a_k|s_k) R_k \right] \end{aligned} \tag{3}$$

This last expression above gives us an unbiased gradient estimator. We sample the agent action based on the currently learned policy at each dialog turn and compute the gradient. In the experiments (Liu et al., 2017) on a movie booking task domain, we show that the proposed RL based optimization leads to significant improvement on task success rate and reduction of dialog turn size comparing to supervised training model. RL after imitation learning with human teaching not only improves dialog policy, but also improves the underlying system components (e.g. state tracking) in the end-to-end training framework.

6.2 Co-Training of Dialog Agent and Simulated User

We aim to design a dialog agent that can not only learn from user feedback, but also to understand the user dynamics and predict the change of user states. Thus, we need to build a user model, which can be used to simulate conversation between an agent and a user to help the agent to learn better policies. Similar to how a dialog agent acts in task-oriented dialogs, a simulated user picks actions based on the dialog state. In addition, the user policy also depends on the user's goal. In modeling the user (Liu and Lane, 2017c), we design a hierarchical LSTM model, similar to the design of dialog agent described in section 3.2, with additional user goal encoding as the model input. The simulated user is firstly trained in a supervised manner using task-oriented dialog corpora, similar to how we train the dialog agent as described in section 4.2. After bootstrapping a dialog agent and a simulated user with supervised training, we improve them further by simulating task-oriented dialogs between the two agents and iteratively optimizing their policies with deep RL. The reward for RL can either be obtained from the learned reward function described in section 5.2 or given by the human users. The intuition behind the co-training framework is that we model task-oriented dialog as a goal fulfilling process, in which we let the dialog agent and the modeled user to positively collaborate to achieve the goal. The modeled user is given a goal to complete, and it is expected to demonstrate coherent but diverse user behavior. The agent, on the other hand, attempts to estimate the user's goal and fulfill his request.

6.3 Learning from Simulation and Interaction with RL

Learning dialog model from user interaction by collecting user feedback (as in section 6.1) is effective but can be very sample inefficient. One might have to employ a large number of users to interact with the agent before the system can reach a satisfactory performance level. On the other hand, learning from dialog simulation internally to the dialog agent (as in section 6.2) is relatively cheap to conduct, but the performance is limited to the modeling capacity learned from

the limited labeled dialog samples. In this section, we describe our proposed method in combining the learning-from-user approach and learning-from-simulation approach, with expectation to improve the online interactive dialog learning efficiency with real users.

We let the dialog agent to conduct dialog with real users using its learned policy and collect feedback (reward) from the user. The newly collected dialog sample and reward are then used to update the dialog agent with the RL algorithm described in section 6.1. Before letting the agent to start a new session of interactive learning with users, we perform a number of learning-from-simulation training cycles. We let the updated dialog agent to "imagine" its conversation with the modeled user, and fine-tune both of them with RL using the reward obtained from the learned reward function (section 5.2). The intuition behind this proposed integrated learning method is that we want to enforce the dialog agent to fully digest the knowledge learned from the interaction with real user by simulating similar dialogs internally. Such integrated learning method may effectively improve dialog learning efficiency and reduce the number of interactive learning attempts with real users.

7 Conclusions

In this thesis proposal, we design an end-to-end learning framework for task-oriented dialog system. We present our proposed neural network based end-to-end dialog model architecture and discuss the proposed learning methods using offline training with dialog corpora and interactive learning with users. The proposed end-to-end dialog learning framework addresses the limitations of the popular pipeline design of task-oriented dialog systems. We show that the proposed model is able to robustly track dialog state, retrieve information from external resources, and produce appropriate system responses to complete task-oriented dialogs. The proposed learning methods achieve promising dialog task success rate and user satisfaction scores. We will further study the effectiveness of the proposed hybrid learning method in improving sample efficiency in online RL policy learning. We believe the work proposed in this thesis will pioneer a new class of end-to-end learning systems for task-oriented dialog and make a significant step towards intelligent conversational human-computer interactions.

References

Antoine Bordes and Jason Weston. 2017. Learning end-to-end goal-oriented dialog. In *ICLR*.

Yun-Nung Chen, Dilek Hakkani-Tür, Gökhan Tür, Jianfeng Gao, and Li Deng. 2016. End-to-end memory networks with knowledge carryover for multi-turn spoken language understanding. In *INTERSPEECH*, pages 3245–3249.

Bhuwan Dhingra, Lihong Li, Xiujun Li, Jianfeng Gao, Yun-Nung Chen, Faisal Ahmed, and Li Deng. 2017. Towards end-to-end reinforcement learning of dialogue agents for information access. In *ACL*.

Mihail Eric and Christopher D Manning. 2017. A copy-augmented sequence-to-sequence architecture gives good performance on task-oriented dialogue. In *EACL*.

Milica Gasic and Steve Young. 2014. Gaussian processes for pomdp-based dialogue manager optimization. *IEEE/ACM Transactions on Audio, Speech, and Language Processing*.

Matthew Henderson, Blaise Thomson, and Steve Young. 2014. Word-based dialog state tracking with recurrent neural networks. In *SIGDIAL*.

Sungjin Lee and Amanda Stent. 2016. Task lineages: Dialog state tracking for flexible interaction. In *SIGDIAL*.

Xuijun Li, Yun-Nung Chen, Lihong Li, and Jianfeng Gao. 2017. End-to-end task-completion neural dialogue systems. In *IJCNLP*.

Bing Liu and Ian Lane. 2016a. Attention-based recurrent neural network models for joint intent detection and slot filling. In *Interspeech*.

Bing Liu and Ian Lane. 2016b. Joint online spoken language understanding and language modeling with recurrent neural networks. In *SIGDIAL*.

Bing Liu and Ian Lane. 2017a. Dialog context language modeling with recurrent neural networks. In *Acoustics, Speech and Signal Processing (ICASSP), 2017 IEEE International Conference on*. IEEE.

Bing Liu and Ian Lane. 2017b. An end-to-end trainable neural network model with belief tracking for task-oriented dialog. In *Interspeech*.

Bing Liu and Ian Lane. 2017c. Iterative policy learning in end-to-end trainable task-oriented neural dialog models. In *IEEE ASRU*.

Bing Liu, Gokhan Tur, Dilek Hakkani-Tur, Pararth Shah, and Larry Heck. 2017. End-to-end optimization of task-oriented dialogue model with deep reinforcement learning. In *NIPS Workshop on Conversational AI*.

Bing Liu, Gokhan Tur, Dilek Hakkani-Tur, Pararth Shah, and Larry Heck. 2018. Dialogue learning with human teaching and feedback in end-to-end trainable task-oriented dialogue systems. In *NAACL*.

Fei Liu and Julien Perez. 2017. Gated end-to-end memory networks. In *EACL*.

Grégoire Mesnil, Yann Dauphin, Kaisheng Yao, Yoshua Bengio, Li Deng, Dilek Hakkani-Tur, Xiaodong He, Larry Heck, Gokhan Tur, Dong Yu, et al. 2015. Using recurrent neural networks for slot filling in spoken language understanding. *Audio, Speech, and Language Processing, IEEE/ACM Transactions on*, 23(3):530–539.

Nikola Mrkšić, Diarmuid O Séaghdha, Tsung-Hsien Wen, Blaise Thomson, and Steve Young. 2016. Neural belief tracker: Data-driven dialogue state tracking. *arXiv preprint arXiv:1606.03777*.

Andrew Y Ng, Stuart J Russell, et al. 2000. Algorithms for inverse reinforcement learning. In *ICML*.

Antoine Raux, Brian Langner, Dan Bohus, Alan W Black, and Maxine Eskenazi. 2005. Lets go public! taking a spoken dialog system to the real world. In *in Proc. of Interspeech 2005*.

Stéphane Ross, Geoffrey J Gordon, and Drew Bagnell. 2011. A reduction of imitation learning and structured prediction to no-regret online learning. In *International Conference on Artificial Intelligence and Statistics*, pages 627–635.

Ruhi Sarikaya, Geoffrey E Hinton, and Anoop Deoras. 2014. Application of deep belief networks for natural language understanding. *IEEE/ACM Transactions on Audio, Speech, and Language Processing*.

Minjoon Seo, Ali Farhadi, and Hannaneh Hajishirzi. 2016. Query-regression networks for machine comprehension. *arXiv preprint arXiv:1606.04582*.

Pei-Hao Su, Milica Gasic, Nikola Mrksic, Lina Rojas-Barahona, Stefan Ultes, David Vandyke, Tsung-Hsien Wen, and Steve Young. 2016. On-line active reward learning for policy optimisation in spoken dialogue systems. In *ACL*.

Tsung-Hsien Wen, David Vandyke, Nikola Mrkšić, Milica Gašić, Lina M. Rojas-Barahona, Pei-Hao Su, Stefan Ultes, and Steve Young. 2017. A network-based end-to-end trainable task-oriented dialogue system. In *EACL*.

Jason D Williams, Kavosh Asadi, and Geoffrey Zweig. 2017. Hybrid code networks: practical and efficient end-to-end dialog control with supervised and reinforcement learning. In *ACL*.

Steve Young, Milica Gašić, Blaise Thomson, and Jason D Williams. 2013. Pomdp-based statistical spoken dialog systems: A review. *Proceedings of the IEEE*.

Towards Generating Personalized Hospitalization Summaries

Sabita Acharya, Barbara Di Eugenio, Andrew Boyd, Richard Cameron, Karen Dunn Lopez,
Pamela Martyn-Nemeth, Carolyn Dickens, Amer Ardati
University of Illinois at Chicago
Chicago, Illinois
`sachar4,bdieugen,boyda,rcameron,kdunnl2,pmartyn,`
`cdickens,aardati@uic.edu`

Abstract

Most of the health documents, including patient education materials and discharge notes, are usually flooded with medical jargons and contain a lot of generic information about the health issue. In addition, patients are only provided with the doctor's perspective of what happened to them in the hospital while the care procedure performed by nurses during their entire hospital stay is nowhere included. The main focus of this research is to generate personalized hospital-stay summaries for patients by combining information from physician discharge notes and nursing plan of care. It uses a metric to identify medical concepts that are *Complex*, extracts definitions for the concept from three external knowledge sources, and provides the simplest definition to the patient. It also takes various features of the patient into account, like their concerns and strengths, ability to understand basic health information, level of engagement in taking care of their health, and familiarity with the health issue and personalizes the content of the summaries accordingly. Our evaluation showed that the summaries contain 80% of the medical concepts that are considered as being important by both doctor and nurses. Three patient advisors (i.e individuals who are trained in understanding patient experience extensively) verified the usability of our summaries and mentioned that they would like to get such summaries when they are discharged from hospital.

1 Introduction

In the current hospital scenario, when a patient is discharged, s/he is provided with a discharge note along with the patient education materials, which contain more information about the health issue as well as the measures that need to be taken by the patient or the care-taker to continue with the much needed care. However, with statistics showing that over a third of US adults have difficulty with common health tasks like adhering to medical instructions (Kutner et al., 2006), not many people will be able to understand basic health information and services needed to make appropriate health decisions. More often, patients end up discarding the health documents that are provided to them, either because they get overwhelmed with a lot of information, or because they find it hard to comprehend the medical jargons that such documents are usually flooded with (Choudhry et al., 2016).

Our solution is to generate concise and comprehensible summaries of what happened to a patient in the hospital. Since patients with chronic health conditions such as heart failure (as is our case) need to continue much of the care that is provided by nurses in the hospital even after they are discharged, we integrate the information from both the physician and nursing documents into a summary. We also develop a metric for determining whether a medical concept (a single word or muli-word term) is *Simple* or *Complex* and provide definitions for *Complex* terms. Unlike the "one size fits all" approach that is used for creating health documents, we generate summaries that are personalized according to the patient's preferences, interests, motivation level, and ability to comprehend health information. In this proposal, we will briefly explain our work on summarizing information and simplifying medical concepts. We will also describe our ongoing efforts on personalizing content and our plans for future evaluations.

2 Related Work

Most of the existing approaches on using natural language generation (NLG) for multi-document summarization work only for homogeneous documents (Yang et al., 2015; Banerjee et al., 2015), unlike our case where the physician and nursing

Proceedings of NAACL-HLT 2018: Student Research Workshop, pages 74–82
New Orleans, Louisiana, June 2 - 4, 2018. ©2017 Association for Computational Linguistics

documentation contain different type of content (free text vs concepts). As concerns identifying terms that are *Complex*, some applications assume that all the terms that appear in specific vocabularies or corpora are difficult to understand (Ong et al., 2007; Kandula et al., 2010). These methods are unreliable because none of the currently available vocabularies are exhaustive. For providing explanations to terms that are identified as difficult, Horn et al. (2014) and Biran et al. (2011) use the replacement that was provided to terms from Wikipedia in the Simple Wikipedia parallel corpus. Elhadad (2006) supplements the selected terminologies with definitions obtained from Google "define". In medical domain, some work has been done in obtaining pairs of medical terms and explanations: Elhadad and Sutaria (2007) prepare pairs of complex medical terms by using a parallel corpus of abstracts of clinical studies and corresponding news stories; Stilo et al. (2013) map medical jargon and everyday language by searching for their occurrence in Wikipedia and Google snippets. Our simplification metric is similar to that of (Shardlow, 2013) but we use five times as many features and a different approach for distinguishing between *Simple* and *Complex* terms. We provide definitions to terms similar to Ramesh et al. (2013), but we are not restricted to single word terms only. Unlike Klavans and Muresan (2000), we refer to multiple knowledge sources for definitions of medical concepts.

There are several existing systems that produce personalized content in biomedical domain (Jimison et al., 1992; DiMarco et al., 1995) as well as in non-medical domains (Paris, 1988; Moraes et al., 2014). However, only a few of the existing biomedical systems generate personalized content for the patients (Buchanan et al., 1995; Williams et al., 2007). PERSIVAL system takes in a natural language query and provides customized summaries of medical literature for patients or doctors (Elhadad et al., 2005). BabyTalk system (Mahamood and Reiter, 2011) generates customized descriptions of patient status for people occupying different roles in Neonatal Intensive Care Unit. However, this system relies on handcrafted ontologies, which are very time intensive to create. Our approach to personalization uses several parameters that determine the content to be included in our summary, similarly to the PERSONAGE system (Mairesse and Walker, 2011), a parameteriz-

Attending: Dr. PHYSICIAN.
Admission diagnosis: acute subcortical CVA.
Secondary diagnosis: hypertension.
Discharge diagnosis: Right sided weakness of unknown etiology.
Consultations:. Physical Medicine Rehabilitation.
Physical Therapy.
Occupational Therapy.
General Medicine.
Nutrition.
HPI (per chart):. The patient is a AGE y/o AAF with H/o HTN, DM, CVA in past transferred from MRH for evaluation for possible stroke. per patient, she was ne until saturday at around 700 pm, while attempting to go to bathroom, she fell down as her body below chest suddenly gave away.[...]

Figure 1: Portion of the doctor's discharge note for Patient 149.

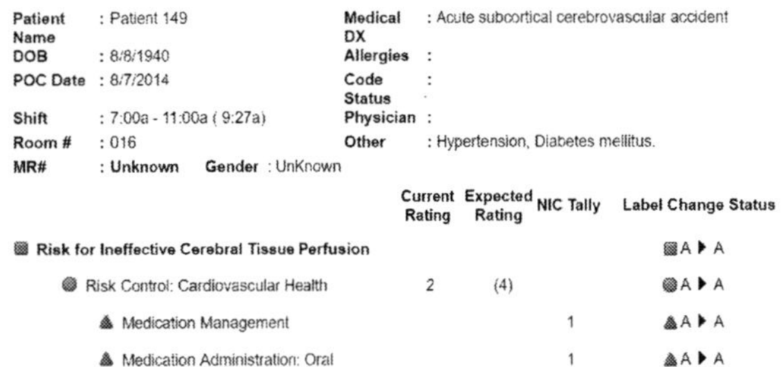

Figure 2: Part of HANDS POC for Patient 149.

able language generator that takes the user's linguistic style into account and generates restaurant recommendations. To the best of our knowledge, there are no existing systems that generate comprehensible and personalized hospital-stay summaries for patients. Moreover, the combination of the four different factors (patient health literacy, motivation to self-care, strengths and concerns, and the patient's familiarity with the health issue) that guide our personalization process has not been explored before.

3 Dataset

Our dataset consists of the doctor's discharge note and shift-by-shift update of the nursing care plan for 60 patients. Discharge note is an unstructured plain text document that usually contains details about the patient, along with other information like the diagnosis, findings, medications, and follow-up information. However, no uniform structure of discharge note is known to be followed by all physicians (Doyle, 2011). Figure 1 shows around 5% of our discharge note for Patient 149. On the other hand, nurses record the details in a standardized electric platform called

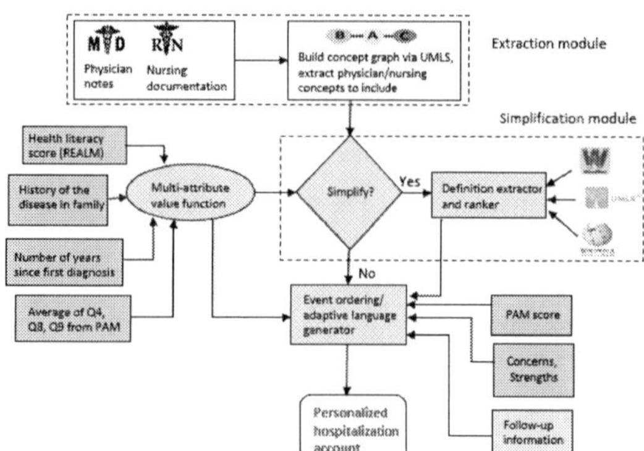

Figure 3: The inputs, output, and workflow of our personalized summary generation system.

HANDS(Keenan et al., 2002), which uses structured nursing taxonomies: *NANDA-I* for nursing diagnosis (Herdman, 2011), *NIC* for nursing intervention (Butcher et al., 2013), and *NOC* for outcomes (Strandell, 2000). Figure 2 shows 15% of a HANDS plan of care (POC) for Patient 149.

4   Approach

The workflow of our presonalized summary generation system is shown in Figure 3. The *Extraction module* is responsible for extracting concepts from physician and nursing documentation and exploring relationship between them. The functioning of this module is explained in Section 4.1. *Simplification module* distinguishes *Complex* terms from *Simple* terms and provides simple explanations to *Complex* terms. This module is explained in Section 4.2. Most of the remaining components of the workflow play a role in producing personalized content and are explained in Section 4.3.

4.1   Exploring relationship between physician and nursing terms

We use MedLEE (Friedman et al., 2004), a medical information extraction tool for extracting medical concepts from the discharge notes and nursing POC. MedLEE maps the concepts to the Unified Medical Language System (UMLS) vocabulary (NIH, 2011). UMLS is a resource that includes more than 3 million concepts from over 200 health and biomedical vocabularies. The knowledge sources provided by UMLS allow us to query about different concepts, their Concept Unique Identifier (CUI), meaning, definitions, along with the relationships between concepts. We begin with

Category	Features
Lexical features	Number of vowels, consonants, prefixes, suffixes,letters, syllables per word
Counts of each POS type	Number of nouns, verbs, adjectives, prepositions, conjunctions, determiners, adverbs, numerals (using Stanford parser)
Vocabulary based	Normalized frequency of the term in Google n-gram corpus, presence of the term in Wordnet
UMLS derived features	Number of semantic types, synonyms, CUIs that are identified for the term; if the term is present in CHV; if the entire term has a CUI; if the semantic type of the term is one of the 16 semantic types from (Ramesh et al., 2013)

Table 1: Features that are extracted for modeling complexity

the nursing concepts (because they are lesser in number as compared to physician concepts) and explore UMLS to identify the physician concepts that are either directly related to the nursing concept or are related through one intermediate node. We restrict ourself to only one intermediate node because going beyond that will lead to reaching up to around 1 million terms in the UMLS graph (Patel et al., 2007), which is not useful for our study. Hence, as shown in Figure 3, the input to this module are all the medical concepts present in the physician and nursing documentation and the output is a list of medical concepts, which comprises of all the concepts from the nursing POC, concepts from the discharge note that are either directly related to a nursing concept or are related through an intermediate concept, and the intermediate concepts themselves. All the concepts that have been explored in this step are candidates for inclusion in our summary. These concepts are then sent to the *Simplification module*, which is briefly described in Section 4.2. For more details on the *Extraction module*, please refer to (Di Eugenio et al., 2014).

4.2   Simplification

The *Simplification module* functions in two steps: 1) it determines whether a concept is *Simple* or *Complex*, and 2) it provides the simplest available definition to a *Complex* concept. Since the existing metrics for assessing health literacy (REALM, TOFHLA, NAALS) and reading level (Felsch, Fry Graph, SMOG) work only on sentences and not on terms (that might consist of a single word or multiple words like *arrhythmia, heart failure*), we set out to develop a new metric for determining term complexity. Our training dataset consists of 600 terms; 300 of which were randomly

Given: i) term T

      ii) linear regression function LR from Section 4.2

1) Assign variable $D=0$

2) Extract all the features for T

3) Supply feature values to LR to obtain a score Z

4) If $Z<0.4$, $D=0$

  If $Z>0.66$, $D=1$

  If $Z>=0.4$ and $Z<=0.66$:

    If semantic type of T falls in our shortlisted types, $D=1$

    Else $D=0$

5) If $D=1$:

  i) Obtain definitions for T from UMLS, Wikipedia, Google

  ii) Extract the medical terms in each definition

  iii) For each term, repeat step 1, 2, and 3 and get a score.

  iv) Add scores of the terms in each definition

  v) Append the definition with the least score to T

  vi) Return T

Else return T with no definition attached

Figure 4: Algorithm for simplifying a term T.

selected from the Dale-Chall list[1], while the remaining 300 terms were randomly chosen from our database of 3164 terms that were explored in Section 4.1. We labeled all the terms from the Dale-Chall list as *Simple* and the terms from our database were annotated as *Simple* or *Complex* by two non-native English speaking undergraduate students who have never had any medical conditions (Cohen's Kappa k=0.786). We assume that non-native English speakers without medical conditions are less familiar with any kind of medical term as compared to native English speakers without medical conditions. Disagreements between the annotators were resolved via mutual consultation. The remaining 2564 terms from our database were used as the testing data.

We extracted all the features enlisted in Table 1 for our terms in training and test dataset. We then used a two step approach for developing our metric. In the first step, we performed linear regression on the training dataset with *Complexity* as the dependent variable. This helped us to identify the features that do not contribute to the complexity of a term. It also provided us with a linear regression function (which we will call as LR) that includes only the important features. In the second step, we performed clustering on the test dataset, using

[1]This list consists of 3000 terms that are known to be understood by 80% of 4th grade students

You were admitted for acute subcortical cerebrovascular accident. During your hospitalization, you were monitored for chances of ineffective cerebral tissue perfusion, risk for falls, problem in verbal communication and walking. We treated difficulty walking related to nervous system disorder with body mechanics promotion. Mobility as a finding has improved appreciably. We provided treatment for risk for ineffective cerebral tissue perfusion with medication management and medication administration. As a result, risk related to cardio-vascular health has reduced slightly. We worked to improve verbal impairment related to communication impairment with speech therapy.[...] With your nurse and doctors, you learned about disease process and medication.

Follow-up: Can follow-up with General Neurology clinic and Medicine clinic as outpatient if desired.

Figure 5: Part of the summary for Patient 149

the 600 terms from our training dataset as cluster seeds. This process resulted in 3 clusters. Out of the 600 cluster seeds, 70% of those in Cluster1 had *Simple* label; 58% of those in Cluster2 had *Simple* label and 42% had Complex label; while 79% of those in Cluster3 had *Complex* label. This indicates the presence of three categories of terms: some that can be identified as *Simple* (Cluster1), some that are *Complex* (Cluster3), and the rest for which there is no clear distinction between *Simple* and *Complex* (Cluster2). For the terms in each of these clusters, we further supplied feature values to LR and analyzed the corresponding scores. We found that across all clusters, 88% of the terms labeled as *Simple* have scores below 0.4 while 96% of the terms whose score was above 0.66 were labeled *Complex*. For the terms whose score was between 0.4 and 0.66, no clear majority of *Simple* or *Complex* labeled terms was observed in any of the clusters. These observations led to the development of our metric, whose functioning is summarized in Figure 4 and is explained in detail in (Acharya et al., 2016). Hence, the *Simplification module* takes a medical concept as input and determines whether it is *Simple* or *Complex*. For the concepts that are identified as being *Complex*, the simplest definition is extracted from the knowledge sources and is appended to the concept, while the *Simple* concepts are directly sent to the language generator.

4.3 Personalized summary generation

4.3.1 Summarizing hospital-stay information

We summarize the information from the discharge note and HANDS POC by using a language generation approach. We use a Java based API called SimpleNLG (Gatt and Reiter, 2009), which uses the supplied constituents like the subject, verb, object, tense, and produces a grammatically correct sentence. It can also compute inflected forms of the content and can aggregate syntactic constituents like phrases and sentences together. The medical concepts with or without definitions appended to them (i.e the output of the *Simplification module*), along with suitable verbs are our input to SimpleNLG. The group of *NANDA-I*, *NIC*, and *NOC* terms are explained in exactly the same order as they are present in the HANDS note. For each group, we begin by explaining the diagnosis (*NANDA-I*), followed by the treatment that was provided (*NIC* term), and the outcome of the treatment (*NOC*) i.e how effective the intervention was in treating the problem. The *NANDA-I* term is used as the subject of the sentence, followed by the physician terms that are directly connected to it or the intermediate concepts that were extracted while exploring the relationship in Section 4.1. The *NIC* intervention is supplied as the object for the diagnosis and a verb "treat" is used for this purpose. We use the current and expected rating values that are associated with each *NOC* concept and use the percentage improvement to decide on the adverb for the sentence. Some portion of the summary generated for Patient 149 is shown in Figure 5. The terms that are underlined in Figure 5 were determined as being *Complex* by our metric and have a definition appended to them. The definitions can be displayed in different forms (like tool-tip text or footnote) depending upon the medium in which the summary will be presented.

We also provide the follow-up information that was mentioned by the physician in the discharge note, if any. Since the patient follow-up information may appear as a separate section or may be spread across various other sections, we use 67 keywords and 15 regular expressions to algorithmically recognize such information. The last paragraph in Figure 5 shows the follow-up information that was obtained for Patient 149.

4.3.2 Personalizing the summary

So far, we have a reasonable summary that contains the important content from both the physician and nursing documentations. However, our summaries still do not include the patient's perspective. Studies have shown that patients' perspective is essential for patient education (Shapiro,

Dear Patient 149, we are sorry to know that you were admitted for acute subcortical <u>cerebrovascular accident</u>. Cerebrovascular accident is a medical condition in which poor blood flow to the brain results in cell death. Dealing with this issue must have been tough for you, we hope you are feeling much better now.

During your hospitalization, we provided treatment for <u>difficulty walking</u> related to <u>nervous system disorder</u> and <u>risk for ineffective cerebral tissue perfusion</u>. We worked to improve <u>verbal impairment</u> and risk for falls.

We can understand that you have to make changes in your way of living, diet and physical activity as a result of your health condition. You have said that you are concerned about your family and friends. We are very glad to know that you have sources to support you and it is really good that you are working on this. Being committed to solving this problem is so important.

Follow-up: Can follow-up with General Neurology clinic and Medicine clinic as outpatient if desired.

Figure 6: Version of a summary for a patient with low PAM score and low level of health literacy.

1993) and that engaging the patients in their own care reduces hospitalizations and improves the quality of life (Riegel et al., 2011). Our work on personalizing patient summary is motivated by these studies. We expect that including patient-specific information such as social-emotional status, preferences, and needs in a summary will encourage patients to read and understand its content, and will make them more informed and active in understand and improving their health status.

There are four different factors that guide our personalization process: health literacy, patient engagement level, patient's familiarity with the health issue, and their strength/concerns. We also introduce several parameters, whose values depend upon the response given by the patient to these four factors.

A) Health literacy: Health literacy is the measure of an individual's ability to gain access to and use information in ways that promote and maintain good health (Nutbeam, 1998). We use the Rapid Estimate of Adult Literacy (REALM) (Davis et al., 1993) test for assessing the health literacy of the patients. REALM consists of 66-itemed word recognition and pronunciation test. Depending upon how correctly a participant pronounces the words in the list, a score is provided. This score tells us whether the health literacy level of the patient is of *third grade or below*, *fourth to sixth grade*, *seventh to eighth grade*, or of *high school level*.

Dear Patient 149, you were admitted for acute subcortical cerebrovascular accident. Cerebrovascular accident is a medical condition in which poor blood flow to the brain results in cell death. During your hospitalization, you were monitored for chances of ineffective cerebral tissue perfusion, risk for falls, problem in verbal communication and walking.

We treated difficulty walking related to nervous system disorder with body mechanics promotion. We provided treatment for risk for ineffective cerebral tissue perfusion with medication management and medication administration. We worked to improve verbal impairment related to communication impairment with speech therapy. We treated risk for falls by managing environment to provide safety.

As a result of these interventions, mobility has improved appreciably. Risk related to cardiovascular health has reduced slightly. On the other hand, communication and fall prevention behavior have improved slightly. With your nurse and doctors, you learned about disease process, medication and fall prevention.

We appreciate your efforts in making changes in your way of living, diet and physical activity for maintaining your health. Keep up the good work. We are very glad to know that you have sources to support you. We hope that you feel better so that you can spend time with your family and friends and return back to your work.

Follow-up: Can follow-up with General Neurology clinic and Medicine clinic as outpatient if desired.

For more information on cerebrovascular accident, please refer to the following website: https://www.healthline.com/health/cerebrovascular-accident

Figure 7: Version of a summary for patient with high PAM score and high level of health literacy.

B) Patient engagement level: In order to determine how motivated a patient is in taking care of his/her health, we use a metric called Patient Activation Measure (PAM) (Hibbard et al., 2005). PAM consists of 13 questions that can be used to determine the patient's stage of activation. We represent patients at stage 1 or 2 as having *low PAM* and those at stage 3 or 4 as having *high PAM*.

C) Strengths/concerns of the patient: We are also interested in identifying the patient's sources of strength and how the disease has affected their lives. For this purpose, we have conducted interviews of 21 patients with heart issues. These interviews are open-ended and the patients are asked to talk about their experiences since they were first diagnosed. We used a pure inductive, grounded theory method for coding the interviews of 9 patients. We found several categories of strength/concern that most of the patients frequently mention, such as: a) priorities in life, b) changes in lifestyle because of the health issue, c)

means of support, and d) ability to cope up with health issues. These topics as well as the possible responses that were collected from the interviews will be phrased as multiple choice questions and will be used for eliciting the strengths and concerns of the patients in real time.

D) Patient's familiarity with the health issue: We are also interested in capturing the patient's disease-specific knowledge. After thoroughly analyzing all the patient interviews, we noticed that patients who have either been having the health issue for some time, or have a history of the health issue in the family, use more disease-specific terminologies during their conversation. Based on this observation, we introduced two parameters: *number of years since first diagnosis*, and *history of the health issue in the family*.

Hence, before a patient gets discharged, s/he will take the health literacy test and answer the following: 1)13 questions from PAM, 2) questions regarding their strengths and concerns, and 3) questions that will assess the patient's familiarity with the health issue. We also introduce a parameter called *health proficiency*, whose value depends upon 4 other parameters: *health literacy, number of years since first diagnosis, history of the health issue in the family*, and *self-efficacy score* (i.e. an average of the scores for questions 4, 8, 9 from PAM). Currently, these 4 constituent parameters are combined in such a way that *health proficiency* can have a value of 1, 2, or 3. We provide maximum weightage to *health literacy*, while the remaining three features are equally weighted. We have developed several rules that take the scores for all the four parameters into account and assign a value to *health proficiency*. Based on the value of *health proficiency*, we make decisions on whether to include more or less details about the medical procedures in the patient summary. Similarly, depending upon whether a patient has *high PAM* or *low PAM*, we decide on whether more or less empathy should be included in the summary.

The phrases that have been used for expressing empathy and encouragement, and the statements for reinforcing patient participation have been derived from the literature on physician-patient and nurse-patient communication (Keller, 1989; Cassell, 1985), as well as some online sources.[2,3,4]

---

[2]www.thedoctors.com/KnowledgeCenter/PatientSafety/ Appendix-2-Examples-Empathetic-Statements-to-Use

[3]myheartsisters.org/2013/02/ 24/empathy-101

[4]www.kevinmd.com/empathy-patient-interactions.html

We have also collected samples of statements from working nursing professionals. Figure 6 shows the personalized version of the summary in Figure 5 for a patient with low health literacy and *low PAM*. Similarly, Figure 7 shows the high health literacy and *high PAM* version of the same summary. As seen from the two samples, the low health literacy version provides information about the health issues of the patient (see second paragraph in Figure 6) and does not include further details about the interventions, while the high literacy version includes details of the health issues, interventions that were done, and the outcomes of the interventions (see second and third paragraph in Figure 7). The patient's response to the questions on their strengths and concerns (as discussed in Section 4.3.2) are described in the third and fourth paragraph of Figure 6 and Figure 7 respectively. For patients with *low PAM* (see Figure 6), we include empathetic phrases like "we are sorry to know that", "we can understand that" and highlight the importance of patient participation with sentences like "Being committed to solving this problem is so important". For *high PAM* patients, we appreciate their efforts in taking care of themselves and include encouraging sentences like "Keep up the good work".

5 Evaluation and Results

We have performed two qualitative evaluations of our summaries, where we measured the coverage of medical terminologies, and obtained feedback on the content and organization of information in the personalized summaries.

5.1 Coverage of medical terminologies

In order to determine whether our summaries have proper representation of the important information from the physician and nursing notes, we asked a nursing student to read both the physician and nursing notes and generate hand-written summaries for 35 patients. A doctor and a nurse highlighted the important contents from 5 out of the 35 handwritten summaries, which were then compared with the corresponding computer generated versions. This evaluation showed that on average, our summaries contain 80% of the concepts that were considered as important by both the doctor and nurse. Similarly, 70% of the concepts from the entire handwritten summary are present in our automatically generated summaries.

5.2 Feedback on the personalized summaries

We asked three patient advisors for their feedback on our attempts for personalization. Patient advisors are a good representative of the patient views because their job role is to communicate with patients first hand. The main aspect that were evaluated are the appearance of our personalized summaries in terms of their feasibility, readability, consistency of style and formatting, and the clarity of the language used.

All the patient advisors liked the personalized summaries as compared to the original ones because they thought that it had a better flow of information. They were able to distinguish between the low literacy and high literacy version of our summaries. All of them said that they would like to get such a summary when they are discharged from the hospital. One interesting thing that we observed is that even within such a small group of evaluators that have almost similar medical knowledge and experiences, we found that there was no uniformity in the sample of summary they preferred, nor were their reasons behind choosing the particular sample alike. This further demonstrates the need for producing personalized summaries, because the preferences and interests of individuals vary from each other.

6 Conclusion and Future Work

In this paper, we described our efforts on summarizing information from physician and nursing documentation and simplifying medical terms. We explored different factors that can guide a personalization system for producing adaptive health content for patients. We also proposed a personalization system that can incorporate the beliefs, interests, and preferences of different patients into the same text.

Our next immediate goal is to further improve our personalization algorithm by performing several iterations of evaluations with nurses and patient advisors. We are also in the process of conducting a more thorough analysis of our patient interviews to identify other features that can be useful for improving the content and quality of our personalized summaries. We also plan to conduct an evaluation on a fairly large population so that we can get insights into whether the decisions taken by our algorithm on the kind of content to include/exclude in different situations aligns with that of a more general population.

References

Sabita Acharya, Barbara Di Eugenio, Andrew D Boyd, Karen Dunn Lopez, Richard Cameron, and Gail M Keenan. 2016. Generating summaries of hospitalizations: A new metric to assess the complexity of medical terms and their definitions. In *The 9th International Natural Language Generation conference*, page 26.

Siddhartha Banerjee, Prasenjit Mitra, and Kazunari Sugiyama. 2015. Multi-document abstractive summarization using ilp based multi-sentence compression. In *IJCAI*, pages 1208–1214.

Or Biran, Samuel Brody, and Noémie Elhadad. 2011. Putting it simply: a context-aware approach to lexical simplification. In *Proceedings of the 49th Annual Meeting of the Association for Computational Linguistics: Human Language Technologies: short papers-Volume 2*, pages 496–501. Association for Computational Linguistics.

Bruce G Buchanan, Johanna D Moore, Diana E Forsythe, Giuseppe Carenini, Stellan Ohlsson, and Gordon Banks. 1995. An intelligent interactive system for delivering individualized information to patients. *Artificial intelligence in medicine*, 7(2):117–154.

Howard K Butcher, Gloria M Bulechek, Joanne M McCloskey Dochterman, and Cheryl Wagner. 2013. *Nursing interventions classification (NIC)*. Elsevier Health Sciences.

Eric J Cassell. 1985. Talking with patients: The theory of doctor-patient communication.(vol. 1).

Asad J Choudhry, Yaser MK Baghdadi, Amy E Wagie, Elizabeth B Habermann, Stephanie F Heller, Donald H Jenkins, Daniel C Cullinane, and Martin D Zielinski. 2016. Readability of discharge summaries: with what level of information are we dismissing our patients? *The American Journal of Surgery*, 211(3):631–636.

Terry C Davis, Sandra W Long, Robert H Jackson, EJ Mayeaux, Ronald B George, Peggy W Murphy, and Michael A Crouch. 1993. Rapid estimate of adult literacy in medicine: a shortened screening instrument. *Family medicine*, 25(6):391–395.

Barbara Di Eugenio, Andrew D Boyd, Camillo Lugaresi, Abhinaya Balasubramanian, Gail M Keenan, Mike Burton, Tamara G Rezende Macieira, Karen Dunn Lopez, Carol Friedman, Jianrong Li, et al. 2014. Patientnarr: Towards generating patient-centric summaries of hospital stays. *INLG 2014*, page 6.

Chrysanne DiMarco, Graeme Hirst, Leo Wanner, and John Wilkinson. 1995. Healthdoc: Customizing patient information and health education by medical condition and personal characteristics. In *Workshop on Artificial Intelligence in Patient Education*.

Edward Doyle. 2011. The wrong stuff: big gaps in discharge communications.

Noémie Elhadad. 2006. Comprehending technical texts: predicting and defining unfamiliar terms. In *AMIA*.

Noemie Elhadad, M-Y Kan, Judith L Klavans, and KR McKeown. 2005. Customization in a unified framework for summarizing medical literature. *Artificial intelligence in medicine*, 33(2):179–198.

Noemie Elhadad and Komal Sutaria. 2007. Mining a lexicon of technical terms and lay equivalents. In *Proceedings of the Workshop on BioNLP 2007: Biological, Translational, and Clinical Language Processing*, pages 49–56. Association for Computational Linguistics.

Carol Friedman, Lyudmila Shagina, Yves Lussier, and George Hripcsak. 2004. Automated encoding of clinical documents based on natural language processing. *Journal of the American Medical Informatics Association*, 11(5):392–402.

Albert Gatt and Ehud Reiter. 2009. Simplenlg: A realisation engine for practical applications. In *Proceedings of the 12th European Workshop on Natural Language Generation*, pages 90–93. Association for Computational Linguistics.

T Heather Herdman. 2011. *Nursing Diagnoses 2012-14: Definitions and Classification*. John Wiley & Sons.

Judith H Hibbard, Eldon R Mahoney, Jean Stockard, and Martin Tusler. 2005. Development and testing of a short form of the patient activation measure. *Health services research*, 40(6p1):1918–1930.

Colby Horn, Cathryn Manduca, and David Kauchak. 2014. Learning a lexical simplifier using wikipedia. In *ACL (2)*, pages 458–463.

Holly B Jimison, Lawrence M Fagan, RD Shachter, and Edward H Shortliffe. 1992. Patient-specific explanation in models of chronic disease. *Artificial Intelligence in Medicine*, 4(3):191–205.

Sasikiran Kandula, Dorothy Curtis, and Qing Zeng-Treitler. 2010. A semantic and syntactic text simplification tool for health content. In *AMIA annual symposium proceedings*, volume 2010, page 366. American Medical Informatics Association.

Gail M Keenan, Julia R Stocker, Annie T Geo-Thomas, Nandit R Soparkar, Violet H Barkauskas, and Jan L Lee. 2002. The hands project: studying and refining the automated collection of a cross-setting clinical data set. *Computers Informatics Nursing*, 20(3):89–100.

Mary L Keller. 1989. Interpersonal relationships: Professional communication skills for nurses.

Judith L Klavans and Smaranda Muresan. 2000. Definder: Rule-based methods for the extraction of medical terminology and their associated definitions from on-line text. In *Proceedings of the AMIA Symposium*, page 1049. American Medical Informatics Association.

Mark Kutner, Elizabeth Greenburg, Ying Jin, and Christine Paulsen. 2006. The health literacy of america's adults: Results from the 2003 national assessment of adult literacy. nces 2006-483. *National Center for Education Statistics*.

Saad Mahamood and Ehud Reiter. 2011. Generating affective natural language for parents of neonatal infants. In *Proceedings of the 13th European Workshop on Natural Language Generation*, pages 12–21. Association for Computational Linguistics.

François Mairesse and Marilyn A Walker. 2011. Controlling user perceptions of linguistic style: Trainable generation of personality traits. *Computational Linguistics*, 37(3):455–488.

Priscilla Moraes, Kathleen McCoy, and Sandra Carberry. 2014. Adapting graph summaries to the users reading levels. *INLG 2014*, page 64.

NIH. 2011. Umls quick start guide. Unified Medical Language System, https://www.nlm.nih.gov/research/umls/quickstart.html. Last accessed on 10/10/2016.

D Nutbeam. 1998. Health promotion glossary1. *Health promotion international*, 13(4):349–64.

Ethel Ong, Jerwin Damay, Gerard Lojico, Kimberly Lu, and Dex Tarantan. 2007. Simplifying text in medical literature. *Journal of Research in Science, Computing and Engineering*, 4(1).

Cecile L Paris. 1988. Tailoring object descriptions to a user's level of expertise. *Computational Linguistics*, 14(3):64–78.

Chintan O Patel, James J Cimino, et al. 2007. A scale-free network view of the umls to learn terminology translations. In *Medinfo 2007: Proceedings of the 12th World Congress on Health (Medical) Informatics; Building Sustainable Health Systems*, page 689. IOS Press.

Balaji Polepalli Ramesh, Thomas K Houston, Cynthia Brandt, Hua Fang, and Hong Yu. 2013. Improving patients' electronic health record comprehension with noteaid. In *MedInfo*, pages 714–718.

Barbara Riegel, Christopher S Lee, Nancy Albert, Terry Lennie, Misook Chung, Eun Kyeung Song, Brooke Bentley, Seongkum Heo, Linda Worrall-Carter, and Debra K Moser. 2011. From novice to expert: confidence and activity status determine heart failure self-care performance. *Nursing research*, 60(2):132–138.

Johanna Shapiro. 1993. The use of narrative in the doctor-patient encounter. *Family Systems Medicine*, 11(1):47.

Matthew Shardlow. 2013. A comparison of techniques to automatically identify complex words. In *ACL (Student Research Workshop)*, pages 103–109.

Giovanni Stilo, Moreno De Vincenzi, Alberto E Tozzi, and Paola Velardi. 2013. Automated learning of everyday patients' language for medical blogs analytics. In *RANLP*, pages 640–648.

Corrine Strandell. 2000. Nursing outcomes classification. *Rehabilitation Nursing*, 25(6):236.

Sandra Williams, Paul Piwek, and Richard Power. 2007. Generating monologue and dialogue to present personalised medical information to patients. In *Proceedings of the Eleventh European Workshop on Natural Language Generation*, pages 167–170. Association for Computational Linguistics.

Guangbing Yang, Dunwei Wen, Nian-Shing Chen, Erkki Sutinen, et al. 2015. A novel contextual topic model for multi-document summarization. *Expert Systems with Applications*, 42(3):1340–1352.

Read and Comprehend by Gated-Attention Reader with More Belief

Haohui Deng[*]
Department of Computer Science
ETH Zurich
8092 Zurich, Switzerland
hadeng@student.ethz.ch

Yik-Cheung Tam[*]
WeChat AI
Tencent
200234 Shanghai, China
wilsontam@tencent.com

Abstract

Gated-Attention (GA) Reader has been effective for reading comprehension. GA Reader makes two assumptions: (1) a uni-directional attention that uses an input query to gate token encodings of a document; (2) encoding at the cloze position of an input query is considered for answer prediction. In this paper, we propose Collaborative Gating (CG) and Self-Belief Aggregation (SBA) to address the above assumptions respectively. In CG, we first use an input document to gate token encodings of an input query so that the influence of irrelevant query tokens may be reduced. Then the filtered query is used to gate token encodings of an document in a collaborative fashion. In SBA, we conjecture that query tokens other than the cloze token may be informative for answer prediction. We apply self-attention to link the cloze token with other tokens in a query so that the importance of query tokens with respect to the cloze position are weighted. Then their evidences are weighted, propagated and aggregated for better reading comprehension. Experiments show that our approaches advance the state-of-the-art results in CNN, Daily Mail, and Who Did What public test sets.

1 Introduction

Recently, machine reading has received a lot of attention in the research community. Several large-scale datasets of cloze-style query-document pairs have been introduced to measure machine reading capability. Deep leaning has been used for text comprehension with state-of-the-art approaches using attention mechanism. One simple and effective approach is based on Gated Attention (GA) (Dhingra et al., 2017). Viewing the attention mechanism as word alignment, GA uses document-to-query attention to align each word

position of a document with a word token in a query in a "soft" manner. Then the expected encoding of the query, which can be viewed as a masking vector, is computed for each word position of a document. Through a gating function such as the element-wise product, each dimension of a token encoding in a document is interacted with the query for information filtering. Intuitively, each token of a document becomes query-aware. Through the gating mechanism, only relevant information in the document is kept for further processing. Moreover, multi-hop reasoning is applied that performs layer-wise information filtering to improve machine reading performance.

In this paper, we propose Collaborative Gating (CG) that attempts to model bi-directional information filtering between query-document pairs. We first apply query-to-document attention so that each token encoding of a query becomes *document-aware*. Then we use the filtered query and apply usual document-to-query attention to filter the document. Bi-directional attention mechanisms are performed in a collaborative manner. Multi-hop reasoning is then applied like in the GA Reader. Intuitively, bi-directional attention may capture complementary information for better machine comprehension (Seo et al., 2017; Cui et al., 2017). By filtering query-document pairs, we hope that feature representation at the final layer will be more precise for answer prediction. Our experiments have shown that CG can yield further improvement compared to GA Reader.

Another contribution is the introduction of self-attention mechanism in GA Reader. One assumption made by GA Reader is that at the final layer for answer prediction, only the cloze position of a query is considered for computing the evidence scores of entity candidates. We conjecture that surrounding words in a query may be related to the cloze position and thus provide addition-

---

[*] indicates equal contribution

Proceedings of NAACL-HLT 2018: Student Research Workshop, pages 83–91
New Orleans, Louisiana, June 2 - 4, 2018. ©2017 Association for Computational Linguistics

al evidence for answer prediction. Therefore, we employ self-attention to weight each token of the query with respect to the cloze token. Our proposed Self-Belief Aggregation (SBA) amounts to compute the expected encoding at the cloze position which can be viewed as evidence propagation from other word positions. Then similarity scores between the expected cloze token and the candidate entities of the document are computed and aggregated at the final layer. Our experiments have shown that SBA can improve machine reading performance over GA Reader.

This paper is organized as follows: In Section 2, we briefly describe related work. Section 3 gives our proposed approaches to improve GA Reader. We present experimental results in Section 4. In Section 5, we summarize and conclude with future work.

2 Related Work

The cloze-style reading comprehension task can be formulated as: Given a document-query pair (d, q), select $c \in C$ that answers the cloze position in q where C is the candidate set. Each candidate answer c appears at least once in the document d. Below are related approaches to address reading comprehension problem.

Hermann et al. (2015) employed Attentive Reader that computes a document vector via attention using q, giving a joint representation $g(d(q), q)$. In some sense, $d(q)$ becomes a query-aware representation of a document. Impatient Reader was proposed in the same paper to model the joint representation but in a incremental fashion. Stanford Reader (Chen et al., 2016) further simplified Attentive Reader with shallower recurrent units and a bilinear attention. Attention-Sum (AS) Reader introduced a bias towards frequently occurred entity candidates via summation of the probabilities of the same entity instances in a document (Kadlec et al., 2016). Cui et al. (2017) proposed Attention-over-Attention (AoA) Reader that employed a two-way attention for reading comprehension. Multi-hop architecture for text comprehension was also investigated in (Hill et al., 2016; Sordoni et al., 2016; Shen et al., 2017; Munkhdalai and Yu, 2017; Dhingra et al., 2017). Kobayashi et al. (2016) and Trischler et al. (2016) built dynamic representations for candidate answers while reading the document, sharing the same spirit to GA Reader (Dhingra et al., 2017) where token encod-

ings of a document become query-aware. Brarda et al. (2017) proposed sequential attention to make the alignment of query and document tokens context-aware. Wang et al. (2017a) showed that additional linguistic features improve reading comprehension.

Self-attention has been successfully applied in various NLP applications including neural machine translation (Vaswani et al., 2017), abstractive summarization (Paulus et al., 2017) and sentence embedding (Lin et al., 2017). Self-attention links different positions of a sequence to generate a structural representation for the sequence. In reading comprehension literature, self-attention has been investigated. (Wang et al., 2017b) proposed a Gated Self-Matching mechanism which produced context-enhanced token encodings in a document. In this paper, we have a different angle for applying self-attention. We employ self-attention to weight and propagate evidences from different positions of a query to the cloze position to enhance reading comprehension performance.

3 Proposed Approaches

To enhance the performance of GA Reader, we propose: (1) Collaborative Gating and (2) Self-Belief Aggregation described in Section 3.1 and Section 3.2 respectively. The notations are consistent to which in original GA Reader paper (see Appendix A).

3.1 Collaborative Gating

In GA Reader, document-to-query attention is applied to obtain query-aware token encodings of a document. The attention flow is thus uni-directional. Seo et al. (2017) and Cui et al. (2017) showed that bi-directional attention can be helpful for reading comprehension. Inspired by their idea, we propose a Collaborative Gating (CG) approach under GA Reader, where *query-to-document* and *document-to-query* attention are applied in a collaborative manner. We first use query-to-document attention to generate *document-aware* query token encodings. Intuitively, we use the document to create a mask for each query token. In this step, the query is said to be "filtered" by the document. Then we use the filtered query to gate document tokens like in GA Reader. The document is said to be "filtered" by the filtered query in the previous step. The output document token encodings are fed into the nex-

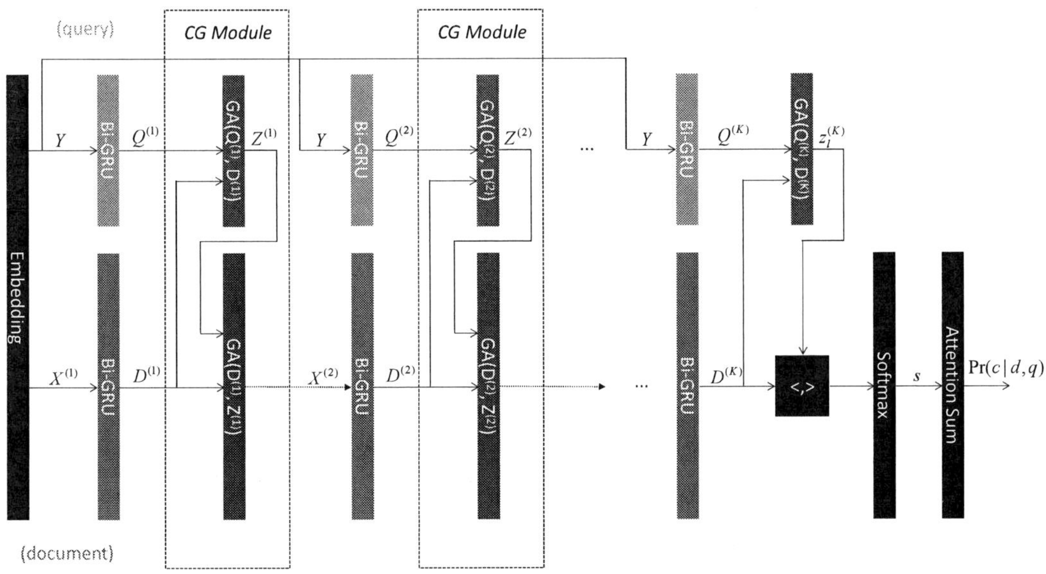

Figure 1: Collaborative Gating with a multi-hop architecture.

t computation layer. Figure 1 illustrates CG under a multi-hop architecture, showing that CG fits naturally into GA Reader. The mathematical notations are consistent to GA Reader described in Appendix A. Dashed lines represent dropout connections. CG modules are circled. At each layer, document tokens X and query tokens Y are fed into Bi-GRUs to obtain token encodings Q and D. Then we apply query-to-document attention to obtain a document-aware query representation using $GA(Q, D)$:

$$\beta_j = softmax(D^T q_j) \tag{1}$$
$$\tilde{d}_j = D\beta_j \tag{2}$$
$$z_j = q_j \odot \tilde{d}_j \tag{3}$$

Upon this, we get the filtered query tokens $Z = [z_1, z_2, ..., z_{|Q|}]$. Then we apply document-to-query attention using Z to obtain a query-aware document representation using $GA(D, Z)$:

$$\alpha_i = softmax(Z^T d_i) \tag{4}$$
$$\tilde{z}_i = Z\alpha_i \tag{5}$$
$$x_i = d_i \odot \tilde{z}_i \tag{6}$$

The resulting sequence $X = [x_1, x_2, ..., x_{|D|}]$ are fed into the next layer. We also explore another way to compute the term $\tilde{z}$ in equation 5. In particular, we may replace Z by Q in equation 5 since

Q is in the unmodified encoding space compared to Z. We will study this effect in detail in Section 4.

At the final layer of GA Reader, encoding at the cloze position is used to calculate similarity score for each word token in a document. We evaluate whether applying the query-to-document attention to filter the query is crucial before computing the similarity scores. In other words, we use $D^{(K)}$ to filter the query producing $Z^{(K)}$. Then the score vector of document positions s is calculated as:

$$s = softmax((z_l^{(K)})^T D^{(K)}) \tag{7}$$

where index l is the cloze position. Similar to GA Reader, the prediction then can be obtained using equation 19 and equation 20 in Appendix A. We will study the effect of this final filtering in detail in Section 4.

3.2 Self Belief Aggregation

In this section, we introduce self-attention for GA Reader to aggregate beliefs from positions other than the cloze position. The motivation is that surrounding words other than the cloze position of a query may be informative so that beliefs from the surrounding positions can be propagated into the cloze position in a weighted manner. We employ self-attention to measure the weight between the cloze and surrounding positions. Figure 2 shows

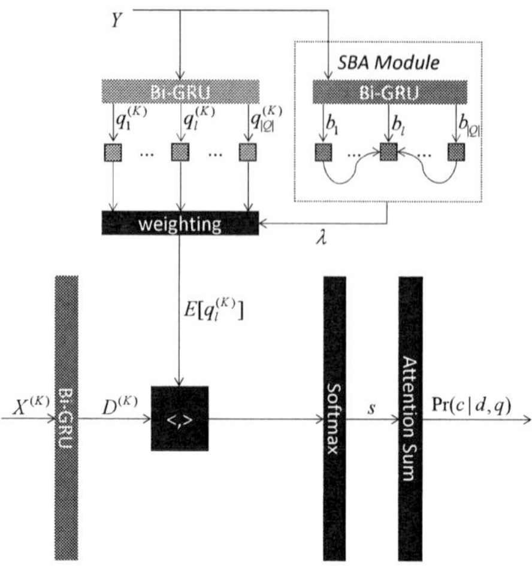

Figure 2: Self Belief Aggregation.

the Self-Belief Aggregation module at the final layer of GA Reader. Query Y is fed into the S-BA module that uses another Bi-directional GRU to obtain token encodings $B = [b_1, b_2, ..., b_{|Q|}]$. Then attention weights are computed using:

$$B = \overleftrightarrow{GRU}(Y) \tag{8}$$

$$\lambda = softmax(B^T b_l) \tag{9}$$

where l is the cloze position. λ measures the importance of each query word with respect to the cloze position. We compute weighted-sum $E[q_l^{(K)}]$ using λ so that beliefs from surrounding words can be propagated and aggregated upon similarity score computation. Finally, scores at word positions of a document are calculated using:

$$s = softmax((E[q_l^{(K)}])^T D^{(K)}) \tag{10}$$

When CG is applied jointly with SBA, the filtered query $Z^{(K)}$ is used instead of $Q^{(K)}$. Namely, $E[q_l^{(K)}])$ is replaced by $E[z_l^{(K)}])$ in equation 10.

Note that self-attention can also be applied on documents to model correlation among words in documents. Considering a document sentence *"Those efforts helped him earn the 2013 CNN Hero of the Year"* and query *"@placeholder was the 2013 CNN Hero of the Year"*. Obviously, the entity co-referenced by *him* is the answer. So we hope that self-attention may have the co-reference resolution effect for "him". We will provide empirical results in Section 4.

4 Experiments

We provide experimental evaluation on our proposed approaches on public datasets in this section.

4.1 Datasets

News stories from CNN and Daily Mail (Hermann et al., 2015)[1] were used to evaluate our approaches. In particular, a query was generated by replacing an entity in the summary with @placeholder. Furthermore, entities in the news articles were anonymized to erase the world knowledge and co-occurrence effect for reading comprehension. Word embeddings of these anonymized entities are thus less informative.

Another dataset was Who Did What[2] (WD-W) (Onishi et al., 2016), constructed from the LD-C English Gigaword newswire corpus. Document pairs appeared around the same time period and with shared entities were chosen. Then, one article was selected as document and another article formed a cloze-style query. Queries that were answered easily by the baseline were removed to make the task more challenging. Two versions of the WDW datasets were considered for experiments: a smaller "strict" version and a larger but noisy "relaxed" version. Both shared the same validation and test sets.

4.2 Collaborative Gating Results

We evaluated Collaborative Gating under various settings. Recall from Section 3.1, we proposed two schemes for calculating the gates: Using Q or Z in equation 5. When using Z for computation, the semantics of the query are altered. When using the original Q, the semantics of the query are not altered. Moreover, we also investigate whether to apply query filtering at the final layer (denoted as "+final filtering" in Table 2).

Results show that CG helps compared to the baseline GA Reader. This may be due to the effect of query-to-document attention which makes the token encodings of a query more discriminable. Moreover, it is crucial to apply query filtering at the final layer. Using the original Q to compute the gates brought us the best results with an absolute gain of 0.7% compared to GA Reader on both the validation and test sets. Empirically, we found

---

[1] https://github.com/deepmind/rc-data
[2] https://tticnlp.github.io/who_did_what/

Model	CNN		Daily Mail		WDW Strict		WDW Relaxed	
	Val	Test	Val	Test	Val	Test	Val	Test
Deep LSTM Reader †	55.0	57.0	63.3	62.2	-	-	-	-
Attentive Reader †	61.6	63.0	70.5	69.0	-	53	-	55
Impatient Reader †	61.8	63.8	69.0	68.0	-	-	-	-
MemNets †	63.4	66.8	-	-	-	-	-	-
AS Reader †	68.6	69.5	75.0	73.9	-	57	-	59
DER Network †	71.3	72.9	-	-	-	-	-	-
Stanford AR †	73.8	73.6	77.6	76.6	-	64	-	65
Iterative AR †	72.6	73.3	-	-	-	-	-	-
EpiReader †	73.4	74.0	-	-	-	-	-	-
AoA Reader †	73.1	74.4	-	-	-	-	-	-
ReasoNet †	72.9	74.7	77.6	76.6	-	-	-	-
NSE †	-	-	-	-	66.5	66.2	67.0	66.7
BiDAF †	76.3	76.9	80.3	79.6	-	-	-	-
GA Reader †	77.9	77.9	81.5	80.9	71.6	71.2	72.6	72.6
MemNets (ensemble) †	66.2	69.4	-	-	-	-	-	-
AS Reader (ensemble) †	73.9	75.4	78.7	77.7	-	-	-	-
Stanford AR (ensemble) †	77.2	77.6	80.2	79.2	-	-	-	-
Iterative AR (ensemble) †	75.2	76.1	-	-	-	-	-	-
CG	**78.6**	78.6	81.9	**81.4**	**72.4**	71.9	73.0	72.6
SBA	78.5	**78.9**	**82.0**	81.2	71.5	71.5	72.3	71.3
CG + SBA	78.5	78.2	81.9	81.2	**72.4**	**72.0**	**73.1**	**72.8**

Table 1: Validation and test accuracies on CNN, Daily Mail and WDW. Results marked with † are previously published results.

Model	Accuracy	
	Val	Test
GA Reader	77.9	77.9
CG (by Z)	78.4	78.1
CG (by Q)	77.9	78.1
CG (by Z, +final filtering)	**78.7**	77.9
CG (by Q, +final filtering)	78.6	**78.6**

Table 2: Performance of Collaborative Gating under different settings on the CNN corpus.

Model	Accuracy	
	Val	Test
GA Reader	77.9	77.9
SBA on $Q^{(K)}$ (tanh)	77.1	77.1
SBA on $Q^{(K)}$	**78.5**	**78.9**
SBA on $D^{(K)}$	78.1	78.3
SBA on $D^{(K)}\&Q^{(K)}$	78.1	78.2

Table 3: Performance of Self-Belief Aggregation under different settings on the CNN corpus.

that CG using Z for gate computation seems easier to overfit. Therefore, we use CG with the setting "by Q, +final filtering" for further comparison.

4.3 Self-Belief Aggregation Results

To study the effect of SBA, we disabled CG in the reported experiments of this section. Furthermore, we compare the attention functions using dot product and a feed forward neural network with $tanh()$ activation (Wang et al., 2017b). Results are shown in Table 3.

SBA yielded performance gain on all settings when the attention function was dot product. On the other hand, attention function using feed-forward neural network degraded accuracy compared to the baseline GA Reader which was surprising to us. Although SBA on $Q^{(K)}$ and $D^{(K)}$ individually yielded performance gain, combining them together did not bring further improvement. Even a slight drop in test accuracy was observed. Applying SBA on both query and document may make the training more difficult. From the empirical results, it seems that the learning process was led solely by document self-attention. In future work, we will consider a stepwise approach where the previous best model of a simpler network architecture will be used for initialization to avoid

Query: *in a video , @placeholder says he is sick of @entity3 being discriminated against in @entity5* (**Correct Answer:** @entity18)

GA Reader (Prediction: @entity4):

@entity4 *, the leader of the* @entity5 @entity9 *(* @entity9 *) , complains that* @entity5 *'s membership of the* @entity11 *means it is powerless to stop a flow of foreign immigrants , many from impoverished* @entity15 *, into his " small island " nation . in a video posted on* @entity20 *, prince* @entity18 *said he was fed up with discrimination against* @entity3 *living in* @entity5 *.*

Collaborative Gating (Prediction: @entity18):

@entity4 *, the leader of the* @entity5 @entity9 *(* @entity9 *) , complains that* @entity5 *'s membership of the* @entity11 *means it is powerless to stop a flow of foreign immigrants , many from impoverished* @entity15 *, into his " small island " nation . in a video posted on* @entity20 *, prince* @entity18 *said he was fed up with discrimination against* @entity3 *living in* @entity5 *.*

Self Belief Aggregation (Prediction: @entity18):

@entity4 *, the leader of the* @entity5 @entity9 *(* @entity9 *) , complains that* @entity5 *'s membership of the* @entity11 *means it is powerless to stop a flow of foreign immigrants , many from impoverished* @entity15 *, into his " small island " nation . in a video posted on* @entity20 *, prince* @entity18 *said he was fed up with discrimination against* @entity3 *living in* @entity5 *.*

Figure 3: Comparison between GA Reader and our proposed approaches. Entities with more red color receives higher softmax scores.

joint training from scratch. Self-attention over a long document may be difficult. Constraints such as locality may be imposed to restrict the number of word candidates in self-attention. We conjecture that modeling co-reference between entities and pronouns may be helpful compared to the full-blown self-attention over all word tokens in a document.

Figure 4 shows self-attention on two sample queries using a trained model. Surprisingly, the attention weight at the cloze position is almost

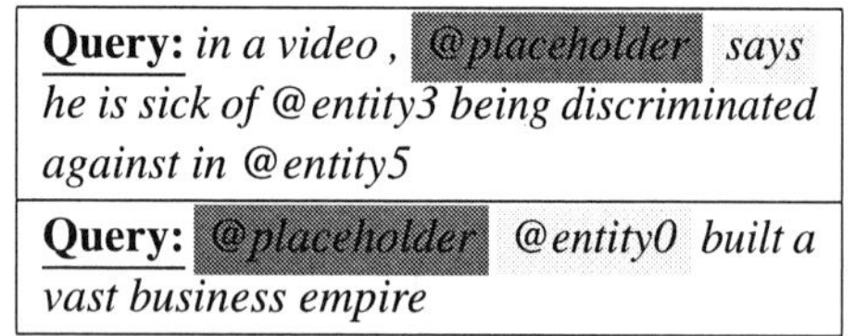

Query: *in a video ,* @placeholder *says he is sick of @entity3 being discriminated against in @entity5*

Query: @placeholder @entity0 *built a vast business empire*

Figure 4: Self beliefs on each query positions with respect to @placeholder.

equal to unity. As a result, the weighted-sum of encodings at the cloze position reduces to encoding at the cloze position, that is the assumption of GA Reader. This may imply that SBA somehow

contributes to better GA Reader training. Since the attention weight at the cloze position is almost unity, SBA can be removed during test. On the other hand, SBA did not work well on smaller datasets such as WDW.

4.4 Overall Results

We compare our approaches with previous published models as shown in Table 1. Note that CG and SBA are under the best settings reported in previous sections. CG+SBA denotes the combination of the best settings of our proposed approaches described in earlier sections. Overall, our approaches achieved the best validation and test accuracies on all datasets. On CNN and Daily Mail, CG or SBA performed similarly. But the combination of them did not always yield additional gain on all datasets. CG exploited information from query and document while SBA only used query. Although these two approaches are quite different, CG and SBA may not have strong complementary relationship for combination from the empirical results.

4.5 Significance Testing

We conducted McNemar's test on the best results
we achieved using sclite toolkit [3]. The test showed
the gains we achieved were all significant at 95%
confidence level. To complete the test, we repeated the baseline GA Reader. Our repetition of GA
Reader yielded almost the same accuracies reported by the original GA Reader paper.

5 Conclusion

We presented Collaborative Gating and Self-
Belief Aggregation to optimize Gated-Attention
Reader. Collaborative Gating employs document-
to-query and query-to-document attentions in a
collaborative and multi-hop manner. With gating
mechanism, both document and query are filtered
to achieve more fine-grained feature representation for machine reading. Self-Belief Aggregation
attempts to propagate encodings of other query
words into the cloze position using self-attention
to relax the assumption of GA Reader. We e-
valuated our approaches on standard datasets and
achieved state-of-the-art results compared to the
previously published results. Collaborative Gating
performed well on all datasets while SBA seems to
work better on large datasets. The combination of
Collaborative Gating and Self-Belief Aggregation
did not bring significant additive improvements,
which may imply that they are not complementary.
We hope that self-attention mechnism may capture the effect of co-reference among words. So
far, experimental results did not bring gain more
than we hope for. Perhaps more constraints in self-
attention should be imposed to learn a better model for future work. Another future investigation
would be to apply SBA at each layer of GA Reader
and further investigate better interaction with Collaborative Gating.

References

Rami Al-Rfou, Guillaume Alain, Amjad Almahairi,
Christof Angermueller, Dzmitry Bahdanau, Nicolas
Ballas, Frédéric Bastien, Justin Bayer, Anatoly Be-
likov, Alexander Belopolsky, et al. 2016. Theano:
A python framework for fast computation of mathe-
matical expressions. *arXiv preprint* .

Dzmitry Bahdanau, Kyunghyun Cho, and Yoshua Bengio. 2015. Neural machine translation by jointly
learning to align and translate. In *Proceedings of
the International Conference on Learning Representations.*

Sebastian Brarda, Philip Yeres, and Samuel R. Bowman. 2017. Sequential attention: A context-aware
alignment function for machine reading. In *ACL
2017 2nd Workshop on Representation Learning for
NLP.*

Danqi Chen, Jason Bolton, and Christopher D Manning. 2016. A thorough examination of the cn-
n/daily mail reading comprehension task. In *Proceedings of the 54th Annual Meeting of the Association for Computational Linguistics.*

Kyunghyun Cho, Bart Van Merriënboer, Caglar Gulcehre, Dzmitry Bahdanau, Fethi Bougares, Holger
Schwenk, and Yoshua Bengio. 2014. Learning
phrase representations using rnn encoder-decoder
for statistical machine translation. In *Proceedings
of the Empirical Methods in Natural Language Processing.*

Yiming Cui, Zhipeng Chen, Si Wei, Shijin Wang, T-
ing Liu, and Guoping Hu. 2017. Attention-over-
attention neural networks for reading comprehension. In *Proceedings of the 55th Annual Meeting
of the Association for Computational Linguistics.*

Bhuwan Dhingra, Hanxiao Liu, Zhilin Yang,
William W Cohen, and Ruslan Salakhutdinov.
2017. Gated-attention readers for text comprehension. In *Proceedings of the 55th Annual Meeting of
the Association for Computational Linguistics.*

Bhuwan Dhingra, Zhong Zhou, Dylan Fitzpatrick,
Michael Muehl, and William W Cohen. 2016.
Tweet2vec: Character-based distributed representa-
tions for social media. In *Proceedings of the 54th
Annual Meeting of the Association for Computation-
al Linguistics.*

Karl Moritz Hermann, Tomas Kocisky, Edward
Grefenstette, Lasse Espeholt, Will Kay, Mustafa Suleyman, and Phil Blunsom. 2015. Teaching machines to read and comprehend. In *Advances in Neural Information Processing Systems.* pages 1693–
1701.

Felix Hill, Antoine Bordes, Sumit Chopra, and Jason
Weston. 2016. The goldilocks principle: Reading
children's books with explicit memory representations. In *Proceedings of the 4th International Conference on Learning Representations.*

Rudolf Kadlec, Martin Schmid, Ondrej Bajgar, and Jan
Kleindienst. 2016. Text understanding with the attention sum reader network. In *Proceedings of the
54th Annual Meeting of the Association for Computational Linguistics.*

Diederik Kingma and Jimmy Ba. 2015. Adam: A
method for stochastic optimization. In *Proceedings
of the International Conference on Learning Representations.*

---

[3] `http://www1.icsi.berkeley.edu/Speech/
docs/sctk-1.2/sclite.htm`

Sosuke Kobayashi, Ran Tian, Naoaki Okazaki, and Kentaro Inui. 2016. Dynamic entity representation with max-pooling improves machine reading. In *HLT-NAACL*. pages 850–855.

Peng Li, Wei Li, Zhengyan He, Xuguang Wang, Ying Cao, Jie Zhou, and Wei Xu. 2016. Dataset and neural recurrent sequence labeling model for open-domain factoid question answering. *arXiv preprint arXiv:1607.06275* .

Zhouhan Lin, Minwei Feng, Cicero Nogueira dos Santos, Mo Yu, Bing Xiang, Bowen Zhou, and Yoshua Bengio. 2017. A structured self-attentive sentence embedding. In *Proceedings of the International Conference on Learning Representations*.

Tsendsuren Munkhdalai and Hong Yu. 2017. Reasoning with memory augmented neural networks for language comprehension. In *Proceedings of the 5th International Conference on Learning Representations*.

Takeshi Onishi, Hai Wang, Mohit Bansal, Kevin Gimpel, and David McAllester. 2016. Who did what: A large-scale person-centered cloze dataset. In *Proceedings of the Empirical Methods in Natural Language Processing*.

Razvan Pascanu, Tomas Mikolov, and Yoshua Bengio. 2013. On the difficulty of training recurrent neural networks. In *International Conference on Machine Learning*. pages 1310–1318.

Romain Paulus, Caiming Xiong, and Richard Socher. 2017. A deep reinforced model for abstractive summarization. *arXiv preprint arXiv:1705.04304* .

Jeffrey Pennington, Richard Socher, and Christopher Manning. 2014. Glove: Global vectors for word representation. In *Proceedings of the empirical methods in natural language processing*. pages 1532–1543.

Minjoon Seo, Aniruddha Kembhavi, Ali Farhadi, and Hannaneh Hajishirzi. 2017. Bidirectional attention flow for machine comprehension. In *Proceedings of the International Conference on Learning Representations*.

Yelong Shen, Po-Sen Huang, Jianfeng Gao, and Weizhu Chen. 2017. Reasonet: Learning to stop reading in machine comprehension. In *Proceedings of the 23rd ACM SIGKDD International Conference on Knowledge Discovery and Data Mining*. ACM, pages 1047–1055.

Alessandro Sordoni, Philip Bachman, Adam Trischler, and Yoshua Bengio. 2016. Iterative alternating neural attention for machine reading. *arXiv preprint arXiv:1606.02245* .

Sainbayar Sukhbaatar, Jason Weston, Rob Fergus, et al. 2015. End-to-end memory networks. In *Advances in neural information processing systems*. pages 2440–2448.

Adam Trischler, Zheng Ye, Xingdi Yuan, and Kaheer Suleman. 2016. Natural language comprehension with the epireader. In *Proceedings of the Empirical Methods in Natural Language Processing*.

Ashish Vaswani, Noam Shazeer, Niki Parmar, Jakob Uszkoreit, Llion Jones, Aidan N. Gomez, Lukasz Kaiser, and Illia Polosukhin. 2017. Attention is all you need. In *Advances in neural information processing systems*.

Hai Wang, Takeshi Onishi, Kevin Gimpel, and McAllester David. 2017a. Emergent predication structure in hidden state vectors of neural readers. In *Proceedings of the 55th Annual Meeting of the Association for Computational Linguistics*.

Wenhui Wang, Nan Yang, Furu Wei, Baobao Chang, and Ming Zhou. 2017b. Gated self-matching networks for reading comprehension and question answering. In *Proceedings of the 55th Annual Meeting of the Association for Computational Linguistics*. volume 1, pages 189–198.

Jason Weston, Sumit Chopra, and Antoine Bordes. 2014. Memory networks. *arXiv preprint arXiv:1410.3916* .

A Gated-Attention Reader

Dhingra et al. (2017) proposed Gated-Attention Reader that combined two successful factors for text comprehension: *Multi-hop architecture* (Weston et al., 2014; Sukhbaatar et al., 2015) and *attention mechanism* (Bahdanau et al., 2015; Cho et al., 2014). At each layer, the Gated-Attention module applies attention to interact with each dimension of token encodings of a document, generating query-aware token encodings. The gated token encodings were then fed as inputs to the next layer. After a multi-hop representation learning, dot product was applied to measure the relevance between each word position in a document and the cloze position of a query. The score of each candidate entity token was calculated and summed like in the Attention-Sum Reader. Below are the details describing GA Reader computation.

Gated Recurrent Units (GRU) are used for text encoding. For an input sequence $X = [x_1, x_2, ..., x_T]$, the output sequence $H = [h_1, h_2, ..., h_T]$ can be computed as follows:

$$r_t = \sigma(W_r x_t + U_r h_{t-1} + b_r)$$
$$z_t = \sigma(W_z x_t + U_z h_{t-1} + b_z)$$
$$\tilde{h}_t = tanh(W_h x_t + U_h(r_t \odot h_{t-1}) + b_h)$$
$$h_t = (1 - z_t) \odot h_{t-1} + z_t \odot \tilde{h}_t$$

where $\odot$ denotes the element-wise multiplication. r_t and z_t are *reset* and *update* gates respectively. A Bi-directional GRU (Bi-GRU) is used to process the sequence in both forward and backward directions. The produced output sequences $[h_1^f, h_2^f, ..., h_T^f]$ and $[h_1^b, h_2^b, ..., h_T^b]$ are concatenated as output encodings:

$$\overleftrightarrow{GRU}(X) = [h_1^f || h_T^b, ..., h_T^f || h_1^b] \qquad (11)$$

Let $X^{(1)} = [x_1^{(1)}, x_2^{(1)}, ..., x_{|D|}^{(1)}]$ denote token embeddings of a document, and $Y = [y_1, y_2, ..., y_{|Q|}]$ denote token embeddings of a query. $|D|$ and $|Q|$ are the length of a document and a query respectively. The multi-hop architecture can be formulated as follows:

$$D^{(k)} = \overleftrightarrow{GRU}_D^{(k)}(X^{(k)}) \qquad (12)$$

$$Q^{(k)} = \overleftrightarrow{GRU}_Q^{(k)}(Y) \qquad (13)$$

$$X^{(k+1)} = GA(D^{(k)}, Q^{(k)}) \qquad (14)$$

where $GA(D, Q)$ is a Gated-Attention module. Mathematically, it is defined as:

$$\alpha_i = softmax(Q^T d_i) \qquad (15)$$

$$\tilde{q}_i = Q\alpha_i \qquad (16)$$

$$x_i = d_i \odot \tilde{q}_i \qquad (17)$$

where d_i is the i-th token in D. Let K be the index of the final layer, GA Reader predicts an answer using:

$$s = softmax((q_l^{(K)})^T D^{(K)}) \qquad (18)$$

$$Pr(c|d, q) \propto \sum_{i \in \mathcal{I}(c,d)} s_i \qquad (19)$$

$$c^* = argmax_{c \in \mathcal{C}} Pr(c|d, q) \qquad (20)$$

where l is the cloze position, c is a candidate and $\mathcal{I}(c, d)$ is the set of positions where a token c appears in document d. c^* is the predicted answer.

B Implementation Details

We used the optimal configurations for CNN, Daily Mail and WDW datasets provided by (Dhingra et al., 2017) for our experiments. Our code was implemented based on the source code [4] using Theano (Al-Rfou et al., 2016). Character embedding (Dhingra et al., 2016) and the token-level indicator feature (Li et al., 2016) were used for WDW. For CNN and Daily Mail, GloVe vectors (Pennington et al., 2014) were used for word embedding initialization. We employed gradient clipping to stabilize GRU training (Pascanu et al., 2013). ADAM (Kingma and Ba, 2015) optimizer was used in all of our experiments.

---

[4] https://github.com/bdhingra/ga-reader

ListOps: A Diagnostic Dataset for Latent Tree Learning

Nikita Nangia[1]

nikitanangia@nyu.edu

Samuel R. Bowman[1,2,3]

bowman@nyu.edu

[1]Center for Data Science
New York University
60 Fifth Avenue
New York, NY 10011

[2]Dept. of Linguistics
New York University
10 Washington Place
New York, NY 10003

[3]Dept. of Computer Science
New York University
60 Fifth Avenue
New York, NY 10011

Abstract

Latent tree learning models learn to parse a sentence without syntactic supervision, and use that parse to build the sentence representation. Existing work on such models has shown that, while they perform well on tasks like sentence classification, they do not learn grammars that conform to any plausible semantic or syntactic formalism (Williams et al., 2018a). Studying the parsing ability of such models in natural language can be challenging due to the inherent complexities of natural language, like having several valid parses for a single sentence. In this paper we introduce ListOps, a toy dataset created to study the parsing ability of latent tree models. ListOps sequences are in the style of prefix arithmetic. The dataset is designed to have a single correct parsing strategy that a system needs to learn to succeed at the task. We show that the current leading latent tree models are unable to learn to parse and succeed at ListOps. These models achieve accuracies worse than purely sequential RNNs.

1 Introduction

Recent work on *latent tree learning* models (Yogatama et al., 2017; Maillard et al., 2017; Choi et al., 2018; Williams et al., 2018a) has introduced new methods of training tree-structured recurrent neural networks (TreeRNNs; Socher et al., 2011) without ground-truth parses. These latent tree models learn to parse with indirect supervision from a downstream semantic task, like sentence classification. They have been shown to perform well at sentence understanding tasks, like textual entailment and sentiment analysis, and they generally outperform their TreeRNN counterparts that use parses from conventional parsers.

Latent tree learning models lack direct syntactic supervision, so they are not being pushed to conform to expert-designed grammars, like the

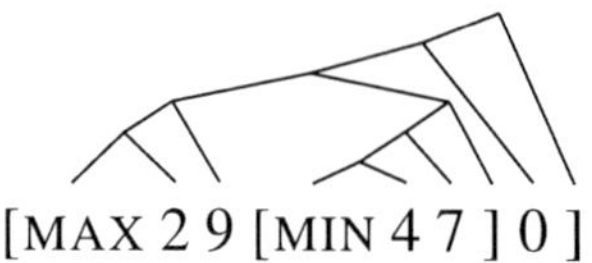

Figure 1: Example of a parsed ListOps sequence. The parse is left-branching within each list, and each constituent is either a partial list, an integer, or the final closing bracket.

Penn Treebank (PTB; Marcus et al., 1999). Theoretically then, they have the freedom to learn whichever grammar is best suited for the task at hand. However, Williams et al. (2018a) show that current latent tree learning models do not learn grammars that follow recognizable semantic or syntactic principles when trained on natural language inference. Additionally, the learned grammars are not consistent across random restarts. This begs the question, do these models fail to learn useful grammars because it is unnecessary for the task? Or do they fail because they are incapable of learning to parse? In this paper we introduce the ListOps datasets which is designed to address this second question.

Since natural language is complex, there are often multiple valid parses for a single sentence. Furthermore, as was shown in Williams et al. (2018a), using sensible grammars is not necessary to do well at some existing natural language datasets. Since our primary objective is to study a system's ability to learn a correct parsing strategy, we build a toy dataset, ListOps, that primarily tests a system's parsing ability. ListOps is in the style of prefix arithmetic; it is comprised of deeply nested lists of mathematical operations and a list of single-digit integers.

The ListOps sequences are generated with a reference parse, and this parse corresponds to the

Proceedings of NAACL-HLT 2018: Student Research Workshop, pages 92–99
New Orleans, Louisiana, June 2 - 4, 2018. ©2017 Association for Computational Linguistics

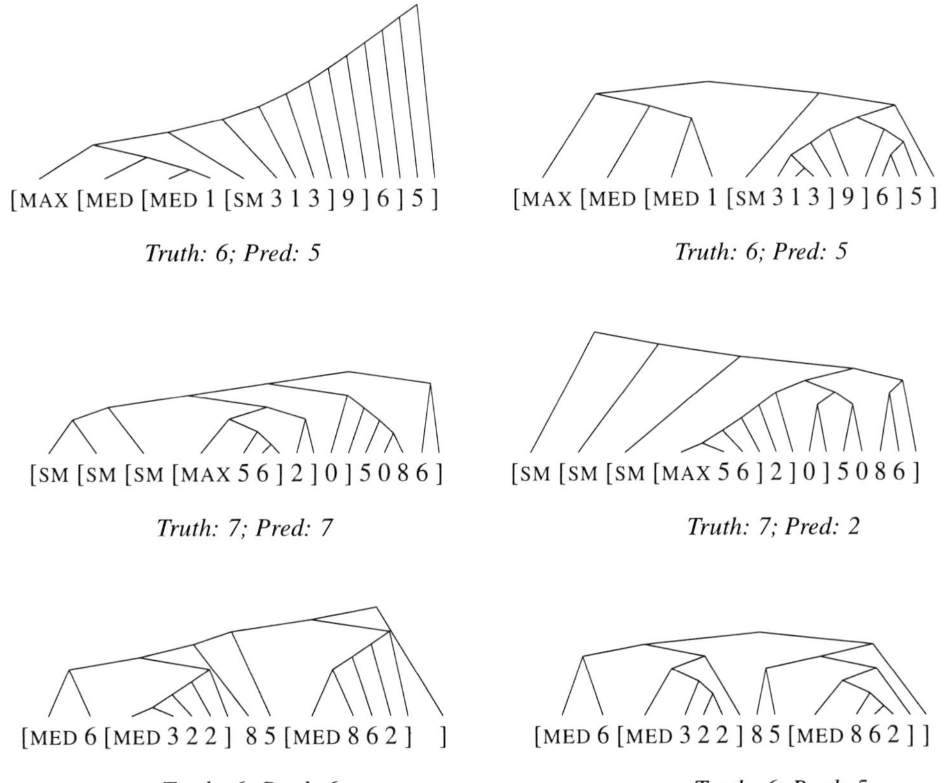

Figure 2: *Left:* Parses from RL-SPINN model. *Right:* Parses from ST-Gumbel model. For the first set of examples in the top row, both each models predict the wrong value *(truth: 6, pred: 5)*. In the second row, RL-SPINN predicts the correct value *(truth: 7)* while ST-Gumbel does not *(pred: 2)*. In the third row, RL-SPINN predicts the correct value *(truth: 6)* and generates the same parse as the ground-truth tree; ST-Gumbel predicts the wrong value *(pred: 5)*.

simplest available strategy for interpretation. We are unaware of reasonably effective strategies that differ dramatically from our reference parses. If a system is given the ground-truth parses, it is trivially easy to succeed at the task. However, if the system does not have the reference parses, or is unable to learn to parse, doing well on ListOps becomes dramatically more difficult. Therefore, we can use ListOps as a litmus test and diagnostic tool for studying latent tree learning models. ListOps is an environment where parsing is essential to success. So if a latent tree model is able to achieve high accuracy in this rigid environment, it indicates that the model is able to learn a sensible parsing strategy. Conversely, if it fails on ListOps, it may suggest that the model is simply incapable of learning to parse.

2 Related Work

To the best of our knowledge, all existing work on latent tree models studies them in a natural language setting. Williams et al. (2018a) experiment with two leading latent tree models on the textual entailment task, using the SNLI (Bowman et al., 2015) and MultiNLI corpora (Williams et al., 2018b). The Williams et al. (2018a) analysis studies the models proposed by Yogatama et al. (2017) (which they call RL-SPINN) and Choi et al. (2018) (which they call ST-Gumbel). A third latent tree learning model, which is closely related to ST-Gumbel, is presented by Maillard et al. (2017).

All three models make use of TreeLSTMs (Tai et al., 2015) and learn to parse with distant supervision from a downstream semantic objective. The RL-SPINN model uses the REINFORCE algorithm (Williams, 1992) to train the model's parser.

The parser makes discrete decisions and cannot be trained with backpropogation.

The model Maillard et al. (2017) present uses a CYK-style (Cocke, 1969; Younger, 1967; Kasami, 1965) chart parser to compute a soft combination of all valid binary parse trees. This model computes $O(N^2)$ possible tree nodes for N words, making it computationally intensive, particularly on ListOps which has very long sequences.

The ST-Gumbel model uses a similar data structure to Maillard et al., but instead utilizes the Straight-Through Gumbel-Softmax estimator (Jang et al., 2016) to make discrete decisions in the forward pass and select a single binary parse.

Our work, while on latent tree learning models, is with a toy dataset designed to study parsing ability. There has been some previous work on the use of toy datasets to closely study the performance of systems on natural language processing tasks. For instance, Weston et al. (2015) present bAbI, a set of toy tasks for to testing Question-Answering systems. The tasks are designed to be prerequisites for any system that aims to succeed at language understanding. The bAbI tasks have influenced the development of new learning algorithms (Sukhbaatar et al., 2015; Kumar et al., 2016; Peng et al., 2015).

3   Dataset

Description   The ListOps examples are comprised of summary operations on lists of single-digit integers, written in prefix notation. The full sequence has a corresponding solution which is also a single-digit integer, thus making it a ten-way balanced classification problem. For example, [MAX 2 9 [MIN 4 7] 0] has the solution 9. Each operation has a corresponding closing square bracket that defines the list of numbers for the operation. In this example, MIN operates on $\{4, 7\}$, while MAX operates on $\{2, 9, 4, 0\}$. The correct parse for this example is shown in Figure 1. As with this example, the reference parses in ListOps are left-branching within each list. If they were right-branching, the model would always have to maintain the entire list in memory. This is because the summary statistic for each list is dependent on the type of operation, and the operation token appears first in prefix notation.

Furthermore, we select a small and easy operation space to lower output set difficulty. The operations that appear in ListOps are:

- MAX: the largest value of the given list. For the list $\{8, 12, 6, 3\}$, 12 is the MAX.

- MIN: the smallest value of the given list. For the list $\{8, 12, 6, 3\}$, 3 is the MIN.

- MED: the median value of the given list. For the list $\{8, 12, 6, 3\}$, 7 is the MED.

- SUM_MOD (SM): the sum of the items in the list, constrained to a single digit by the use of the modulo-10 operator. For the list $\{8, 12, 6, 3\}$, 9 is the SM.

ListOps is constructed such that it is trivially easy to solve if a model has access to the ground-truth parses. However, if a model does not have the parses, or is unable to learn to parse correctly, it may have to maintain a large stack of information to arrive at the correct solution. This is particularly true as the sequences become long and have many nested lists.

Efficacy   We take an empirical approach to determine the efficacy of the ListOps dataset to test parsing capability. ListOps should be trivial to solve if a model is given the ground-truth parses. Therefore, a tree-structured model that is provided with the parses should be able to achieve near 100% accuracy on the task. So, to establish the upper-bound and solvability of the dataset, we use a TreeLSTM as one of our baselines.

Conversely, if the ListOps dataset is adequately difficult, then a strong sequential model should not perform well on the dataset. We use an LSTM (Hochreiter and Schmidhuber, 1997) as our sequential baseline.

We run extensive experiments on the ListOps dataset to ensure that the TreeLSTM does consistently succeed while the LSTM fails. We tune the model size, learning rate, L2 regularization, and decay of learning rate (the learning rate is lowered at every epoch when there has been no gain). We require that the TreeLSTM model does well at a relatively low model size. We further ensure that the LSTM, at an order of magnitude greater model size, is still unable to solve ListOps. Therefore, we build the dataset and establish its effectiveness as a diagnostic task by maximizing this RNN–TreeRNN gap.

Theoretically, this RNN–TreeRNN gap arises because an RNN of fixed size does not have the capacity to store all the necessary information. More concretely, we know that each of the operations in ListOps can be computed by passing over the list of integers with a constant amount of memory. For example, to compute the MAX, the system only needs to remember the largest number it has seen in the operation's list. As an RNN reads a sequence, if it is in the middle of the sequence, it will have read many operations without closed parentheses, i.e. without terminating the lists. Therefore, it has to maintain the state of all the open operations it has read. So the amount of information the RNN has to maintain grows linearly with tree depth. As a result, once the trees are deep enough, an RNN with a fixed-size memory cannot effectively store and retrieve all the necessary information.

For a TreeRNN, every constituent in ListOps is either a partial list, an integer, or the final closing bracket. For example, in Figure 1, the first constituent, ([MAX, 2, 9), is a partial list. So, the amount of information the TreeLSTM has to store at any given node is no greater than the small amount needed to process one list. Unlike with an RNN, this small amount of information at each node does not grow with tree depth. Consequently, TreeRNNs can achieve high accuracy at ListOps with very low model size, while RNNs require higher capacity to do well.

Generation The two primary variables that determine the difficulty of the ListOps dataset are tree depth and the function space of mathematical operations. We found tree depth to be an essential variable in stressing model performance, and in maximizing the RNN–TreeRNN gap. While creating ListOps, we clearly observe that with increasing recursion in the dataset the performance of sequential models falls. Figure 3 shows the distribution of tree depths in the ListOps dataset; the average tree depth is 9.6.

As discussed previously, since we are concerned with a model's ability to learn to parse, and not its ability to approximate mathematical operations, we choose a minimal number of operations (MAX, MIN, MED, SM). In our explorations, we find that these easy-to-compute operations yield bigger RNN–TreeRNN gaps than operations like multiplication.

The ListOps dataset used in this paper has 90k training examples and 10k test examples. During data generation, the operations are selected at random, and their frequency is balanced in the final

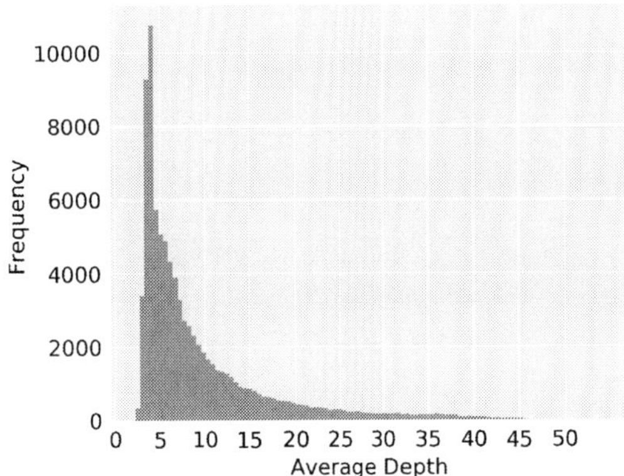

Figure 3: Distribution of average tree depth in the ListOps training dataset.

dataset. We wrote a simple Python script to generate the ListOps data. Variables such as maximum tree-depth, as well as number and kind of operations, can be changed to generate variations on ListOps. One might want to increase the average tree depth if a model with much larger hidden states is being tested. With a very large model size, an RNN, in principle, can succeed at the ListOps dataset presented in this paper. The dataset and data generation script are available on GitHub.[1]

4 Models

We use an LSTM for our sequential baseline, and a TreeLSTM for our tree-structured baseline. For the latent tree learning models, we use two leading models discussed in Section 2: RL-SPINN (Yogatama et al., 2017) and ST-Gumbel (Choi et al., 2018). We are borrowing the model names from Williams et al. (2018a).

Training details All models are implemented in a shared codebase in PyTorch 0.3, and the code is available on GitHub.[1] We do extensive hyperparameter tuning for all baselines and latent tree models. We tune the learning rate, L2 regularization, and rate of learning rate decay. We tune the model size for the baselines in our endeavor to establish the RNN–TreeRNN gap, wanting to ensure that the TreeLSTM, with reference parses, can solve ListOps at a low hidden dimension size, while the LSTM can not solve the dataset at significantly larger hidden sizes. We test model sizes from 32D to 1024D for the baselines. The model

---

[1]`https://github.com/NYU-MLL/spinn/tree/listops-release`

Model	ListOps	SNLI
Prior Work: Baselines		
100D LSTM (Yogatama)	–	80.2
300D BiLSTM (Williams)	–	81.5
300D TreeLSTM (Bowman)	–	80.9
Prior Work: Latent Tree Learning		
300D RL-SPINN (Williams)	–	83.3
300D ST-Gumbel (Choi)	–	**84.6**
100D Soft-Gating (Maillard)	–	81.6
This Work: Baselines		
128D LSTM	73.3	–
1024D LSTM	74.4	–
48D TreeLSTM	94.7	–
128D TreeLSTM	**98.7**	–
This Work: Latent Tree Learning		
48D RL-SPINN	62.3	–
128D RL-SPINN	64.8	–
48D ST-Gumbel	58.5	–
128D ST-Gumbel	61.0	–

Table 1: *SNLI* shows test set results of models on the Stanford Natural Language Inference Corpus, a sentence classification task. We see that the latent tree learning models outperform the supervised TreeLSTM model. However, on *ListOps*, RL-SPINN and ST-Gumbel have worse performance accuracy than the LSTM baseline.

size for latent tree models is tuned to a lesser extent, since a model with parsing ability should have adequate representational power at lower dimensions. We choose the narrower range of model sizes based on how well the TreeLSTM baseline performs at those sizes. We consider latent tree model sizes from 32D to 256D. Note that the latent tree models we train with sizes greater than 128D do not show significant improvement in performance accuracy.

For all models, we pass the representation through a 2-layer MLP, followed by a ten-way softmax classifier. We use the Adam optimizer (Kingma and Ba, 2014) with default values for the beta and epsilon parameters.

5 ListOps Results

Baseline models   The results for the LSTM and TreeLSTM baseline models are shown in Table 1. We clearly see the RNN–TreeRNN gap. The TreeLSTM model does well on ListOps at embedding dimensions as low as 48D, while the LSTM model shows low performance even at 1024D, and with heavy hyperparameter tuning. With this

large performance gap ($\sim$25%) between our tree-based and sequential baselines, we conclude that ListOps is an ideal setting to test the parsing ability of latent-tree learning models that are deprived of syntactic supervision.

Latent tree models   Prior work (Yogatama et al., 2017; Choi et al., 2018; Maillard et al., 2017; Williams et al., 2018a) has established that latent tree learning models often outperform standard TreeLSTMs at natural language tasks. In Table 1 we summarize results for baseline models and latent tree models on SNLI, a textual entailment corpus. We see that all latent tree models outperform the TreeLSTM baseline, and ST-Gumbel does so with a sizable margin. However, the same models do very poorly on the ListOps dataset. A TreeLSTM model, with its access to ground truth parses, can essentially solve ListOps, achieving an accuracy of 98.7% with 128D model size. The RL-SPINN and ST-Gumbel models exhibit very poor performance, achieving 64.8% and 61.0% accuracy with 128D model size. These latent tree models are designed to learn to parse, and use the generated parses to build sentence representations. Theoretically then, they should be able to find a parsing strategy that enables them to succeed at ListOps. However, their poor performance in this setting indicates that they can not learn a sensible parsing strategy.

Interestingly, the latent tree models perform substantially worse than the LSTM baseline. We theorize that this may be because the latent tree models do not settle on a single parsing strategy. The LSTM can thoroughly optimize given its fully sequential approach. If the latent tree models keep changing their parsing strategy, they will not be able to optimize nearly as well as the LSTM.

To test repeatability and each model's robustness to random initializations, we do four runs of each 128D model (using the best hyperparameter settings); we report the results in Table 2. We find that the LSTM maintains the highest accuracy with an average of 71.5. Both latent tree learning models have relatively high standard deviation, indicating that they may be more susceptible to bad initializations.

Ultimately, ListOps is a setting in which parsing correctly is strongly encouraged, and doing so ensures success. The failure of both latent tree models suggests that, in-spite their architectures, they may be incapable of learning to parse.

Model	Accuracy		Self
	$\mu(\sigma)$	max	F1
LSTM	71.5 (1.5)	**74.4**	-
RL-SPINN	60.7 (2.6)	64.8	30.8
ST-Gumbel	57.6 (2.9)	61.0	**32.3**
Random Trees	-	-	30.1

Table 2: *Accuracy* shows accuracy across four runs of the models (expressed as mean, standard deviation, and maximum). *Self F1* shows how well each of these four model runs agrees in its parsing decisions with the other three.

		F1 wrt.		Avg.
Model	LB	RB	GT	Depth
48D RL-SPINN	**64.5**	**16.0**	32.1	**14.6**
128D RL-SPINN	43.5	13.0	**71.1**	10.4
48D ST-Gumbel	52.2	15.3	55.3	11.1
128D ST-Gumbel	56.5	9.8	57.3	12.7
Ground-Truth Trees	41.6	8.8	100.0	9.6
Random Trees	24.0	24.0	24.2	5.2

Table 3: *F1 wrt.* shows F1 scores on ListOps with respect to left-branching (LB), right-branching (RB), and ground-truth (GT) trees. *Avg. Depth* shows the average across sentences of the average depth of each token in its tree.

6 Analysis

Given that the latent tree models perform poorly on ListOps, we take a look at what kinds of parses these models produce.

F1 scores In Table 3, we show the F1 scores between each model's predicted parses and fully left-branching, right-branching, and ground-truth trees. We use the best run for each model in the reported statistics.

Overall, the RL-SPINN model produces parses that are most consistent with the ground-truth trees. The ListOps ground-truth trees have a high F1 of 41.6 with left-branching trees, compared to 9.8 with right-branching trees. Williams et al. (2018a) show that RL-SPINN tends to settle on a left-branching strategy when trained on MultiNLI. We observe a similar phenomena here at 48D. Since ListOps is more left-branching, this tendency of RL-SPINN's could offer it an advantage. Furthermore, as might be expected, increasing model size from 48D to 128D helps improve RL-SPINN's parsing quality. At 128D, it has a

high F1 score of 71.1 with ground-truth trees. The 128D model also produces parses with an average tree depth (10.4) closer to that of ground-truth trees (9.6).

The parses from the 128D ST-Gumbel have a significantly lower F1 score with ground-truth trees than the parses from RL-SPINN. This result corresponds with the performance on the ListOps task where RL-SPINN outperforms ST-Gumbel by $\sim$4%. Even though the trees ST-Gumbel generates are of a worse quality than RL-SPINN's, the trees are consistently better than random trees on F1 with ground-truth trees.

It's important to note that the F1 scores have very high variance from one run to the next. Table 2 shows the self F1 scores across random restarts of both models. Both have very poor agreement in parsing decisions across restarts, their self F1 is comparable to that of randomly generated trees. For RL-SPINN, the F1 with ground-truth trees ranges from 18.5 to 71.1, with an average of 39.8 and standard deviation of 19.4. While ST-Gumbel has an average of 44.5, and a standard deviation of 11.8. This high variance in F1 scores is reflective of the high variance in accuracy across random restarts, and it supports our hypothesis that these latent tree models do not find and settle on a single parsing strategy.

Parse trees In Figure 2, we show some examples of trees generated by both models. We use the best runs for the 128D versions of the models. Parses generated by RL-SPINN are in the left column, and those generated by ST-Gumbel are on the right.

For the pair of examples in the top row of Figure 2, both models incorrectly predict 5 as the solution. Both parses compose the first three operations together, and it is not clear how these models arrive at that solutions given their chosen parses.

In the second pair of examples, RL-SPINN predicts the correct value of 7, while ST-Gumbel wrongly predicts 2. The parse generated by RL-SPINN is not the same as the ground-truth tree but it finds some of the correct constituent boundaries: ([MAX 5 6) are composed with a right-branching tree, and (2]) are composed together. Since the first three operations are all SUM_MOD, their strange composition does not prevent the model from correctly predicting 7.

For the third pair of examples, the RL-SPINN model generates the same parse as the ground-

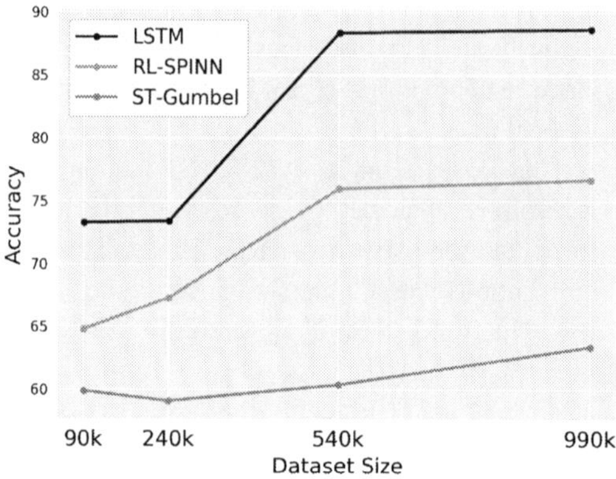

Figure 4: Model accuracy on ListOps test set by size of training dataset.

truth reference and rightly predicts 6. While ST-Gumbel gets some of the correct constituent boundaries, it produces a fairly balanced tree, and falters by predicting 5. Overall, the generated parses are not always interpretable, particularly when the model composes several operations together.

Dataset size ListOps is intended to be a simple dataset that can be easily solved with the correct parsing strategy. One constraint on ListOps is the dataset size. With a large enough dataset, in principle an RNN with enough capacity should be able to solve ListOps. As we stated in Section 3, a requirement for ListOps is having a large RNN–TreeRNN gap to ensure the efficacy of the dataset.

However, it is possible that the latent tree models we discuss in this paper could greatly benefit from a larger dataset size, and may indeed be able to learn to parse given more data. To test this hypothesis, and to ensure that data volume is not critical to solving ListOps, we generate three expansions on the training data, keeping the original test set. The new training datasets have 240k, 540k, and 990k examples, with each dataset being a subset of the next larger one. We train and tune the 128D LSTM, RL-SPINN, and ST-Gumbel models on these datasets. Model accuracies for all training sets are plotted in Figure 4. We see that while accuracy does go up for the latent tree models, it's not at a rate comparable to the LSTM. Even with an order of magnitude more data, the two models are unable to learn how to parse successfully, and remain thoroughly outstripped by the LSTM. Clearly then, data volume is not a critical issue

keeping these latent tree models from success.

7 Conclusion

In this paper we introduce ListOps, a new toy dataset that can be used as a diagnostic tool to study the parsing ability of latent tree learning models. ListOps is an ideal setting for testing a system's parsing ability since it is explicitly designed to have a large RNN–TreeRNN performance gap. While ListOps may not be the simplest type of dataset to test a system's parsing capability, it is certainly simpler than natural language, and it fits our criteria.

The experiments conducted on ListOps with leading latent tree learning models show that these models are unable to learn to parse, even in a setting that strongly encourages it. We only test two latent tree models, and are unable to train and analyse some other leading models, like Maillard et al.'s (2017) due to its high computational complexity. In the future, we would like to develop a version of ListOps with shorter sequence lengths, while maintaining the RNN–TreeRNN gap. With such a version, we can experiment with more computationally intensive models.

Ultimately, we aim to develop a latent tree learning model that is able to succeed at ListOps. If the model can succeed in this setting, then perhaps it will discover interesting grammars in natural language that differ from expert designed grammars. If those discovered grammars are principled and systematic, they may lead to improved sentence representations. We hope that this work will inspire more research on latent tree learning and lead to rigorous testing of such models' parsing abilities.

Acknowledgments

This project has benefited from financial support to Sam Bowman by Google, Tencent Holdings, and Samsung Research. We thank Andrew Drozdov, who contributed to early discussions that motivated this work.

References

Samuel R. Bowman, Gabor Angeli, Christopher Potts, and Christopher D. Manning. 2015. A large annotated corpus for learning natural language inference. In *Proceedings of the 2015 Conference on Empirical Methods in Natural Language Processing (EMNLP)*.

Jihun Choi, Kang Min Yoo, and Sang-goo Lee. 2018. Learning to compose task-specific tree structures. In *Proceedings of the 2018 Association for the Advancement of Artificial Intelligence (AAAI)*.

John Cocke. 1969. *Programming Languages and Their Compilers: Preliminary Notes*. Courant Institute of Mathematical Sciences, New York University.

Sepp Hochreiter and Jürgen Schmidhuber. 1997. Long short-term memory. *Neural computation*, 9(8):1735–1780.

Eric Jang, Shixiang Gu, and Ben Poole. 2016. Categorical reparameterization with gumbel-softmax. In *Proceedings of the International Conference on Learning Representations (ICLR)*.

Tadao Kasami. 1965. *An efficient recognition and syntax analysis algorithm for context-free languages*. Air Force Cambridge Research Laboratory, Bedford, MA.

Diederik P. Kingma and Jimmy Ba. 2014. Adam: A method for stochastic optimization. In *Proceedings of the International Conference for Learning Representations (ICLR)*.

Ankit Kumar, Ozan Irsoy, Peter Ondruska, Mohit Iyyer, James Bradbury, Ishaan Gulrajani, Victor Zhong, Romain Paulus, and Richard Socher. 2016. Ask me anything: Dynamic memory networks for natural language processing. In *Proceedings of the 33rd International Conference on Machine Learning (ICML)*.

Jean Maillard, Stephen Clark, and Dani Yogatama. 2017. Jointly learning sentence embeddings and syntax with unsupervised tree-lstms. *arXiv preprint 1705.09189*.

Mitchell P. Marcus, Beatrice Santorini, Mary Ann Marcinkiewicz, and Ann Taylor. 1999. Treebank-3. LDC99T42. Linguistic Data Consortium.

Baolin Peng, Zhengdong Lu, Hang Li, and Kam-Fai Wong. 2015. Towards neural network-based reasoning. *arXiv preprint 1508.05508*.

Richard Socher, Jeffrey Pennington, Eric H. Huang, Andrew Y. Ng, and Christopher D. Manning. 2011. Semi-supervised recursive autoencoders for predicting sentiment distributions. In *Proceedings of the 2011 Conference on Empirical Methods in Natural Language Processing (EMNLP)*.

Sainbayar Sukhbaatar, Arthur Szlam, Jason Weston, and Rob Fergus. 2015. End-to-end memory networks. In *Proceedings of the 2015 Conference on Advances in Neural Information Processing Systems (NIPS)*.

Kai Sheng Tai, Richard Socher, and Christopher D. Manning. 2015. Improved semantic representations from tree-structured long short-term memory networks. In *Proceedings of the 53rd Annual Meeting of the Association for Computational Linguistics and the 7th International Joint Conference on Natural Language Processing (ACL-IJCNLP)*.

Jason Weston, Antoine Bordes, Sumit Chopra, and Tomas Mikolov. 2015. Towards AI-complete question answering: A set of prerequisite toy tasks. *arXiv preprint 1502.05698*.

Adina Williams, Andrew Drozdov, and Samuel R. Bowman. 2018a. Learning to parse from a semantic objective: It works. is it syntax? In *Proceedings of the Transactions of the Association for Computational Linguistics (TACL)*.

Adina Williams, Nikita Nangia, and Samuel R Bowman. 2018b. A broad-coverage challenge corpus for sentence understanding through inference. In *Proceedings of the 2018 Conference of the North American Chapter of the Association for Computational Linguistics (NAACL)*.

Ronald J. Williams. 1992. Simple statistical gradient-following algorithms for connectionist reinforcement learning. *Machine learning*, 8(3-4):229–256.

Dani Yogatama, Phil Blunsom, Chris Dyer, Edward Grefenstette, and Wang Ling. 2017. Learning to compose words into sentences with reinforcement learning. In *Proceedings of the International Conference on Learning Representations (ICLR)*.

Daniel H. Younger. 1967. Recognition and parsing of context-free languages in time n3. *Information and Control*, 10:10:189–208.

Japanese Predicate Conjugation for Neural Machine Translation

Michiki Kurosawa, Yukio Matsumura, Hayahide Yamagishi and Mamoru Komachi

Tokyo Metropolitan University

Hino city, Tokyo, Japan

{*kurosawa-michiki, matsumura-yukio, yamagishi-hayahide*}@ed.tmu.ac.jp

komachi@tmu.ac.jp

Abstract

Neural machine translation (NMT) has a drawback in that can generate only high-frequency words owing to the computational costs of the softmax function in the output layer.

In Japanese-English NMT, Japanese predicate conjugation causes an increase in vocabulary size. For example, one verb can have as many as 19 surface varieties. In this research, we focus on predicate conjugation for compressing the vocabulary size in Japanese. The vocabulary list is filled with the various forms of verbs. We propose methods using predicate conjugation information without discarding linguistic information. The proposed methods can generate low-frequency words and deal with unknown words. Two methods were considered to introduce conjugation information: the first considers it as a token (**conjugation token**) and the second considers it as an embedded vector (**conjugation feature**).

The results using these methods demonstrate that the vocabulary size can be compressed by approximately 86.1% (Tanaka corpus) and the NMT models can output the words not in the training data set. Furthermore, BLEU scores improved by 0.91 points in Japanese-to-English translation, and 0.32 points in English-to-Japanese translation with ASPEC.

1 Introduction

Neural machine translation (NMT) is gaining significant attention in machine translation research because it produces high-quality translation (Bahdanau et al., 2015; Luong et al., 2015a). However, because NMT requires massive computational time to select output words, it is necessary to reduce the vocabulary in practice by using only high-frequency words in the training corpus. Therefore, NMT treated not only **unknown words**, which do not exist in the training corpus, but also **OOV**, which can not consider words to NMT's computational ability, as unknown word token[1].

Two approaches were proposed to address this problem: backoff dictionary (Luong et al., 2015b) and byte pair encoding, or BPE (Sennrich et al., 2016). However, because the backoff dictionary is a post-processing method to replace OOV, it is not a fundamental solution. BPE can eliminate unknown words by dividing a word into partial strings; however, there is a possibility of loss of linguistic information such as loss of the meaning of words.

In Japanese grammar, the surfaces of verb, adjective, and auxiliary verb change into different forms by the neighboring words. This phenomenon is called "conjugation," and 18 conjugation patterns can be formed at maximum for each word. We consider the conjugation forms as the vocabulary of NMT using Japanese language because the Japanese morphological analyzer divides a sentence into words based on conjugation forms. The vocabulary set in the NMT model must have all conjugation forms for generating fluent sentences.

In this research, we propose two methods using predicate conjugation information without discarding linguistic information. These methods can not only reduce OOV words, but also deal with unknown words. In addition, we consider a method to introduce part-of-speech (POS) information other than predicate. We found this method is related to source head information.

The main contributions of this paper are as follows:

---

[1] In this paper, we denote a word not appearing in the training corpus as "unknown word," and a word treated as an unknown low-frequency word as "OOV."

Proceedings of NAACL-HLT 2018: Student Research Workshop, pages 100–105
New Orleans, Louisiana, June 2 - 4, 2018. ©2017 Association for Computational Linguistics

語幹 Stem	未然形 Irrealis	連用形 Continuative	終止形 Terminal	連体形 Attributive	仮定形 Hypothetical	命令形 Imperative
走る (*hashi-ru*; run)	走ら (*hashi-ra*) 走ろ (*hashi-ro*)	走り (*hashi-ri*)	走る (*hashi-ru*)	走る (*hashi-ru*)	走れ (*hashi-re*)	走れ (*hashi-re*)
歩く (*aru-ku*; walk)	歩か (*aru-ka*) 歩こ (*aru-ko*)	歩き (*aru-ki*)	歩く (*aru-ku*)	歩く (*aru-ku*)	歩け (*aru-ke*)	歩け (*aru-ke*)
する (*su-ru*; do)	せ (*se*) し (*shi*)	し (*shi*)	する (*su-ru*)	する (*su-ru*)	すれ (*su-re*)	しろ (*shi-ro*) せよ (*se-yo*)

Table 1: Leverage table of verb.

- The proposed NMT reduced the vocabulary size and improved BLEU scores particularly in small- and medium-sized corpora.

- We found that conjugation features are best exploited as tokens rather than embeddings and suggested the connection between the position of the token and linguistic properties.

2 Related work

Backoff dictionary. Luong et al. (2015b) proposed a method of rewriting an unknown word token in the output into an appropriate word using a dictionary. This method determines a corresponding word using alignment information between an output sentence and an input sentence and rewrites the unknown word token in the output using the dictionary. Therefore, it does not allow NMT to consider the meaning of OOVs. However, this method can be used together with the proposed method, which results in the further reduction of unknown words.

Byte pair encoding. Sennrich et al. (2016) proposed a method to construct vocabulary by splitting all the words into characters and re-combining them based on their frequencies to make sub-word unit. Because all words can be split into known words based on characters, this method has an advantage in that OOV words disappear. However, because coupling of subwords depends on frequency, grammatical and semantic information is not taken into consideration. Incidentally, Japanese has many characters especially kanji; therefore, there might exist unknown characters that do not exist in the training corpus even after applying BPE.

Input feature. Sennrich and Haddow (2016) proposed a method to add POS information and dependency structure as embeddings with the aim of explicitly learning syntax information in NMT. However, it can only be applied to the input side.

3 Japanese predicate conjugation

Japanese predicates consist of stems and conjugation suffixes. In the vocabulary set obtained by conventional word segmentation, they are treated as different words. Therefore, the vocabulary set is occupied with predicates which have similar meaning but different conjugation.

As an example, a three-type conjugation table is shown in Table 1. In this way, conjugation represents many expressions with only a subtle difference in meaning. Due to the Japanese writing system, most of the predicates do not share conjugation suffixes even though they share the same conjugation patterns. Comparing "走る (run)" and "歩く (walk)", if one wants to share the conjugation suffixes using BPE, it is necessary to represent these words using Latin alphabets instead of phonetic characters, or kana. In addition, a special verb "する (do)" cannot share the conjugation suffixes with these words even using BPE. Therefore, we cannot divide the predicates into the stems and shared conjugation suffixes using BPE.

In the proposed method, we handle them collectively. Since types of conjugation are limited, we can deal with every types. All conjugation forms can be consolidated into one lemma, and OOV can be reduced[2]. Furthermore, by treating a lemma and conjugation forms as independent words, it is possible to represent the predicates which we were observed a few times on the training corpus by combining lemmas and conjugation forms found in the training corpus.

In this research, MeCab[3] is used as a Japanese morphological analyzer, and the morpheme information adopts the standard of IPADic. Specifically, "*surface form*", "*POS (coarse-grained)*", "*POS (fine-grained)*", "*conjugation type*", "*conju-*

---

[2]Derivational grammar (Ogawa et al., 1998) to unify multiple conjugation forms, but it cannot distinguish between plain and attributive forms and imperfective and continuative forms if they have the same surface.

[3]https://github.com/taku910/mecab

gation form", and "*lemma*" are used. Hereafter, predicates represent verbs, adjectives, and auxiliary verbs.

4 Introducing Japanese predicate conjugation for NMT

We propose two methods to introduce conjugation information: in the first method, it is treated as a token (**conjugation token**) and in the second, it is treated as concatenation of embeddings (**conjugation feature**). Moreover we considere to introduce POS information into all words (**POS token**).

4.1 Conjugation token

In this method, lemmas and conjugation forms are treated as tokens. A conjugation form is introduced as a special token with which its POS can be distinguished from other tokens.

In this method, the special token also occupies a part of the vocabulary. However, as there are only 55 tokens[4] at maximum in the IPADic standard, the influence is negligible compared to the vocabulary size that can be reduced. Moreover, because the stem and its conjugation suffix are explicitly retrieved, the output can be restored at any time. For example, these are converted as follows.

走る	→	走る	<動詞・基本形>
		(run)	(verb–plain)
走れ	→	走る	<動詞・命令形>
		(run)	(verb–imperative)
だ	→	だ	<助動詞・体言接続>
		(COPULA)	(aux.verb–attributive)

4.2 Conjugation feature

In this method, we use a conjugation form as a feature of input side. Specifically, "*POS (coarse-grained)*", "*POS (fine-grained)*", and "*conjugation forms*" are used in addition to the lemma. Moreover, this information is added to words other than predicates. These features are first represented as one-hot vectors, and the learned embedding vectors are concatenated and used.

This method has an advantage in that it does not waste vocabulary size; however, because it is not trivial to restore a word from embeddings, it can be adopted to the source side only.

4.3 POS token

As a natural extension to Conjugation token, we introduce POS information into all words in addition to conjugation information. We use POS

Corpus	train	dev	test	Max length
NTCIR	1,638,742	2,741	2,300	60
ASPEC	827,503	1,790	1,812	40
Tanaka	50,000	500	500	16

Table 2: Details of each corpus.

information and conjugation information in the same manner to Conjugation token. We propose three methods to incorporate POS information as special tokens.

Suffix token. This method introduces POS and conjugation information behind each word as a token.

Prefix token. This method introduces POS and conjugation information in front of each word as a token.

Circumfix token. This method introduces POS information in front of each word and conjugation information behind each word as a token.

Example sentences are shown below:

Baseline
> 私 は 走る 。 (I run .)

Suffix token
> 私 <noun> は <particle> 走る <verb-plain> <verb> 。 <symbol>

Prefix token
> <noun> 私 <particle> は <verb> <verb-plain> 走る <symbol> 。

Circumfix token
> <noun> 私 <particle> は <verb> 走る <verb-plain> <symbol> 。

5 Experiment

We experimented two baseline methods (with and without BPE) and two proposed methods. Each experiment was conducted four times with different initializations. We report the average performance over all experiments.

We used three data sets: NTCIR PatentMT Parallel Corpus - 10 (Goto et al., 2013), Asian Scientific Paper Excerpt Corpus (Nakazawa et al., 2016), and Tanaka Corpus (Excerpt, Preprocessed)[5]. The details of each corpus are shown in Table 2. Only in Tanaka, English sentences were

---

[4]Verb: 18, Adjective: 14, Auxiliary verb: 22

[5]`http://github.com/odashi/small_parallel_enja`

Method		Japanese - English			English - Japanese		
		NTCIR	ASPEC	Tanaka	NTCIR	ASPEC	Tanaka
Baseline	w/o BPE	33.87	20.98	30.23	36.41	29.57	30.25
	BPE only Japanese	**34.17**	21.10	30.43	35.96	28.96	28.66
	BPE both sides	-	21.43	30.45	-	30.93	29.27
	BPE only English	-	20.55	30.13	-	30.59	29.15
Only predicate conjugation information	(4.1) Conjugation token	33.96	21.47	32.47	**36.48**	**29.89**	30.46
	(4.2) Conjugation feature	33.84	21.33	30.35	N/A	N/A	N/A
Using predicate conjugation information and all POS information	(4.3) Suffix token	-	21.49	31.82	-	29.77	**31.47**
	(4.3) Prefix token	-	21.61	32.16	-	29.02	30.36
	(4.3) Circumfix token	-	**21.89**	**32.96**	-	28.89	31.07

Table 3: BLEU scores of each experiment (average of four runs). The best score in each corpus is made bold (expect for BPE "both" and "only English").

already lowercased; hence, truecase was not used. As for ASPEC, we used only the first one million sentences sorted by sentence alignment confidence. Japanese sentences were tokenized by the morphological analyzer MeCab (IPADic), and English sentences were preprocessed by Moses[6] (tokenizer, truecaser). As for the training corpus, we deleted sentences that exceeded the maximum number of tokens each sentence shown in Table 2.

We used our implementation[7] based on Luong et al. (2015a) as the baseline. Hyperparameters are as follows. If the setting differs in the corpus, it is written in the order of NTCIR / ASPEC / Tanaka.

Optimization: AdaGrad, Learning rate: 0.01,

Embed size: 512, Hidden size: 1,024,

Batch size: 128, Maximum epoch: 15 / 15 / 30,

Vocab size: 30,000 / 30,000 / 5,000,

Output limit: 100 / 100 / 40

The setting of each experiment except the baseline is shown below. We used the same setting as the baseline unless otherwise specified.

Byte pair encoding. We conducted an experiment using BPE as the comparative method. BPE was applied to the Japanese side only for making a fair comparison with the proposed method.

The number of merge operations in both NTCIR and ASPEC was set to 16,000 and in Tanaka, the number was set to 2,000. As a result, OOV did not exist in all corpora because the size of Japanese vocabulary is smaller than that of BPE.

Conjugation token. Because the output of English–Japanese translation includes special tokens, we evaluate it by restoring the results with rules using IPADic. The restoration accuracy is

100%. If the output has only a lemma, it is converted into the plain form, and if it has a conjugation token only, the token is deleted from the output.

Conjugation feature. Because this method can solely be adopted to the source side, only Japanese-to-English translation was performed. To restrict the embed size to 512, the size of each feature was set to POS (coarse-grained): 4, POS (fine-grained): 8, conjugation form: 8, lemma: 492.

POS token. We increased the output limit by 2.5 times in English-to-Japanese translation because of additional POS tokens attached to all words.

We used the same restoration rules as for Conjugation token to treat special tokens.

We evaluated POS features in only ASPEC and Tanaka owing to time constraints.

6 Discussion

6.1 Translation quality

The results of BLEU score (Papineni et al., 2002) are shown in Table 3. Compared to the baseline without BPE, Conjugation token improved in BLEU score on all corpora and in both translation directions. In addition, Conjugation token outperformed the baselines with BPE with an exception on NTCIR in Japanese-to-English direction. When the POS token was introduced, BLEU scores improved by 1.82 points on average from the baseline in Japanese-to-English translation. (ASPEC : 0.91, Tanaka : 2.73)

Furthermore, we compared proposed methods with the baseline that adopted BPE to the Japanese side only[8]. Table 3 shows the results of baseline

[6] http://www.statmt.org/moses/
[7] http://github.com/yukio326/nmt-chainer

[8] Owing to time limitations, we performed comparison with ASPEC and Tanaka corpora only, and experimented only once on each corpus.

Corpus	Baseline	Conjugation token	Conjugation feature
NTCIR	26.48%	27.43%	27.46%
ASPEC	18.56%	18.96%	18.96%
Tanaka	46.46%	53.95%	54.41%

Table 4: Vocabulary coverage.

src	彼 は 古来[10] まれ な 大 政治 家 で ある 。
ref	he is as great a statesman as ever lived .
w/o BPE	he is as great a statesman as any .
BPE	he is as great a statesman as ever lived .
C_token[9]	he is as great a statesman as ever lived .

Table 5: Output example 1.

src	これ を 下ろす[10] の てつだって ください 。
ref	please give me help in taking this down .
w/o BPE	please take this for me .
BPE	please take this to me .
C_token[9]	please take this down .

Table 6: Output example 2.

with BPE to both English and Japanese sides. According to the results, Japanese-only BPE was inferior to the baseline without BPE.

6.2 Vocabulary coverage

The proposed method is effective in reducing the vocabulary size. The coverage of each training corpus is shown in Table 4. As for Conjugation feature, we evaluate only the number of lemmas.

It can be seen that OOV is reduced in all corpora. In particular, a significant improvement was found in the small Tanaka corpus. It can partly account for the improvement in BLEU scores in the proposed methods.

6.3 Effect of conjugation information

Experimental results showed that Conjugation token improved the BLEU score. However, Conjugation feature exhibited little or no improvement over the baselines with and without BPE. It was shown that conjugation information consists of useful features, but we should exploit the information as Conjugation token.

In the Conjugation token method, we found that the scores are influenced by the corpus size. In particular, the largest improvement was seen in a small Tanaka corpus. Conversely, Conjugation token had a small effect in a large NTCIR corpus, where both proposed methods were inferior compared to the baseline using BPE in Japanese-to-English translation. This is because the size of the corpus was sufficient to learn frequent words to produce fluent translations. Also, our method is superior to BPE in small corpus because it can compress the vocabulary without relying on frequency.

6.4 Output example

Tables 5 and 6 show the output examples in Japanese-to-English translation results.

Table 5 depicts the handling of OOV. The baseline without BPE treated "古来" (ever lived) in this source sentence as OOV, so it could not translate the word. However, BPE and Conjugation token could translate it because it was included in each vocabulary.

Table 6 shows the handling of an unknown word. In the baseline without BPE, "下ろす" (take down) in the source sentence was represented as an unknown word token because it did not appear on the training corpus, and therefore, it failed to generate "take down" correctly. However, the conjugation token could successfully translate it because the lemma ("下ろす") which appears on the training corpus as the conditional form ("下ろせ"), continuative form ("下ろし"), and plain form ("下ろす") could be used to generate the plain form ("下ろす").

6.5 Effect of POS information

Experimental results showed that the Circumfix token (4.3) achieved the best score in Japanese-to-English translation, whereas the Conjugation token (4.1) or suffix token (4.3) was the best in English-to-Japanese translation.

We suppose that the reason for this tendency derives from the head-directionality of the target language. Because the target language in English-to-Japanese translation is Japanese, which is a head-final language, the POS token as the suffix seems to improve the translation accuracy more than the others.

However, experimental results in Japanese-to-English translation contradict this hypothesis. We assume that it is because of the right-hand head rule (Ziering and van der Plas, 2016) in English. According to this rule, basic linguistic information should be introduced before a word whereas inflection information should be placed after the word. This accounts for the different tendency in

---

[9] Abbreviation for Conjugation token.

[10] OOV or unknown word in the baseline.

the performance of the POS token.

7 Conclusion

In this paper, we proposed two methods using predicate conjugation information for compressing Japanese vocabulary size. The experimental results confirmed improvements in both vocabulary coverage and translation performance by using Japanese predicate conjugation information. It is important for the NMT systems to retain the grammatical property of the target language when injecting linguistic information as a special token. Moreover, it was confirmed that the proposed method is effective not only for OOV but also for unknown words.

References

Dzmitry Bahdanau, Kyunghyun Cho, and Yoshua Bengio. 2015. Neural machine translation by jointly learning to align and translate. In *Proc. of ICLR*.

Isao Goto, Ka Po Chow, Bin Lu, Eiichiro Sumita, and Benjamin K. Tsou. 2013. Overview of the patent machine translation task at the NTCIR-10 workshop. In *Proc. of NTCIR*, pages 260–286.

Thang Luong, Hieu Pham, and Christopher D. Manning. 2015a. Effective approaches to attention-based neural machine translation. In *Proc. of EMNLP*, pages 1412–1421.

Thang Luong, Ilya Sutskever, Quoc Le, Oriol Vinyals, and Wojciech Zaremba. 2015b. Addressing the rare word problem in neural machine translation. In *Proc. of ACL*, pages 11–19.

Toshiaki Nakazawa, Manabu Yaguchi, Kiyotaka Uchimoto, Masao Utiyama, Eiichiro Sumita, Sadao Kurohashi, and Hitoshi Isahara. 2016. ASPEC: Asian scientific paper excerpt corpus. In *Proc. of LREC*, pages 2204–2208.

Yasuhiro Ogawa, Mahsut Muhtar, Katsuhiko Toyama, and Yasuyoshi Inagaki. 1998. Derivational grammar approach to morphological analysis of Japanese sentences. In *Proc. of PRICAI*, pages 424–435.

Kishore Papineni, Salim Roukos, Todd Ward, and Wei-Jing Zhu. 2002. BLEU: a method for automatic evaluation of machine translation. In *Proc. of ACL*, pages 311–318.

Rico Sennrich and Barry Haddow. 2016. Linguistic input features improve neural machine translation. In *Proc. of WMT*, pages 83–91.

Rico Sennrich, Barry Haddow, and Alexandra Birch. 2016. Neural machine translation of rare words with subword units. In *Proc. of ACL*, pages 1715–1725.

Patrick Ziering and Lonneke van der Plas. 2016. Towards unsupervised and language-independent compound splitting using inflectional morphological transformations. In *Proc. of NAACL*, pages 644–653.

Metric for Automatic Machine Translation Evaluation based on Universal Sentence Representations

Hiroki Shimanaka[†]   **Tomoyuki Kajiwara**[††]   **Mamoru Komachi**[†]

[†]Graduate School of Systems Design, Tokyo Metropolitan University, Tokyo, Japan

`shimanaka-hiroki@ed.tmu.ac.jp, komachi@tmu.ac.jp`

[‡]Institute for Datability Science, Osaka University, Osaka, Japan

`kajiwara@ids.osaka-u.ac.jp`

Abstract

Sentence representations can capture a wide range of information that cannot be captured by local features based on character or word N-grams. This paper examines the usefulness of universal sentence representations for evaluating the quality of machine translation. Although it is difficult to train sentence representations using small-scale translation datasets with manual evaluation, sentence representations trained from large-scale data in other tasks can improve the automatic evaluation of machine translation. Experimental results of the WMT-2016 dataset show that the proposed method achieves state-of-the-art performance with sentence representation features only.

1 Introduction

This paper describes a segment-level metric for automatic machine translation evaluation (MTE). MTE metrics having a high correlation with human evaluation enable the continuous integration and deployment of a machine translation (MT) system. Various MTE metrics have been proposed in the metrics task of the Workshops on Statistical Machine Translation (WMT) that was started in 2008. However, most MTE metrics are obtained by computing the similarity between an MT hypothesis and a reference translation based on character N-grams or word N-grams, such as SentBLEU (Lin and Och, 2004), which is a smoothed version of BLEU (Papineni et al., 2002), Blend (Ma et al., 2017), MEANT 2.0 (Lo, 2017), and chrF++ (Popović, 2017), which achieved excellent results in the WMT-2017 Metrics task (Bojar et al., 2017). Therefore, they can exploit only limited information for segment-level MTE. In other words, MTE metrics based on character N-grams or word N-grams cannot make full use of sentence representations; they only check for word matches.

We propose a segment-level MTE metric by using universal sentence representations capable of capturing information that cannot be captured by local features based on character or word N-grams. The results of an experiment in segment-level MTE conducted using the datasets for to-English language pairs on WMT-2016 indicated that the proposed regression model using sentence representations achieves the best performance.

The main contributions of the study are summarized below:

- We propose a novel supervised regression model for segment-level MTE based on universal sentence representations.

- We achieved state-of-the-art performance on the WMT-2016 dataset for to-English language pairs without using any complex features and models.

2 Related Work

DPMF$_{comb}$ (Yu et al., 2015a) achieved the best performance in the WMT-2016 Metrics task (Bojar et al., 2016). It incorporates 55 default metrics provided by the Asiya MT evaluation toolkit[1] (Giménez and Màrquez, 2010), as well as three other metrics, namely, DPMF (Yu et al., 2015b), REDp (Yu et al., 2015a), and ENTFp (Yu et al., 2015a), using ranking SVM to train parameters of each metric score. DPMF evaluates the syntactic similarity between an MT hypothesis and a reference translation. REDp evaluates an MT hypothesis based on the dependency tree of the reference translation that comprises both lexical and syntactic information. ENTFp (Yu et al., 2015a) evaluates the fluency of an MT hypothesis.

---

[1]http://asiya.lsi.upc.edu/

Proceedings of NAACL-HLT 2018: Student Research Workshop, pages 106–111

New Orleans, Louisiana, June 2 - 4, 2018. ©2017 Association for Computational Linguistics

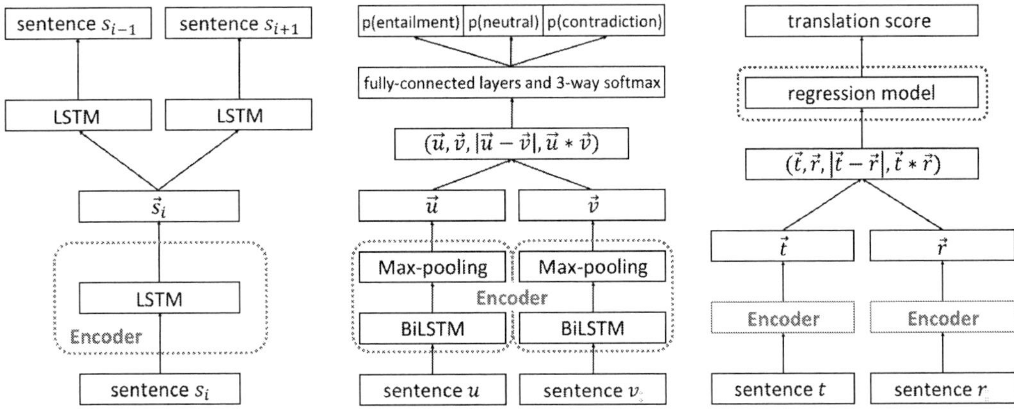

Figure 1: Outline of Skip-Thought. Figure 2: Outline of InferSent. Figure 3: Outline of our metric.

After the success of $\text{DPMF}_{\text{comb}}$, Blend[2] (Ma et al., 2017) achieved the best performance in the WMT-2017 Metrics task (Bojar et al., 2017). Similar to $\text{DPMF}_{\text{comb}}$, Blend is essentially an SVR (RBF kernel) model that uses the scores of various metrics as features. It incorporates 25 lexical metrics provided by the Asiya MT evaluation toolkit, as well as four other metrics, namely, BEER (Stanojević and Sima'an, 2015), CharacTER (Wang et al., 2016), DPMF and ENTFp. BEER (Stanojević and Sima'an, 2015) is a linear model based on character N-grams and replacement trees. CharacTER (Wang et al., 2016) evaluates an MT hypothesis based on character-level edit distance.

$\text{DPMF}_{\text{comb}}$ is trained through relative ranking of human evaluation data in terms of relative ranking (RR). The quality of five MT hypotheses of the same source segment are ranked from 1 to 5 via comparison with the reference translation. In contrast, Blend is trained through direct assessment (DA) of human evaluation data. DA provides the absolute quality scores of hypotheses, by measuring to what extent a hypothesis adequately expresses the meaning of the reference translation. The results of the experiments in segment-level MTE conducted using the datasets for to-English language pairs on WMT-2016 showed that Blend achieved a better performance than $\text{DPMF}_{\text{comb}}$ (Table 2). In this study, we use Blend and propose a supervised regression model trained using DA human evaluation data.

Instead of using local and lexical features,

ReVal[3] (Gupta et al., 2015a,b) proposes using sentence-level features. It is a metric using Tree-LSTM (Tai et al., 2015) for training and capturing the holistic information of sentences. It is trained using datasets of pseudo similarity scores, which is generated by translating RR data, and out-domain datasets of similarity scores of SICK[4]. However, the training dataset used in this metric consists of approximately 21,000 sentences; thus, the learning of Tree-LSTM is unstable and accurate learning is difficult (Table 2). The proposed metric uses sentence representations trained using LSTM as sentence information. Further, we apply universal sentence representations to this task; these representations were trained using large-scale data obtained in other tasks. Therefore, the proposed approach avoids the problem of using a small dataset for training sentence representations.

3 Regression Model for MTE Using Universal Sentence Representations

The proposed metric evaluates MT results with universal sentence representations trained using large-scale data obtained in other tasks. First, we explain two types of sentence representations used in the proposed metric in Section 3.1. Then, we explain the proposed regression model and feature extraction for MTE in Section 3.2.

3.1 Universal Sentence Representations

Several approaches have been proposed to learn sentence representations. These sentence representations are learned through large-scale data so

---

[2]http://github.com/qingsongma/blend

[3]https://github.com/rohitguptacs/ReVal
[4]http://clic.cimec.unitn.it/composes/sick.html

	cs-en	de-en	fi-en	ro-en	ru-en	tr-en
WMT-2015	500	500	500	-	500	-
WMT-2016	560	560	560	560	560	560

Table 1: Number of DA human evaluation datasets for to-English language pairs[8] in WMT-2015 (Stanojević et al., 2015) and WMT-2016 (Bojar et al., 2016).

that they constitute potentially useful features for MTE. These have been proved effective in various NLP tasks such as document classification and measurement of semantic textual similarity, and we call them universal sentence representations.

First, Skip-Thought[5] (Kiros et al., 2015) builds an unsupervised model of universal sentence representations trained using three consecutive sentences, such as s_{i-1}, s_i, and s_{i+1}. It is an encoder-decoder model that encodes sentence s_i and predicts previous and next sentences s_{i-1} and s_{i+1} from its sentence representation $\vec{s_i}$ (Figure 1). As a result of training, this encoder can produce sentence representations. Skip-Thought demonstrates high performance, especially when applied to document classification tasks.

Second, InferSent[6] (Conneau et al., 2017) constructs a supervised model computing universal sentence representations trained using Stanford Natural Language Inference (SNLI) datasets[7] (Bowman et al., 2015). The Natural Language Inference task is a classification task of sentence pairs with three labels, *entailment*, *contradiction* and *neutral*; thus, InferSent can train sentence representations that are sensitive to differences in meaning. This model encodes sentence pairs u and v and generates features by sentence representations $\vec{u}$ and $\vec{v}$ with a bi-directional LSTM architecture with max pooling (Figure 2). InferSent demonstrates high performance across various document classification and semantic textual similarity tasks.

3.2 Regression Model for MTE

In this paper, we propose a segment-level MTE metric for to-English language pairs. This problem can be treated as a regression problem that estimates translation quality as a real number from an MT hypothesis t and a reference translation r. Once d-dimensional sentence vectors $\vec{t}$ and $\vec{r}$ are generated, the proposed model applies the follow-

ing three matching methods to extract relations between t and r (Figure 3).

- Concatenation: $(\vec{t}, \vec{r})$

- Element-wise product: $\vec{t} * \vec{r}$

- Absolute element-wise difference: $|\vec{t} - \vec{r}|$

Thus, we perform regression using $4d$-dimensional features of $\vec{t}, \vec{r}, \vec{t} * \vec{r}$ and $|\vec{t} - \vec{r}|$.

4 Experiments of Segment-Level MTE for To-English Language Pairs

We performed experiments using evaluation datasets of the WMT Metrics task to verify the performance of the proposed metric.

4.1 Setups

Datasets. We used datasets for to-English language pairs from the WMT-2016 Metrics task (Bojar et al., 2016) as summarized in Table 1. Following Ma et al. (2017), we employed all other to-English DA data as training data (4,800 sentences) for testing on each to-English language pair (560 sentences) in WMT-2016.

Features. Publicly available pre-trained sentence representations such as Skip-Thought[5] and InferSent[6] were used as the features mentioned in Section 3. Skip-Thought is a collection of 4,800-dimensional sentence representations trained on 74 million sentences of the BookCorpus dataset (Zhu et al., 2015). InferSent is a collection of 4,096-dimensional sentence representations trained on both 560,000 sentences of the SNLI dataset (Bowman et al., 2015) and 433,000 sentences of the MultiNLI dataset (Williams et al., 2017).

Model. Our regression model used SVR with the RBF kernel from scikit-learn[9]. Hyperparameters were determined through 10-fold cross

---

[5]https://github.com/ryankiros/skip-thoughts
[6]https://github.com/facebookresearch/InferSent
[7]https://nlp.stanford.edu/projects/snli/

[8]en: English, cs: Czech, de: German, fi: Finnish, ro: Romanian, ru: Russian, tr: Turkish
[9]http://scikit-learn.org/stable/

	cs-en	de-en	fi-en	ro-en	ru-en	tr-en	Avg.
SentBLEU (Bojar et al., 2016)	0.557	0.448	0.484	0.499	0.502	0.532	0.504
Blend (Ma et al., 2017)	0.709	0.601	0.584	0.636	0.633	**0.675**	0.640
DPMF$_{comb}$ (Bojar et al., 2016)	**0.713**	0.584	0.598	0.627	0.615	0.663	0.633
ReVal (Bojar et al., 2016)	0.577	0.528	0.471	0.547	0.528	0.531	0.530
SVR with Skip-Thought	0.665	0.571	0.609	**0.677**	0.608	0.599	0.622
SVR with InferSent	0.679	0.604	0.617	0.640	0.644	0.630	0.636
SVR with InferSent + Skip-Thought	0.686	**0.611**	**0.633**	0.660	**0.649**	0.646	**0.648**

Table 2: Segment-level Pearson correlation of metric scores and DA human evaluations scores for to-English language pairs in WMT-2016 (newstest2016).

validation using the training data. We examined all combinations of hyper-parameters among $C \in \{0.01, 0.1, 1.0, 10\}$, $\epsilon \in \{0.01, 0.1, 1.0, 10\}$, and $\gamma \in \{0.01, 0.1, 1.0, 10\}$.

There are three comparison methods: Blend (Ma et al., 2017), DPMF$_{comb}$ (Yu et al., 2015a), and ReVal (Gupta et al., 2015a,b), as described in Section 2. Blend and DPMF$_{comb}$ are MTE metrics that exhibited the best performance in the WMT-2017 Metrics task (Bojar et al., 2017) and WMT-2016 Metrics task, respectively. We compared the Pearson correlation of each metric score and DA human evaluation scores.

4.2 Result

As can be seen in Table 2, the proposed metric, which combines InferSent and Skip-Thought representations, surpasses the best performance in three out of six to-English languages pairs and achieves state-of-the-art performance on average.

4.3 Discussion

These results indicate that it is possible to adopt universal sentence representations in MTE by training a regression model using DA human evaluation data. Since Blend is an ensemble method using combinations of various MTE metrics as features, our results show that universal sentence representations can consider information more abundantly than a complex model. Since ReVal is also based on sentence representations, we conclude that universal sentence representations trained on a large-scale dataset are more effective for MTE tasks than sentence representations trained on a small or limited in-domain dataset.

4.4 Error Analysis

We re-implemented Blend[10] (Ma et al., 2017) and compared the evaluation results with the proposed metric.[11]

We analyzed 20% of the pairs of MT hypotheses and reference translations (112 sentence pairs × 6 languages = 672 sentence pairs) in descending order of DA human score in each language pair. In other words, the top 20% of MT hypotheses that were close to the meaning of the reference translations for each language pair were analyzed. Among these, only Blend estimates the translation quality as high for 70 sentence pairs, and only our metric estimates the translation quality as high for 88 sentence pairs.

Surface. Among pairs estimated to have high translation quality by each method, there were 26 pairs in Blend and 42 pairs in the proposed method with a low word surface matching rate between MT hypotheses and reference translations. This result shows that the proposed metric can evaluate a wide range of sentence information that cannot be captured by Blend.

Unknown words. There were 26 MT hypotheses consisting of words that were treated as unknown words in Skip-Thought or InferSent that were correctly evaluated in Blend. On the other hand, there were 26 MT hypotheses that were correctly evaluated in the proposed metric. This result shows that the proposed metric is affected by unknown words. However, it is also true that there are some MT hypotheses containing unknown words that can be correctly evaluated.

---

[10]http://github.com/qingsongma/blend

[11]The average Pearson correlation of all language pairs after re-implementing Blend was 0.636, which is a little lower than the value reported in their paper. However, we judged that the following discussion will not be affected by this difference.

Therefore, we analyzed further by focusing on sentence length. There were 17 MT hypotheses consisting of words that were treated as unknown words by either Skip-Thought or InferSent with a short length (15 words or less) that were correctly evaluated in Blend. However, in the proposed metric, there were only two MT hypotheses that were correctly evaluated. This result indicates that the shorter the sentence, the more likely is the proposed metric to be affected by unknown words.

5 Conclusions

In this study, we tried to apply universal sentence representation to MTE based on the DA of human evaluation data. Our segment-level MTE metric achieved the best performance on the WMT-2016 dataset. We conclude that:

- Universal sentence representations can consider information more comprehensively than an ensemble metric using combinations of various MTE metrics based on features of character or word N-grams.

- Universal sentence representations trained on a large-scale dataset are more effective than sentence representations trained on a small or limited in-domain dataset.

- Although a metric based on SVR with universal sentence representations is not good at handling unknown words, it correctly estimates the translation quality of MT hypotheses with a low word matching rate with reference translations.

Following the success of InferSent (Conneau et al., 2017), many works (Wieting and Gimpel, 2017; Cer et al., 2018; Subramanian et al., 2018) on universal sentence representations have been published. Based on the results of our work, we expect that the MTE metric will be further improved using these better universal sentence representations.

References

Ondřej Bojar, Yvette Graham, and Amir Kamran. 2017. Results of the WMT17 Metrics Shared Task. In *Proceedings of the Second Conference on Machine Translation*, pages 489–513.

Ondřej Bojar, Yvette Graham, Amir Kamran, and Miloš Stanojević. 2016. Results of the WMT16 Metrics Shared Task. In *Proceedings of the First Conference on Machine Translation*, pages 199–231.

Samuel R. Bowman, Gabor Angeli, Christopher Potts, and Christopher D. Manning. 2015. A Large Annotated Corpus for Learning Natural Language Inference. In *Proceedings of the 2015 Conference on Empirical Methods in Natural Language Processing*, pages 632–642.

Daniel Cer, Yinfei Yang, Sheng yi Kong, Nan Hua, Nicole Limtiaco, Rhomni St. John, Noah Constant, Mario Guajardo-Cespedes, Steve Yuan, Chris Tar, Yun-Hsuan Sung, Brian Strope, and Ray Kurzweil. 2018. Universal Sentence Encoder. *arXiv preprint arXiv:1803.11175*.

Alexis Conneau, Douwe Kiela, Holger Schwenk, Loïc Barrault, and Antoine Bordes. 2017. Supervised Learning of Universal Sentence Representations from Natural Language Inference Data. In *Proceedings of the 2017 Conference on Empirical Methods in Natural Language Processing*, pages 670–680.

Jesús Giménez and Lluís Màrquez. 2010. Asiya: An Open Toolkit for Automatic Machine Translation (Meta-) Evaluation. *The Prague Bulletin of Mathematical Linguistics*, (94):77–86.

Rohit Gupta, Constantin Orasan, and Josef van Genabith. 2015a. ReVal: A Simple and Effective Machine Translation Evaluation Metric Based on Recurrent Neural Networks. In *Proceedings of the 2015 Conference on Empirical Methods in Natural Language Processing*, pages 1066–1072.

Rohit Gupta, Constantin Orasan, and Josef van Genabith. 2015b. Machine Translation Evaluation using Recurrent Neural Networks. In *Proceedings of the Tenth Workshop on Statistical Machine Translation*, pages 380–384.

Ryan Kiros, Yukun Zhu, Ruslan R Salakhutdinov, Richard Zemel, Raquel Urtasun, Antonio Torralba, and Sanja Fidler. 2015. Skip-Thought Vectors. In *Advances in Neural Information Processing Systems 28*, pages 3294–3302.

Chin-Yew Lin and Franz Josef Och. 2004. ORANGE: a Method for Evaluating Automatic Evaluation Metrics for Machine Translation. In *Proceedings of the 20th International Conference on Computational Linguistics*, pages 501–507.

Chi-Kiu Lo. 2017. MEANT 2.0: Accurate semantic MT evaluation for any output language. In *Proceedings of the Second Conference on Machine Translation*, pages 589–597.

Qingsong Ma, Yvette Graham, Shugen Wang, and Qun Liu. 2017. Blend: a Novel Combined MT Metric Based on Direct Assessment —CASICT-DCU submission to WMT17 Metrics Task. In *Proceedings of the Second Conference on Machine Translation*, pages 598–603.

Kishore Papineni, Salim Roukos, Todd Ward, and Wei-Jing Zhu. 2002. BLEU: a Method for Automatic Evaluation of Machine Translation. In *Proceedings of 40th Annual Meeting of the Association for Computational Linguistics*, pages 311–318.

Maja Popović. 2017. chrF++: words helping character n-grams. In *Proceedings of the Second Conference on Machine Translation*, pages 612–618.

Miloš Stanojević, Philipp Koehn, and Ondřej Bojar. 2015. Results of the WMT15 Metrics Shared Task. In *Proceedings of the Tenth Workshop on Statistical Machine Translation*, pages 256–273.

Miloš Stanojević and Khalil Sima'an. 2015. BEER 1.1: ILLC UvA submission to metrics and tuning task. In *Proceedings of the Tenth Workshop on Statistical Machine Translation*, pages 396–401.

Sandeep Subramanian, Adam Trischler, Yoshua Bengio, and Christopher J Pal. 2018. Learning General Purpose Distributed Sentence Representations via Large Scale Multi-task Learning. In *Proceedings of the 6th International Conference on Learning Representations*, pages 1–16.

Weiyue Wang, Jan-Thorsten Peter, Hendrik Rosendahl, and Hermann Ney. 2016. CharacTER: Translation Edit Rate on Character Level. In *Proceedings of the First Conference on Machine Translation*, pages 505–510.

John Wieting and Kevin Gimpel. 2017. Pushing the Limits of Paraphrastic Sentence Embeddings with Millions of Machine Translations. *arXiv preprint arXiv:1711.05732*.

Adina Williams, Nikita Nangia, and Samuel R. Bowman. 2017. A Broad-Coverage Challenge Corpus for Sentence Understanding through Inference. *arXiv preprint arXiv:1704.05426*.

Hui Yu, Qingsong Ma, Xiaofeng Wu, and Qun Liu. 2015a. CASICT-DCU Participation in WMT2015 Metrics Task. In *Proceedings of the Tenth Workshop on Statistical Machine Translation*, pages 417–421.

Hui Yu, Xiaofeng Wu, Wenbin Jiang, Qun Liu, and Shouxun Lin. 2015b. An Automatic Machine Translation Evaluation Metric Based on Dependency Parsing Model. *arXiv preprint arXiv:1508.01996*.

Yukun Zhu, Ryan Kiros, Richard Zemel, Ruslan Salakhutdinov, Raquel Urtasun, Antonio Torralba, and Sanja Fidler. 2015. Aligning Books and Movies: Towards Story-like Visual Explanations by Watching Movies and Reading Books. *arXiv preprint arXiv:1506.06724*.

Neural Machine Translation for Low Resource Languages using Bilingual Lexicon Induced from Comparable Corpora

Sree Harsha Ramesh and **Krishna Prasad Sankaranarayanan**

College of Information and Computer Sciences
University of Massachusetts Amherst
{shramesh, ksankaranara}@cs.umass.edu

Abstract

Resources for the non-English languages are scarce and this paper addresses this problem in the context of machine translation, by automatically extracting parallel sentence pairs from the multilingual articles available on the Internet. In this paper, we have used an end-to-end Siamese bidirectional recurrent neural network to generate parallel sentences from comparable multilingual articles in Wikipedia. Subsequently, we have showed that using the harvested dataset improved BLEU scores on both NMT and phrase-based SMT systems for the low-resource language pairs: English–Hindi and English–Tamil, when compared to training exclusively on the limited bilingual corpora collected for these language pairs.

1 Introduction

Both neural and statistical machine translation approaches are highly reliant on the availability of large amounts of data and are known to perform poorly in low resource settings. Recent crowdsourcing efforts and workshops on machine translation have resulted in small amounts of parallel texts for building viable machine translation systems for low-resource pairs (Post et al., 2012). But, they have been shown to suffer from low accuracy (incorrect translation) and low coverage (high out-of-vocabulary rates), due to insufficient training data. In this project, we try to address the high OOV rates in low-resource machine translation systems by leveraging the increasing amount of multilingual content available on the Internet for enriching the bilingual lexicon.

Comparable corpora such as Wikipedia, are collections of topic-aligned but non-sentence-aligned multilingual documents which are rich resources for extracting parallel sentences from. For example, Figure 1 shows that there are equivalent sentences on the page about Donald Trump in Tamil

Language (*ISO 639-1*)	# Bilingual Wiki articles	# Curated en–xx sent. pairs
Urdu (*ur*)	124,078	35,916
Hindi (*hi*)	121,234	1,495,854
Tamil (*ta*)	113,197	169,871
Telugu (*te*)	67,508	46,264
Bengali (*bn*)	52,518	23,610
Malayalam (*ml*)	52,224	33,248

Table 1: Number of bilingual articles in Wikipedia against the number of parallel sentences in the largest xx–en corpora available.

and English, and the phrase alignment for an example sentence is shown in Table 2.

Table 1 shows that there are at least tens of thousands of bilingual articles on Wikipedia which could potentially have at least as many parallel sentences that could be mined to address the scarcity of parallel sentences as indicated in column 2 which shows the number of sentence-pairs in the largest available bilingual corpora for xx-en[1]. As shown by Irvine and Callison-Burch (2013), the illustrated data sparsity can be addressed by extending the scarce parallel sentence-pairs with those automatically extracted from Wikipedia and thereby improving the performance of statistical machine translation systems.

In this paper, we will propose a neural approach to parallel sentence extraction and compare the BLEU scores of machine translation systems with and without the use of the extracted sentence pairs to justify the effectiveness of this method. Compared to previous approaches which require spe-

---

[1] en–ta : http://ufal.mff.cuni.cz/~ramasamy/parallel/html/
en–hi: http://www.cfilt.iitb.ac.in/iitb_parallel/
en–others:https://github.com/joshua-decoder/indian-parallel-corpora

Proceedings of NAACL-HLT 2018: Student Research Workshop, pages 112–119
New Orleans, Louisiana, June 2 - 4, 2018. ©2017 Association for Computational Linguistics

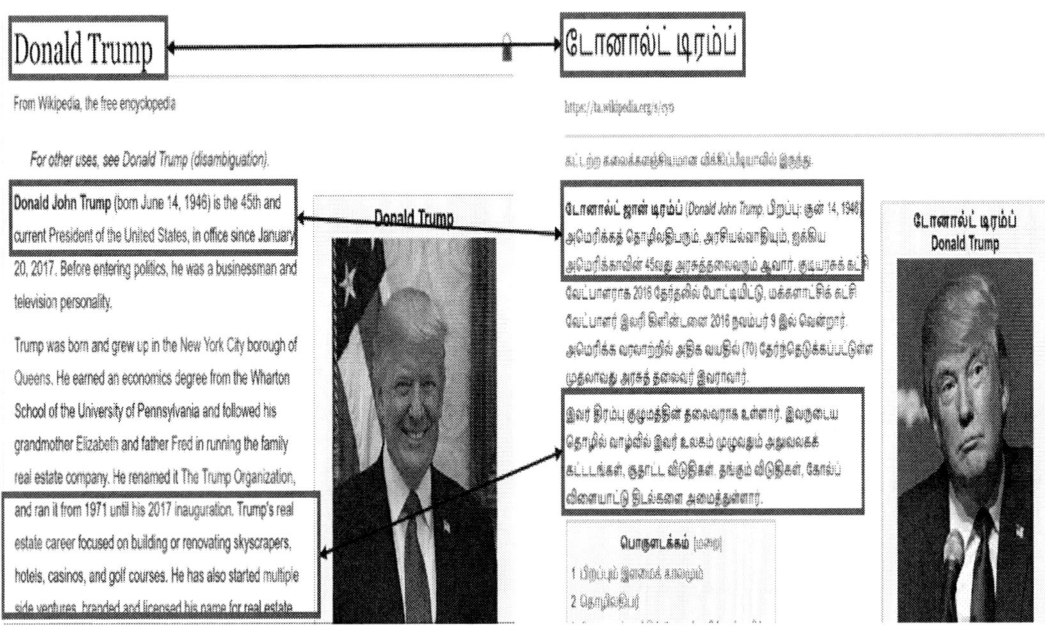

Figure 1: A side-by-side comparison of nearly parallel sentences from bilingual Wikipedia articles about Donald Trump in English and Tamil.

English Word	Tamil Word
Donald Trump	டோனால்ட் டிரம்ப்
President	அரசுத்தலைவர்
United States	ஐக்கிய அமெரிக்கா
Casinos	சூதாட்ட விடுதிகள்
Hotels	தங்கும் விடுதிகள்

Table 2: Phrase-aligned en–ta pairs from Fig 1

cialized meta-data from document structure or significant amount of hand-engineered features, the neural model for extracting parallel sentences is learned end-to-end using only a small bootstrap set of parallel sentence pairs.

2 Related Work

A lot of work has been done on the problem of automatic sentence alignment from comparable corpora, but a majority of them (Abdul-Rauf and Schwenk, 2009; Irvine and Callison-Burch, 2013; Yasuda and Sumita, 2008) use a pre-existing translation system as a precursor to ranking the candidate sentence pairs, which the low resource language pairs are not at the luxury of having; or use statistical machine learning approaches, where a Maximum Entropy classifier is used that relies on surface level features such as word overlap in order to obtain parallel sentence pairs (Munteanu and Marcu, 2005). However, the deep neural network model used in our paper is probably the first of its kind, which does not need any feature engineering and also does not need a pre-existing translation system.

Munteanu and Marcu (2005) proposed a parallel sentence extraction system which used comparable corpora from newspaper articles to extract the parallel sentence pairs. In this procedure, a maximum entropy classifier is designed for all sentence pairs possible from the Cartesian product of a pair of documents and passed through a sentence-length ratio filter in order to obtain candidate sentence pairs. SMT systems were trained on the extracted sentence pairs using the additional features from the comparable corpora like distortion and position of current and previously aligned sentences. This resulted in a state of the art approach with respect to the translation performance of low resource languages.

Similar to our proposed approach, Barrón-Cedeño et al. (2015) showed how using parallel documents from Wikipedia for domain specific alignment would improve translation quality of SMT systems on in-domain data. In this method, similarity between all pairs of cross-language sentences with different text similarity measures are estimated. The issue of domain definition is overcome by the use of IR techniques which use the characteristic vocabulary of the domain to query a Lucene search engine over the entire corpus. The candidate sentences are defined based on word overlap and the decision whether a sentence pair is parallel or not using the maximum entropy classifier. The difference in the BLEU scores between out of domain and domain-specific translation is proved clearly using the word embeddings from characteristic vocabulary extracted using the extracted additional bitexts.

Abdul-Rauf and Schwenk (2009) extract parallel sentences without the use of a classifier. Target language candidate sentences are found using the translation of source side comparable corpora. Sentence tail removal is used to strip the tail parts of sentence pairs which differ only at the end. This, along with the use of parallel sentences enhanced the BLEU score and helped to determine if the translated source sentence and candidate target sentence are parallel by measuring the word and translation error rate. This method succeeds in eliminating the need for domain specific text by using the target side as a source of candidate sentences. However, this approach is not feasible if there isn't a good source side translation system to begin with, like in our case.

Yet another approach which uses an existing translation system to extract parallel sentences from comparable documents was proposed by Yasuda and Sumita (2008). They describe a framework for machine translation using multilingual Wikipedia articles. The parallel corpus is assembled iteratively, by using a statistical machine translation system trained on a preliminary sentence-aligned corpus, to score sentence-level en–jp BLEU scores. After filtering out the unaligned pairs based on the MT evaluation metric, the SMT is retrained on the filtered pairs.

3 Approach

In this section, we will describe the entire pipeline, depicted in Figure 2, which is involved in training a parallel sentence extraction system, and also to infer and decode high-precision nearly-parallel sentence-pairs from bilingual article pages collected from Wikipedia.

3.1 Bootstrap Dataset

The parallel sentence extraction system needs a sentence aligned corpus which has been curated. These sentences were used as the ground truth pairs when we trained the model to classify parallel sentence pair from non-parallel pairs.

3.2 Negative Sampling

The binary classifier described in the next section, assigns a translation probability score to a given sentence pair, after learning from examples of translations and negative examples of non-translation pairs. For, this we make a simplistic assumption that the parallel sentence pairs found in the bootstrap dataset are unique combinations, which fail being translations of each other, when we randomly pick a sentence from both the sets. Thus, there might be cases of false negatives due to the reliance on unsupervised random sampling for generation of negative labels.

Therefore at the beginning of every epoch, we randomly sample m negative sentences of the target language for every source sentence. From a few experiments and also from the literature, we converged on $m = 7$ to be performing the best, given our compute constraints.

3.3 Model

Here, we describe the neural network architecture as shown in Grégoire and Langlais (2017), where the network learns to estimate the probability that the sentences in a given sentence pair, are translations of each other, $p(y_i = 1|s_i^S, s_i^T)$, where s_i^S is the candidate source sentence in the given pair, and s_i^T is the candidate target sentence.

3.3.1 Training

As illustrated in Figure 2 (d), the architecture uses a siamese network (Bromley et al., 1994), consisting of a bidirectional RNN (Schuster and Paliwal, 1997) sentence encoder with recurrent units such as long short-term memory units, or LSTMs (Hochreiter and Schmidhuber, 1997) and gated recurrent units, or GRUs (Cho et al., 2014) learning a vector representation for the source and target sentences and the probability of any given pair of sentences being translations of each other. For seq2seq architectures, especially in translation, we have found the that the recommended recurrent unit is GRU, and all our experiments use this over LSTM.

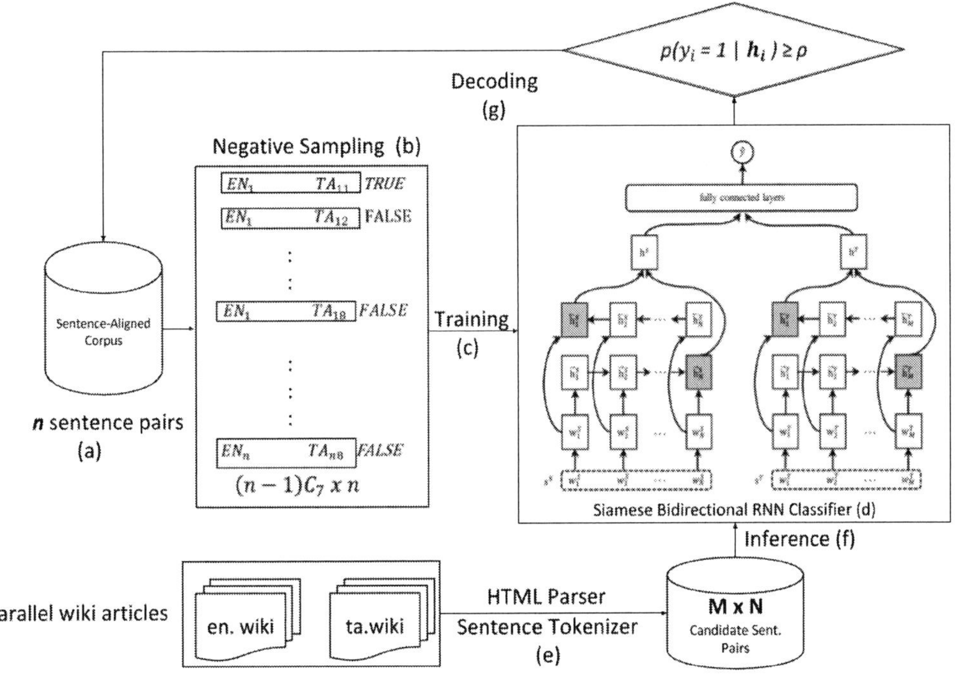

Figure 2: Architecture for the parallel sentence extraction system showing training and inference pipelines. EN - English, TA - Tamil

The forward RNN reads the variable-length sentence and updates its recurrent state from the first token until the last one to create a fixed-size continuous vector representation of the sentence. The backward RNN processes the sentence in reverse. In our experiments, we use the concatenation of the last recurrent state in both directions as a final representation $\mathbf{h}_i^S = [\overrightarrow{\mathbf{h}}_{i,N}^S ; \overleftarrow{\mathbf{h}}_{i,1}^S]$

$$\mathbf{w}_{i,t}^S = \mathbf{E}^{S\top}\mathbf{w}_k \tag{1}$$

$$\overrightarrow{\mathbf{h}}_{i,t}^S = \phi(\overrightarrow{\mathbf{h}}_{i,t-1}^S, \mathbf{w}_{i,t}^S) \tag{2}$$

$$\overleftarrow{\mathbf{h}}_{i,t}^S = \phi(\overleftarrow{\mathbf{h}}_{i,t+1}^S, \mathbf{w}_{i,t}^S) \tag{3}$$

where ϕ is the gated recurrent unit (GRU). After both source and target sentences have been encoded, we capture their matching information by using their element-wise product and absolute element-wise difference. We estimate the probability that the sentences are translations of each other by feeding the matching vectors into fully connected layers:

$$\mathbf{h}_i^{(1)} = \mathbf{h}_i^S \odot \mathbf{h}_i^T \tag{4}$$

$$\mathbf{h}_i^{(2)} = |\mathbf{h}_i^S - \mathbf{h}_i^T| \tag{5}$$

$$\mathbf{h}_i = tanh(\mathbf{W}^{(1)}\mathbf{h}_i^{(1)} + \mathbf{W}^{(2)}\mathbf{h}_i^{(2)} + \mathbf{b}) \tag{6}$$

$$p(y_i = 1|\mathbf{h}_i) = \sigma(\mathbf{W}^{(3)}\mathbf{h}_i + c) \tag{7}$$

where σ is the sigmoid function, $\mathbf{W}^{(1)}$, $\mathbf{W}^{(2)}$, $\mathbf{W}^{(3)}$, $\mathbf{b}$ and c are model parameters. The model is trained by minimizing the cross entropy of our labeled sentence pairs:

$$\mathcal{L} = - \sum_{i=1}^{n(1+m)} y_i \log \sigma(\mathbf{W}^{(3)}\mathbf{h}_i + c) \\ - (1 - y_i) \log(1 - \sigma(\mathbf{W}^{(3)}\mathbf{h}_i + c)) \tag{8}$$

where n is the number of source sentences and m is the number of candidate target sentences being considered.

3.3.2 Inference

For prediction, a sentence pair is classified as parallel if the probability score is greater than or equal to a decision threshold ρ that we need to fix. We found that to get high precision sentence pairs, we

115

Extracted Tamil Sentences from Wikipedia	Model generated Parallel English Sentences From Wikipedia	Translation of Extracted Tamil Sentence for Comparison (Google Translate)	Translation Probability
சிலி , எதியோப்பியா பிஜி , இலங்கை , மற்றும் உஸ்பெகிஸ்தான் ஆகியன தமது முதல் பராலிம்பிக் பதக்கங்களை வென்றன.	Athletes from Chile , Ethiopia , Fiji , Sri Lanka , and Uzbekistan won their first Paralympic medals.	Chile, Ethiopia Fiji, Sri Lanka, and Uzbekistan won their first paralympic medals.	0.991
இந்தியப் பிரதமர் சவகர்லால் நேரு சனவரி 16, 1955இல் புதுச்சேரிக்கு வருகை புரிந்தார்.	Prime Minister of India Jawaharlal Nehru visited Pondicherry on 16 January 1955.	Indian Prime Minister Shivakral Nehru visited Puducherry on January 16, 1955.	0.994
ஜிம்மி டேலி Jimmy Daley , பிறப்பு: செப்டம்பர் 24 1973), இங்கிலாந்து அணியின் துடுப்பாட்டக்காரர்.	Jimmy Daley (born 24 September 1973) is a retired English cricketer .	Jimmy Daley (born September 24, 1973) is an English cricketer.	0.993

Table 3: A sample of parallel sentences extracted from Wiki en–ta articles. The translation of the extracted Tamil sentence in English is also provided. Translation probability corresponds to our model's score of how likely the sentences are translations of each other, as calculated in Equation 8.

had to use $\rho = 0.99$, and if we were able to sacrifice some precision for recall, a lower $\rho = 0.80$ of 0.80 would work in the favor of reducing OOV rates.

$$\hat{y}_i = \begin{cases} 1 & \text{if } p(y_i = 1|\mathbf{h}_i) \geq \rho \\ 0 & \text{otherwise} \end{cases} \quad (9)$$

4 Experiments

4.1 Dataset

We experimented with two language pairs: English – Hindi (en–hi) and English – Tamil (en–ta). The parallel sentence extraction systems for both en–ta and en–hi were trained using the architecture described in 3.2 on the following bootstrap set of parallel corpora:

- An English-Tamil parallel corpus (Ramasamy et al., 2014) containing a total of $169,871$ sentence pairs, composed of $3,984,038$ English Tokens and $2,776,397$ Tamil Tokens.

- An English-Hindi parallel corpus (Kunchukuttan et al., 2017) containing a total of $1,492,827$ sentence pairs, from which a set of $200,000$ sentence pairs were picked randomly.

Subsequently, we extracted parallel sentences using the trained model, and parallel articles collected from Wikipedia[2]. There were $67,449$ bilin-

[2]Tamil: dumps.wikimedia.org/tawiki/latest/
Hindi: dumps.wikimedia.org/hiwiki/latest/

gual English-Tamil and $58,802$ English-Hindi titles on the Wikimedia dumps collected in December 2017.

4.2 Evaluation Metrics

For the evaluation of the performance of our sentence extraction models, we looked at a few sentences manually, and have done a qualitative analysis, as there was no gold standard evaluation set for sentences extracted from Wikipedia. In Table 3, we can see the qualitative accuracy for some parallel sentences extracted from Tamil. The sentences extracted from Tamil, have been translated to English using Google Translate, so as to facilitate a comparison with the sentences extracted from English.

For the statistical machine translation and neural machine translation evaluation we use the BLEU score (Papineni et al., 2002) as an evaluation metric, computed using the *multi-bleu* script from Moses (Koehn et al., 2007).

4.3 Sentence Alignment

Figures 3a shows the number of high precision sentences that were extracted at $\rho = 0.99$ without greedy decoding. Greedy decoding could be thought of as sampling without replacement, where a sentence that's already been extracted on one side of the extraction system, is precluded from being considered again. Hence, the number of sentences without greedy decoding, are of an order of magnitude higher than with decoding, as can be seen in Figure 3b.

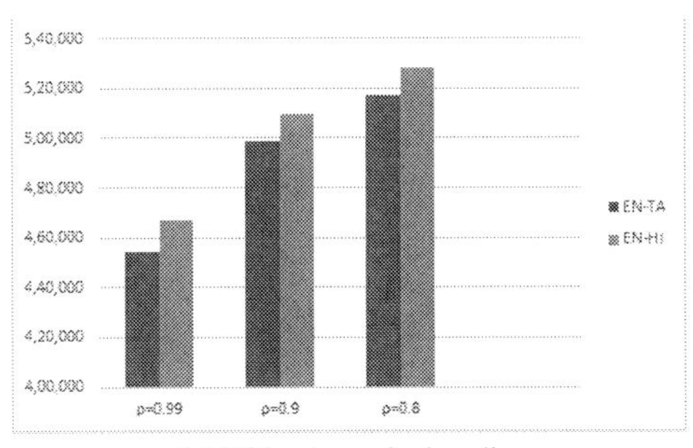

(a) Without greedy decoding

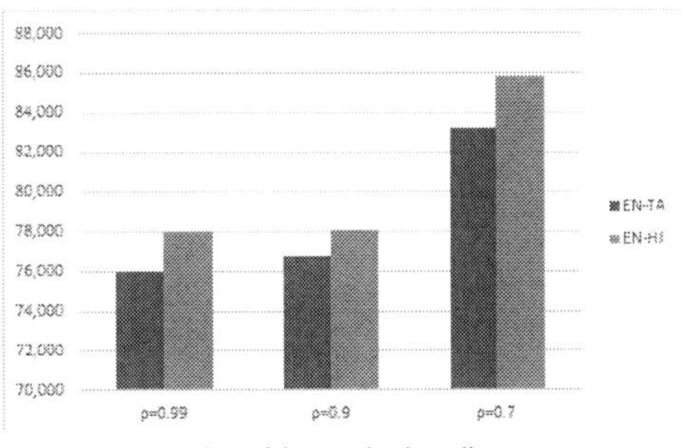

(b) With greedy decoding

Figure 3: Number of parallel sentences extracted from 10,000 parallel Wikipedia article pairs using different thresholds and decoding methods

Training Data	Model	BLEU	#Sents
IIT Bombay en–hi	SMT	2.96	200,000
+ Wiki Extracted =0.99	SMT	3.57(+0.61)	+77,988
IIT Bombay en–hi	NMT	3.46	200,000
+ Wiki Extracted =0.99	NMT	3.97(+0.51)	+77,988
Ramasamy et.al en–ta	SMT	4.02	169,871
+ Wiki Extracted =0.99	SMT	4.57(+0.55)	+75,970
Ramasamy et.al en–ta	NMT	4.53	169,871
+ Wiki Extracted =0.99	NMT	5.03(+0.50)	+75,970

Table 4: BLEU score results for en–hi and en–ta

4.4 Machine Translation

We evaluated the quality of the extracted parallel sentence pairs, by performing machine translation experiments on the augmented parallel corpus.

4.4.1 SMT

As the dataset for training the machine translation systems, we used high precision sentences extracted with greedy decoding, by ranking the sentence-pairs on their translation probabilities. Phrase-Based SMT systems were trained using Moses (Koehn et al., 2007). We used the *grow-diag-final-and* heuristic for extracting phrases, lexicalised reordering and Batch MIRA (Cherry and Foster, 2012) for tuning (the default parameters on Moses). We trained 5-gram language models with Kneser-Ney smoothing using KenLM (Heafield et al., 2013). With these parameters, we trained SMT systems for en–ta and en–hi language pairs, with and without the use of extracted parallel sentence pairs.

4.4.2 NMT

For training neural machine translation models, we used the TensorFlow (Abadi et al., 2016) implementation of OpenNMT (Klein et al.) with attention-based transformer architecture (Vaswani et al., 2017). The BLEU scores for the NMT models were higher than for SMT models, for both en–ta and en–hi pairs, as can be seen in Table 4.

5 Conclusion

In this paper, we evaluated the benefits of using a neural network procedure to extract parallel sentences. Unlike traditional translation systems which make use of multi-step classification procedures, this method requires just a parallel corpus to extract parallel sentence pairs using a Siamese BiRNN encoder using GRU as the activation function.

This method is extremely beneficial for translating language pairs with very little parallel corpora. These parallel sentences facilitate significant improvement in machine translation quality when compared to a generic system as has been shown in our results.

The experiments are shown for English-Tamil and English-Hindi language pairs. Our model achieved a marked percentage increase in the BLEU score for both en–ta and en–hi language pairs. We demonstrated a percentage increase in BLEU scores of 11.03% and 14.7% for en–ta and en–hi pairs respectively, due to the use of parallel-sentence pairs extracted from comparable corpora using the neural architecture.

As a follow-up to this work, we would be comparing our framework against other sentence alignment methods described in (Resnik and Smith, 2003), (Ayan and Dorr, 2006), (Rosti et al., 2007) and (Smith et al., 2010). It has also been interesting to note that the 2018 edition of the Workshop on Machine Translation (WMT) has released a new shared task called Parallel Corpus Filtering [3] where participants develop methods to filter a given noisy parallel corpus (crawled from the web), to a smaller size of high quality sentence pairs. This would be the perfect avenue to test the efficacy of our neural network based approach of extracting parallel sentences from unaligned corpora.

References

Martín Abadi, Ashish Agarwal, Paul Barham, Eugene Brevdo, Zhifeng Chen, Craig Citro, Greg S Corrado, Andy Davis, Jeffrey Dean, Matthieu Devin, et al. 2016. Tensorflow: Large-scale machine learning on heterogeneous distributed systems. *arXiv preprint arXiv:1603.04467*.

Sadaf Abdul-Rauf and Holger Schwenk. 2009. On the use of comparable corpora to improve smt performance. In *Proceedings of the 12th Conference of the European Chapter of the Association for Computational Linguistics*, pages 16–23. Association for Computational Linguistics.

Necip Fazil Ayan and Bonnie J. Dorr. 2006. Going beyond aer: An extensive analysis of word alignments and their impact on mt. In *Proceedings of the 21st International Conference on Computational Linguistics and the 44th Annual Meeting of the Association for Computational Linguistics*, ACL-44, pages 9–16, Stroudsburg, PA, USA. Association for Computational Linguistics.

Alberto Barrón-Cedeño, Cristina España Bonet, Josu Boldoba Trapote, and Luís Márquez Villodre. 2015. A factory of comparable corpora from wikipedia. In *Proceedings of the Eighth Workshop on Building and Using Comparable Corpora*, pages 3–13. Association for Computational Linguistics.

Jane Bromley, Isabelle Guyon, Yann LeCun, Eduard Säckinger, and Roopak Shah. 1994. Signature verification using a" siamese" time delay neural network. In *Advances in Neural Information Processing Systems*, pages 737–744.

Colin Cherry and George Foster. 2012. Batch tuning strategies for statistical machine translation. In *Proceedings of the 2012 Conference of the North American Chapter of the Association for Computational Linguistics: Human Language Technologies*, pages 427–436. Association for Computational Linguistics.

Kyunghyun Cho, Bart Van Merriënboer, Caglar Gulcehre, Dzmitry Bahdanau, Fethi Bougares, Holger Schwenk, and Yoshua Bengio. 2014. Learning phrase representations using rnn encoder-decoder for statistical machine translation. *arXiv preprint arXiv:1406.1078*.

Francis Grégoire and Philippe Langlais. 2017. A deep neural network approach to parallel sentence extraction. *arXiv preprint arXiv:1709.09783*.

Kenneth Heafield, Ivan Pouzyrevsky, Jonathan H Clark, and Philipp Koehn. 2013. Scalable modified kneser-ney language model estimation. In *ACL (2)*, pages 690–696.

Sepp Hochreiter and Jürgen Schmidhuber. 1997. Long short-term memory. *Neural computation*, 9(8):1735–1780.

Ann Irvine and Chris Callison-Burch. 2013. Combining bilingual and comparable corpora for low resource machine translation. In *WMT@ ACL*, pages 262–270.

G. Klein, Y. Kim, Y. Deng, J. Senellart, and A. M. Rush. OpenNMT: Open-Source Toolkit for Neural Machine Translation. *ArXiv e-prints*.

Philipp Koehn, Hieu Hoang, Alexandra Birch, Chris Callison-Burch, Marcello Federico, Nicola Bertoldi, Brooke Cowan, Wade Shen, Christine Moran, Richard Zens, et al. 2007. Moses: Open source toolkit for statistical machine translation. In *Proceedings of the 45th annual meeting of the ACL on interactive poster and demonstration sessions*, pages 177–180. Association for Computational Linguistics.

Anoop Kunchukuttan, Pratik Mehta, and Pushpak Bhattacharyya. 2017. The iit bombay english-hindi parallel corpus. *arXiv preprint arXiv:1710.02855*.

Dragos Stefan Munteanu and Daniel Marcu. 2005. Improving machine translation performance by exploiting non-parallel corpora. *Computational Linguistics*, 31(4):477–504.

Kishore Papineni, Salim Roukos, Todd Ward, and Wei-Jing Zhu. 2002. Bleu: a method for automatic evaluation of machine translation. In *Proceedings of the 40th annual meeting on association for computational linguistics*, pages 311–318. Association for Computational Linguistics.

Matt Post, Chris Callison-Burch, and Miles Osborne. 2012. Constructing parallel corpora for six indian languages via crowdsourcing. In *Proceedings of the*

[3] http://statmt.org/wmt18/parallel-corpus-filtering.html

Seventh Workshop on Statistical Machine Translation, pages 401–409. Association for Computational Linguistics.

Loganathan Ramasamy, Ondřej Bojar, and Zdeněk Žabokrtský. 2014. Entam: An english-tamil parallel corpus (entam v2. 0).

Philip Resnik and Noah A Smith. 2003. The web as a parallel corpus. *Computational Linguistics*, 29(3):349–380.

Antti-Veikko Rosti, Necip Fazil Ayan, Bing Xiang, Spyros Matsoukas, Richard Schwartz, and Bonnie Dorr. 2007. Combining outputs from multiple machine translation systems. In *Human Language Technologies 2007: The Conference of the North American Chapter of the Association for Computational Linguistics; Proceedings of the Main Conference*, pages 228–235.

Mike Schuster and Kuldip K Paliwal. 1997. Bidirectional recurrent neural networks. *IEEE Transactions on Signal Processing*, 45(11):2673–2681.

Jason R Smith, Chris Quirk, and Kristina Toutanova. 2010. Extracting parallel sentences from comparable corpora using document level alignment. In *Human Language Technologies: The 2010 Annual Conference of the North American Chapter of the Association for Computational Linguistics*, pages 403–411. Association for Computational Linguistics.

Ashish Vaswani, Noam Shazeer, Niki Parmar, Jakob Uszkoreit, Llion Jones, Aidan N Gomez, Lukasz Kaiser, and Illia Polosukhin. 2017. Attention is all you need. *arXiv preprint arXiv:1706.03762*.

Keiji Yasuda and Eiichiro Sumita. 2008. Method for building sentence-aligned corpus from wikipedia. In *2008 AAAI Workshop on Wikipedia and Artificial Intelligence (WikiAI08)*, pages 263–268.

Training a Ranking Function for Open-Domain Question Answering

Phu Mon Htut[1]
pmh330@nyu.edu

Samuel R. Bowman[1,2,3]
bowman@nyu.edu

Kyunghyun Cho[1,3]
kyunghyun.cho@nyu.edu

[1]Center for Data Science
New York University
60 Fifth Avenue
New York, NY 10011

[2]Dept. of Linguistics
New York University
10 Washington Place
New York, NY 10003

[3]Dept. of Computer Science
New York University
60 Fifth Avenue
New York, NY 10011

Abstract

In recent years, there have been amazing advances in deep learning methods for machine reading. In machine reading, the machine reader has to extract the answer from the given ground truth paragraph. Recently, the state-of-the-art machine reading models achieve human level performance in SQuAD which is a reading comprehension-style question answering (QA) task. The success of machine reading has inspired researchers to combine information retrieval with machine reading to tackle open-domain QA. However, these systems perform poorly compared to reading comprehension-style QA because it is difficult to retrieve the pieces of paragraphs that contain the answer to the question. In this study, we propose two neural network rankers that assign scores to different passages based on their likelihood of containing the answer to a given question. Additionally, we analyze the relative importance of semantic similarity and word level relevance matching in open-domain QA.

1 Introduction

The goal of a question answering (QA) system is to provide a relevant answer to a natural language question. In reading comprehension-style QA, the ground truth paragraph that contains the answer is given to the system whereas no such information is available in open-domain QA setting. Open-domain QA systems have generally been built upon large-scale structured knowledge bases, such as Freebase or DBpedia. The drawback of this approach is that these knowledge bases are not complete (West et al., 2014), and are expensive to construct and maintain.

Another method for open-domain QA is a corpus-based approach where the QA system looks for the answer in the unstructured text corpus (Brill et al., 2001). This approach eliminates the need to build and update knowledge bases by taking advantage of the large amount of text data available on the web. Complex parsing rules and information extraction methods are required to extract answers from unstructured text. As machine readers are excellent at this task, there have been attempts to combine search engines with machine reading for corpus-based open-domain QA (Chen et al., 2017; Wang et al., 2017). To achieve high accuracy in this setting, the top documents retrieved by the search engine must be relevant to the question. As the top ranked documents returned from search engine might not contain the answer that the machine reader is looking for, re-ranking the documents based on the likelihood of containing answer will improve the overall QA performance. Our focus is on building a neural network ranker to re-rank the documents retrieved by a search engine to improve overall QA performance.

Semantic similarity is crucial in QA as the passage containing the answer may be semantically similar to the question but may not contain the exact same words in the question. For example, the answer to *"What country did world cup 1998 take place in?"* can be found in *"World cup 1998 was held in France."* Therefore, we evaluate the performance of the fixed size distributed representations that encode the general meaning of the whole sentence on ranking. We use a simple feed-forward neural network with fixed size question and paragraph representations for this purpose.

In ad-hoc retrieval, the system aims to return a list of documents that satisfies the user's information need described in the query.[1] Guo et al. (2017) show that, in ad-hoc retrieval, rele-

---

[1]Information Retrieval Glossary:
http://people.ischool.berkeley.edu/ hearst/irbook/glossary.html

Proceedings of NAACL-HLT 2018: Student Research Workshop, pages 120–127
New Orleans, Louisiana, June 2 - 4, 2018. ©2017 Association for Computational Linguistics

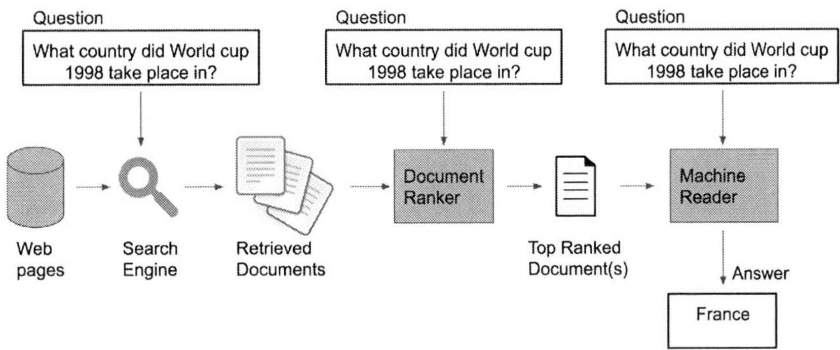

Figure 1: The overall pipeline of the open-domain QA model

vance matching—identifying whether a document is relevant to a given query—matters more than semantic similarity. Unlike semantic similarity, that measures the overall similarity in meaning between a question and a document, relevance matching measures the word or phrase level local interactions between pieces of texts in a question and a document. As fixed size representations encode the general meaning of the whole sentence or document, they lose some distinctions about the keywords that are crucial for retrieval and question answering. To analyze the importance of relevance matching in QA, we build another ranker model that focuses on local interactions between words in the question and words in the document. We evaluate and analyze the performance of the two rankers on QUASAR-T dataset (Dhingra et al., 2017b). We observe that the ranker model that focuses on relevance matching (Relation-Networks ranker) achieves significantly higher retrieval recall but the ranker model that focuses on semantic similarity (InferSent ranker) has better overall QA performance. We achieve 11.6 percent improvement in overall QA performance by integrating InferSent ranker (6.4 percent improvement by Relation-Networks ranker).

2 Related Work

With the introduction of large-scale datasets for machine reading such as CNN/DailyMail (Hermann et al., 2015) and The Stanford Question Answering Dataset (SQuAD; Rajpurkar et al., 2016), the machine readers have become increasingly accurate at extracting the answer from a given paragraph. In machine reading-style question answering datasets like SQuAD, the system has to locate the answer to a question in the given ground truth paragraph. Neural network based models excel at this task and have recently achieved human level accuracy in SQuAD.[2]

Following the advances in machine reading, researchers have begun to apply Deep Learning in corpus-based open-domain QA approach by incorporating information retrieval and machine reading. Chen et al. (2017) propose a QA pipeline named DrQA that consists of a Document Retriever and a Document Reader. The Document Retriever is a TF-IDF retrieval system built upon Wikipedia corpus. The Document Reader is a neural network machine reader trained on SQuAD. Although DrQA's Document Reader achieves the exact match accuracy of 69.5 in reading comprehension-style QA setting of SQuAD, their accuracy drops to 27.1 in the open-domain setting, when the paragraph containing the answer is not given to the reader. In order to extract the correct answer, the system should have an effective retrieval system that can retrieve highly relevant paragraphs. Therefore, retrieval plays an important role in open-domain QA and current systems are not good at it.

To improve the performance of the overall pipeline, Wang et al. (2017) propose Reinforced Ranker-Reader (R^3) model. The pipeline of R^3 includes a Lucene-based search engine, and a neural network ranker that re-ranks the documents retrieved by the search engine, followed by a machine reader. The ranker and reader are trained jointly using reinforcement learning. Qualitative analysis of top ranked documents by the ranker of R^3 shows that the neural network ranker can learn

---

[2]SQuAD leaderboard: https://rajpurkar.github.io/SQuAD-explorer/

to rank the documents based on semantic similarity with the question as well as the likelihood of extracting the correct answer by the reader.

We follow a similar pipeline as Wang et al. (2017). Our system consists of a neural network ranker and a machine reader as shown in Figure 1. The focus of our work is to improve the ranker for QA performance. We use DrQA's Document Reader as our reader. We train our ranker and reader models on QUASAR-T (Dhingra et al., 2017b) dataset. QUASAR-T provides a collection top 100 short paragraphs returned by search engine for each question in the dataset. Our goal is to find the correct answer span for a given question.

3 Model Architecture

3.1 Overall Setup

The overall pipeline consists of a search engine, ranker and reader. We do not build our own search engine as QUASAR-T provides 100 short passages already retrieved by the search engine for each question. We build two different rankers: **InferSent ranker** to evaluate the performance of semantic similarity in ranking for QA, and **Relation-Networks ranker** to evaluate the performance of relevance matching in ranking for QA. We use the Document Reader of DrQA (Chen et al., 2017) as our machine reader.

3.2 Ranker

Given a question and a paragraph, the ranker model acts as a scoring function that calculates the similarity between them. In our experiment, we explore two neural network models as the scoring functions of our rankers: a feed-forward neural network that uses InferSent sentence representations (Conneau et al., 2017), and Relation-Networks (Santoro et al., 2017). We train the rankers by minimizing the margin ranking loss (Bai et al., 2010):

$$\sum_{i=1}^{k} max(0, 1 - f(q, p_{pos}) + f(q, p_{neg}^{i})) \quad (1)$$

where f is the scoring function, p_{pos} is a paragraph that contains the ground truth answer, p_{neg} is a negative paragraph that does not contain the ground truth answer, and k is the number of negative paragraphs. We declare paragraphs that contain the exact ground truth answer string provided

in the dataset as positive paragraphs. For every question, we sample one positive paragraph and five negative paragraphs. Given a question and a list of paragraphs, the ranker will return the similarity scores between the question and each of the paragraphs.

3.2.1 InferSent Ranker

InferSent (Conneau et al., 2017) provides distributed representations for sentences.[3] It is trained on Stanford Natural Language Inference Dataset (SNLI; Bowman et al., 2015) and Multi-Genre NLI Corpus (MultiNLI; Williams et al., 2017) using supervised learning. It generalizes well and outperforms unsupervised sentence representations such as Skip-Thought Vectors (Kiros et al., 2015) in a variety of tasks.

As InferSent representation captures the general semantics of a sentence, we use it to implement the ranker that ranks based on semantic similarity. To compose sentence representations into a paragraph representation, we simply sum the InferSent representations of all the sentences in the paragraph. This approach is inspired by the sum of word representations as composition function for forming sentence representations (Iyyer et al., 2015).

We implement a feed-forward neural network as our scoring function. The input feature vector is constructed by concatenating the question embedding, paragraph embedding, their difference, and their element-wise product (Mou et al., 2016):

$$x_{classifier} = \begin{bmatrix} q \\ p \\ q - p \\ q \odot p \end{bmatrix} \quad (2)$$

$$z = W^{(1)} x_{classifier} + b^{(1)} \quad (3)$$

$$score = W^{(2)} ReLU(z) + b^{(2)} \quad (4)$$

The neural network consists of a linear layer followed by a ReLU activation function, and another scalar-valued linear layer that provides the similarity score between a question and a paragraph.

3.2.2 Relation-Networks (RN) Ranker

We use Relation-Networks (Santoro et al., 2017) as the ranker model that focuses on measuring the relevance between words in the question and words in the paragraph. Relation-Networks are designed to infer the relation between object pairs.

---

[3] https://github.com/facebookresearch/InferSent

In our model, the object pairs are the question word and context word pairs as we want to capture the local interactions between words in the question and words in the paragraph. The word pairs will be used as input to the Relation-Networks:

$$RN(q, p) = f_\phi\left(\sum_{i,j} g_\theta([E(q_i); E(p_j)])\right) \quad (5)$$

where $q = \{q_1, q_2, ..., q_n\}$ is the question that contains n words and $p = \{p_1, p_2, ..., p_m\}$ is the paragraph that contains m words; $E(q_i)$ is a 300 dimensional GloVe embedding (Pennington et al., 2014) of word q_i, and $[\cdot; \cdot]$ is the concatenation operator. f_ϕ and g_θ are 3 layer feed-forward neural networks with ReLU activation function.

The role of g_θ is to infer the relation between two words while f_ϕ serves as the scoring function. As we directly compare the word embeddings, this model will lose the contextual information and word order, which can provide us some semantic information. We do not fine-tune the word embeddings during training as we want to preserve the generalized meaning of GloVe embeddings. We hypothesize that this ranker will achieve a high retrieval recall as relevance matching is important for information retrieval (Guo et al., 2017).

3.3 Machine Reader

The Document Reader of DrQA (Chen et al., 2017) is a multi-layer recurrent neural network model that is designed to extract an answer span to a question from a given document (or paragraphs). We refer readers to the original work for details. We apply the default configuration used in the original work, and train the DrQA on QUASAR-T dataset.[4] As QUASAR-T does not provide the ground truth paragraph for each question, we randomly select 10 paragraphs that contain the ground truth answer span for each question, and use them to train the DrQA reader.

3.4 Paragraph Selection

The ranker provides the similarity score between a question and each paragraph in the article. We select the top 5 paragraphs based on the scores provided by the ranker. We use soft-max over the top 5 scores to find $P(p_j^i)$, the model's estimate of the probability that the passage is the most relevant one from among the top 5.

Furthermore, the machine reader provides the probability of each answer span given a paragraph $P(answer_j|p_j^i)$, where $answer_j$ stands for the answer span of jth question in dataset and p_j^i indicates the corresponding top 5 paragraphs. We can thus calculate the overall confidence of each answer span and corresponding paragraph $P(p_j^i, answer_j)$ by multiplying $P(answer_j|p_j^i)$ with $P(p_j^i)$. We then choose the answer span with the highest $P(answer_j, p_j^i)$ as the output of our model.

4 Experimental Setup

4.1 QUASAR Dataset

The QUestion Answering by Search And Reading (QUASAR) dataset (Dhingra et al., 2017b) includes QUASAR-S and QUASAR-T, each designed to address the combination of retrieval and machine reading. QUASAR-S consists of fill-in-the-gaps questions collected from Stackoverflow using software entity tags. As our model is not designed for fill-in-the-gaps questions, we do not use QUASAR-S. QUASAR-T, which we use, consists of 43,013 open-domain questions based on trivia, collected from various internet sources. The candidate passages in this dataset are collected from a Lucene based search engine built upon ClueWeb09.[5,6]

4.2 Baselines

We consider four models with publicly available results for QUASAR-T dataset. GA: Gated Attention Reader (Dhingra et al., 2017a), BiDAF: Bidirectional Attention Flow (Seo et al., 2016), R^3: Reinforced Ranker-Reader (Wang et al., 2017) and SR^2: Simple Ranker-Reader (Wang et al., 2017) which is a variant of R^3 that jointly trains the ranker and reader using supervised learning.

4.3 Implementation Details

Each InferSent embedding has 4096 dimensions. Therefore, the input feature vector to our InferSent ranker has 16384 dimensions. The dimensions of the two linear layers are 500 and 1.

As for Relation-Networks (RN), g_θ and f_ϕ are three layer feed-forward neural networks with (300, 300, 5) and (5, 5, 1) units respectively.

---

⁴DrQA code available at: https://github.com/facebookresearch/DrQA .

⁵https://lucene.apache.org/
⁶https://lemurproject.org/clueweb09/

Question: Which country's name means "equator"? Answer: Ecuador	
InferSent ranker	**RN ranker**
Ecuador : "Equator" in Spanish , as the country lies on the Equator.	Salinas, is considered the best tourist beach resort in Ecuador's Pacific Coastline.. Quito, **Ecuador** Ecuador's capital and the country's second largest city.
The equator crosses just north of **Ecuador**'s capital, Quito, and the country gets its name from this hemispheric crossroads.	Quito is the capital of **Ecuador** and of Pichincha, the country's most populous Andean province, is situated 116 miles from the Pacific coast at an altitude of 9,350 feet, just south of the equator.
The country that comes closest to the equator without actually touching it is Peru.	The location of the Republic of **Ecuador** Ecuador, known officially as the Republic of Ecuador -LRB- which literally means "Republic of the equator" -RRB- , is a representative democratic republic
The name of the country is derived from its position on the Equator.	The name of the country is derived from its position on the Equator.

Table 1: An example question from the QUASAR-T test set with the top passages returned by the two rankers.

We use NLTK to tokenize words for the RN ranker. [7] We lower-case the words, and remove punctuations and infrequent words that occur less than 5 times in the corpus. We pass untokenized sentence string as input directly to InferSent encoder as expected by it.

We train both the InferSent ranker and the RN ranker using Stochastic Gradient Descent with the Adam optimizer (Kingma and Ba, 2014).[8] A dropout (Srivastava et al., 2014) of p=0.5 is applied to all hidden layers for training both InferSent and RN rankers.

5 Results and Analysis

First, we evaluate the two ranker models based on the recall@K, which measures whether the ground truth answer span is in the top K ranked documents. We then evaluate the performance of machine reader on the top K ranked documents of each ranker by feeding them to DrQA reader and measuring the exact match accuracy and F-1 score produced by the reader. Finally, we do qualitative analysis of top-5 documents produced by each ranker.

5.1 Recall of Rankers

The performance of the rankers is shown in Table 2. Although the recall of the InferSent ranker is

somewhat lower than that of the R^3 ranker at top-1, it still improves upon the recall of search engine provided by raw dataset. In addition, it performs slightly better than the ranker from R^3 for recall at top-3 and top-5. We can conclude that using InferSent as paragraph representation improves the recall in re-ranking the paragraphs for machine reading.

The RN ranker achieves significantly higher recall than R^3 and InferSent rankers. This proves our hypothesis that word by word relevance matching improves retrieval recall. Does high recall mean high question answering accuracy? We further analyze the documents retrieved by the rankers to answer this.

5.2 Machine Reading Performance

For each question, we feed the top five documents retrieved by each ranker to DrQA trained on QUASAR-T to produce an answer. The overall QA performance improves from exact match accuracy of 19.7 to 31.2 when InferSent ranker is used (Table 3). We can also observe that InferSent ranker is much better than RN ranker in terms of overall QA performance despite its low recall for retrieval. InferSent ranker with DrQA provides comparable result to SR^2 despite being a simpler model.

---

[7]https://www.nltk.org/
[8]Learning rate is set to 0.001.

	Top-1	Top-3	Top-5
IR	19.7	36.3	44.3
Ranker from R^3	40.3	51.3	54.5
InferSent ranker	36.1	52.8	56.7
RN ranker	**51.4**	**68.2**	**70.3**

Table 2: Recall of ranker on QUASAR-T test dataset. The recall is calculated by checking whether the ground truth answer appears in top-N paragraphs. IR is the search engine ranking given in QUASAR-T dataset.

	EM	F1
No ranker + DrQA	19.6	24.43
InferSent + DrQA	31.2	37.6
RN + DrQA	26.0	30.7
GA (Dhingra et al., 2017a)	26.4	26.4
BiDAF (Seo et al., 2016)	25.9	28.5
R^3 (Wang et al., 2017)	**35.3**	**41.7**
SR^2 (Wang et al., 2017)	31.9	38.7

Table 3: Exact Match(EM) and F-1 scores of different models on QUASAR-T test dataset. Our InferSent + DrQA model is as competitive as SR^2 which is a supervised variant of the state-of-the-art model, R^3

5.3 Analysis of paragraphs retrieved by the rankers

The top paragraphs ranked by InferSent are generally semantically similar to the question (Table 1). However, we find that there is a significant number of cases where proper noun ground truth answer is missing in the paragraph. An example of such a sentence would be *"The name of the country is derived from its position on the Equator"*. Though this sentence is semantically similar to the question, it does not contain the proper noun answer. As InferSent encodes the general meaning of the whole sentence in a distributed representation, it is difficult for the ranker to decide whether the representation contains the important keywords for QA.

Although the top paragraphs ranked by RN ranker contain the ground truth answer, they are not semantically similar to the question. This behavior is expected as RN ranker only performs matching of words in question with words in the paragraph, and does not have information about the context and word order that is important for learning semantics. However, it is interesting to observe that RN ranker can retrieve the paragraph that contains the ground truth answer span even when the paragraph has little similarity with the question.

In Table 1, the top paragraph retrieved by RN ranker is not semantically similar to the question. Moreover, the only word overlap between the question and paragraph is "**country's**" which is not an important keyword. The fourth paragraph retrieved by RN ranker not only contains the word "**country**" but also has more word overlap with the question. Despite this, RN ranker gives a lower score to the fourth paragraph as it does not contain the ground truth answer span. As RN ranker is designed to give higher ranking score to sentences or paragraphs that has the highest word overlap with the question, this behavior is not intuitive. We notice many similar cases in test dataset which suggests that RN ranker might be learning to predict the possible answer span on its own. As RN ranker compares every word in question with every word in the paragraph, it might learn to give a high score to the word in the paragraph that often co-occurs with all the words in the question. For example, it might learn that *Equador* is the word that has highest co-occurence with *country*, *name*, *means* and *equator*, and gives very high scores to the paragraphs that contain *Equador*.

Nevertheless, it is difficult for machine reader to find answer in such paragraphs that have little or no meaningful overlap with the question. This explains the poor performance of machine reader on documents ranked by RN ranker despite its high recall.

6 Conclusion

We find that word level relevance matching significantly improves retrieval performance. We also show that the ranker with very high retrieval recall may not achieve high overall performance in open-domain QA. Although both semantic similarity and relevance scores are important for open-domain QA, we find that semantic similarity contributes more for a better overall performance of open-domain QA. For the future work, we would like to explore new ranking models that consider both overall semantic similarity and weighted local interactions between words in the question and the document. Moreover, as Relation-Networks are very good at predicting the answer on their own, we would like to implement a model that can do both ranking and answer extraction based on

Relation-Networks.

Acknowledgments

PMH is funded as an AdeptMind Scholar. This project has benefited from financial support to SB by Google, Tencent Holdings, and Samsung Research. KC thanks support by AdeptMind, eBay, TenCent, NVIDIA and CIFAR. This work is partly funded by the Defense Advanced Research Projects Agency (DARPA) D3M program. Any opinions, findings, and conclusions or recommendations expressed in this material are those of the authors and do not necessarily reflect the views of DARPA.

References

Bing Bai, Jason Weston, David Grangier, Ronan Collobert, Kunihiko Sadamasa, Yanjun Qi, Olivier Chapelle, and Kilian Q. Weinberger. 2010. Learning to rank with (a lot of) word features. *Inf. Retr.*, 13(3):291–314.

Samuel R. Bowman, Gabor Angeli, Christopher Potts, and Christopher D. Manning. 2015. A large annotated corpus for learning natural language inference. In *Proceedings of the 2015 Conference on Empirical Methods in Natural Language Processing (EMNLP)*. Association for Computational Linguistics.

Eric Brill, Jimmy J. Lin, Michele Banko, Susan T. Dumais, and Andrew Y. Ng. 2001. Data-intensive question answering. In *Proceedings of The Tenth Text REtrieval Conference, TREC 2001, Gaithersburg, Maryland, USA, November 13-16, 2001*.

Danqi Chen, Adam Fisch, Jason Weston, and Antoine Bordes. 2017. Reading wikipedia to answer open-domain questions. In *Proceedings of the 55th Annual Meeting of the Association for Computational Linguistics, ACL 2017, Vancouver, Canada, July 30 - August 4, Volume 1: Long Papers*, pages 1870–1879.

Alexis Conneau, Douwe Kiela, Holger Schwenk, Loïc Barrault, and Antoine Bordes. 2017. Supervised learning of universal sentence representations from natural language inference data. In *Proceedings of the 2017 Conference on Empirical Methods in Natural Language Processing, EMNLP 2017, Copenhagen, Denmark, September 9-11, 2017*, pages 670–680.

Bhuwan Dhingra, Hanxiao Liu, Zhilin Yang, William W. Cohen, and Ruslan Salakhutdinov. 2017a. Gated-attention readers for text comprehension. In *Proceedings of the 55th Annual Meeting of the Association for Computational Linguistics, ACL 2017, Vancouver, Canada, July 30 - August 4, Volume 1: Long Papers*, pages 1832–1846.

Bhuwan Dhingra, Kathryn Mazaitis, and William W Cohen. 2017b. Quasar: Datasets for question answering by search and reading. *arXiv preprint arXiv:1707.03904*.

Jiafeng Guo, Yixing Fan, Qingyao Ai, and W. Bruce Croft. 2017. A deep relevance matching model for ad-hoc retrieval. *CoRR*, abs/1711.08611.

Karl Moritz Hermann, Tomás Kociský, Edward Grefenstette, Lasse Espeholt, Will Kay, Mustafa Suleyman, and Phil Blunsom. 2015. Teaching machines to read and comprehend. In *Advances in Neural Information Processing Systems 28: Annual Conference on Neural Information Processing Systems 2015, December 7-12, 2015, Montreal, Quebec, Canada*, pages 1693–1701.

Mohit Iyyer, Varun Manjunatha, Jordan L. Boyd-Graber, and Hal Daumé III. 2015. Deep unordered composition rivals syntactic methods for text classification. In *Proceedings of the 53rd Annual Meeting of the Association for Computational Linguistics and the 7th International Joint Conference on Natural Language Processing of the Asian Federation of Natural Language Processing, ACL 2015, July 26-31, 2015, Beijing, China, Volume 1: Long Papers*, pages 1681–1691.

Diederik P. Kingma and Jimmy Ba. 2014. Adam: A method for stochastic optimization. *CoRR*, abs/1412.6980.

Ryan Kiros, Yukun Zhu, Ruslan Salakhutdinov, Richard S. Zemel, Raquel Urtasun, Antonio Torralba, and Sanja Fidler. 2015. Skip-thought vectors. In *Advances in Neural Information Processing Systems 28: Annual Conference on Neural Information Processing Systems 2015, December 7-12, 2015, Montreal, Quebec, Canada*, pages 3294–3302.

Lili Mou, Rui Men, Ge Li, Yan Xu, Lu Zhang, Rui Yan, and Zhi Jin. 2016. Natural language inference by tree-based convolution and heuristic matching. *ACLWeb*, (P16-2022).

Jeffrey Pennington, Richard Socher, and Christopher D. Manning. 2014. Glove: Global vectors for word representation. In *Proceedings of the 2014 Conference on Empirical Methods in Natural Language Processing, EMNLP 2014, October 25-29, 2014, Doha, Qatar, A meeting of SIGDAT, a Special Interest Group of the ACL*, pages 1532–1543.

Pranav Rajpurkar, Jian Zhang, Konstantin Lopyrev, and Percy Liang. 2016. Squad: 100, 000+ questions for machine comprehension of text. In *Proceedings of the 2016 Conference on Empirical Methods in Natural Language Processing, EMNLP 2016, Austin, Texas, USA, November 1-4, 2016*, pages 2383–2392.

Adam Santoro, David Raposo, David G. T. Barrett, Mateusz Malinowski, Razvan Pascanu, Peter

Battaglia, and Tim Lillicrap. 2017. A simple neural network module for relational reasoning. In *Advances in Neural Information Processing Systems 30: Annual Conference on Neural Information Processing Systems 2017, 4-9 December 2017, Long Beach, CA, USA*, pages 4974–4983.

Min Joon Seo, Aniruddha Kembhavi, Ali Farhadi, and Hannaneh Hajishirzi. 2016. Bidirectional attention flow for machine comprehension. *CoRR*, abs/1611.01603.

Nitish Srivastava, Geoffrey E. Hinton, Alex Krizhevsky, Ilya Sutskever, and Ruslan Salakhutdinov. 2014. Dropout: a simple way to prevent neural networks from overfitting. *Journal of Machine Learning Research*, 15(1):1929–1958.

Shuohang Wang, Mo Yu, Xiaoxiao Guo, Zhiguo Wang, Tim Klinger, Wei Zhang, Shiyu Chang, Gerald Tesauro, Bowen Zhou, and Jing Jiang. 2017. R^3: Reinforced reader-ranker for open-domain question answering. *CoRR*, abs/1709.00023.

Robert West, Evgeniy Gabrilovich, Kevin Murphy, Shaohua Sun, Rahul Gupta, and Dekang Lin. 2014. Knowledge base completion via search-based question answering. In *23rd International World Wide Web Conference, WWW '14, Seoul, Republic of Korea, April 7-11, 2014*, pages 515–526.

Adina Williams, Nikita Nangia, and Samuel R. Bowman. 2017. A broad-coverage challenge corpus for sentence understanding through inference. *CoRR*, abs/1704.05426.

Corpus Creation and Emotion Prediction for Hindi-English Code-Mixed Social Media Text

Deepanshu Vijay*, **Aditya Bohra***, **Vinay Singh, Syed S. Akhtar, Manish Shrivastava**
International Institute of Information Technology
Hyderabad, Telangana, India
{deepanshu.vijay, aditya.bohra, vinay.singh, syed.akhtar}@research.iiit.ac.in
m.shrivastava@iiit.ac.in

Abstract

Emotion Prediction is a Natural Language Processing (NLP) task dealing with detection and classification of emotions in various monolingual and bilingual texts. While some work has been done on code-mixed social media text and in emotion prediction separately, our work is the first attempt which aims at identifying the emotion associated with Hindi-English code-mixed social media text. In this paper, we analyze the problem of emotion identification in code-mixed content and present a Hindi-English code-mixed corpus extracted from twitter and annotated with the associated emotion. For every tweet in the dataset, we annotate the source language of all the words present, and also the causal language of the expressed emotion. Finally, we propose a supervised classification system which uses various machine learning techniques for detecting the emotion associated with the text using a variety of character level, word level, and lexicon based features.

1 Introduction

Micro-blogging sites like Twitter and Facebook encourage users to express their daily thoughts in real time, which often result in millions of emotional statements being posted online, everyday. Identification and analysis of emotions in social-media texts are of great significance in understanding the trends, reviews, events and human behaviour. Emotion prediction aims to identify fine-grained emotions, i.e., Happy, Anger, Fear, Sadness, Surprise, Disgust, if any present in the text. Previous research related to this task has mainly been focused only on the monolingual text (Chen et al., 2010; Alm et al., 2005) due to the availability of large-scale monolingual resources. However, usage of code mixed language in online posts is very common, especially in multilingual societies like India, for expressing one's emotions

---

* These authors contributed equally to this work.

and thoughts, particularly when the communication is informal.

Code-Mixing (CM) is a natural phenomenon of embedding linguistic units such as phrases, words or morphemes of one language into an utterance of another (Myers-Scotton, 1993; Muysken, 2000; Duran, 1994; Gysels, 1992). Following are some instances from a Twitter corpus of Hindi-English code-mixed texts also transliterated in English.

T1 : *"I don't want to go to school today, teacher se dar lagta hai mujhe."*
Translation : "I don't want to go to school today, I am afraid of teacher."

T2 : *"Finally India away series jeetne mein successful ho hi gayi :D"*
Translation : "Finally India got success in winning the away series :D"

T3 : *"This is a big surprise that Rahul Gandhi congress ke naye president hain."*
Translation : "This is a big surprise that Rahul Gandhi is the new president of Congress."

The above examples contain both English and Hindi texts. **T1** expresses *fear* through Hindi phrase *"dar lagta hai mujhe"*, *happiness* is expressed in **T2** through a Hindi-English mixed phrase *"jeetne mein successful ho hi gayi"*, while in **T3**, *surprise* is expressed through English phrase *"This is a big surprise"*.

Since very few resources are available for Hindi-English code-mixed text, in this paper we present our initial efforts in constructing the corpus and annotating the code-mixed tweets with associated emotion and the causal language for that emotion. We strongly believe that our initial efforts in constructing the annotated code-mixed emotion corpus will prove to be extremely valuable for researchers working on various natural processing

Proceedings of NAACL-HLT 2018: Student Research Workshop, pages 128–135
New Orleans, Louisiana, June 2 - 4, 2018. ©2017 Association for Computational Linguistics

tasks on social media.

The structure of the paper is as follows. In Section 2, we review related research in the area of code mixing and emotion prediction. In Section 3, we describe the corpus creation and annotation scheme. In Section 4, we discuss the data statistics. In Section 5, we summarize our classification system which includes the pre-processing steps and construction of feature vector. In Section 6, we present the results of experiments conducted using various character-level, word-level and lexicon features. In the last section, we conclude our paper, followed by future work and the references.

2 Background and Related Work

(Bali et al., 2014) performed analysis of data from Facebook posts generated by English-Hindi bilingual users. They created the corpus using posts from Facebook pages in which En-Hin bilinguals are highly active. They also collected the data from BBC Hindi News page. Their final corpus consisted of 6983 posts and 113,578 words. Among the 6983 posts 206 posts were in Devanagari Script, 6544 posts in Roman Script, 246 in Mixed Scripta and 28 in Other Script. After annotating the data with the Named Entities, POS Tags, Word Origin and deleting all such posts which had less than 5 words, they performed analysis on data. Their analysis showed that atleast 4.2% of the data is code-switched. Analysis depicted that significant amount of code-mixing was present in the posts. (Vyas et al., 2014) formalized the problem, created a POS tag annotated Hindi-English code-mixed corpus and reported the challenges and problems in the Hindi-English code-mixed text. They also performed experiments on language identification, transliteration, normalization and POS tagging of the dataset. Their POS tagger accuracy fell by 14% to 65% without using gold language labels and normalization. Thus, language identification and normalization are critical for POS tagging. (Sharma et al., 2016) addressed the problem of shallow parsing of Hindi-English code-mixed social media text and developed a system for Hindi-English code-mixed text that can identify the language of the words, normalize them to their standard forms, assign them their POS tag and segment into chunks. (Barman et al., 2014) addressed the problem of language identification on Bengali-Hindi-English Facebook

comments. They annotated a corpus and achieved an accuracy of 95.76% using statistical models with monolingual dictionaries. (Raghavi et al., 2015) developed a Question Classification system for Hindi-English code-mixed language using word level resources such as language identification, transliteration, and lexical translation.

In addition to information, text also contains some emotional content. (Alm et al., 2005) addressed the problem of text-based emotion prediction in the domain of children's fairy tales using supervised machine learning. (Das and Bandyopadhyay, 2010) deals with the extraction of emotional expressions and tagging of English blog sentences with Ekman's six basic emotion tags and any of the three intensities: low, medium and high. (Xu et al., 2010) built a Chinese emotion lexicon for public use. They adopted a graph-based algorithm which rank words according to a few seed emotion words. (Wang et al., 2016) performed emotion analysis on Chinese-English code-mixed texts using a BAN network. (Joshi et al., 2016; Ghosh et al., 2017) performed Sentiment Identification in Hindi-English code-mixed social media text.

3 Corpus Creation and Annotation

We created the Hindi-English code-mixed corpus using tweets posted online in last 8 years. Tweets were scrapped from Twitter using the Twitter Python API[1] which uses the advanced search option of twitter. We have mined the tweets by selecting certain hashtags from politics, social events, and sports, so that the dataset is not limited to a particular domain. The hashtags used can be found in the appendix section. Tweets retrieved are in the json format which consists all the information such as timestamp, URL, text, user, retweets, replies, full name, id and likes. An extensive semi-automated processing was carried out to remove all the noisy tweets. Noisy tweets are the ones which comprise only of hashtags or urls. Also, tweets in which language other than Hindi or English is used were also considered as noisy and hence removed from the corpus. Furthermore, all those tweets which were written either in pure English or pure Hindi language were removed, and thus, keeping only the code-mixed tweets. In the annotation phase, we further removed all those tweets which were not expressing any emotion.

---

[1]https://pypi.python.org/pypi/twitterscraper/0.2.7

```
<tweet>
<id>954297321843433472</id>
<word lang="other">@sachin_rt</word>
<word lang="hin">sab</word>
<word lang="hin">cheezo</word>
<word lang="hin">ke</word>
<word lang="hin">bare</word>
<word lang="hin">mai</word>
<word lang="eng">tweet</word>
<word lang="hin">kartey</word>
<word lang="hin">ho</word>
<word lang="hin">toh</word>
<word lang="other">#delhiAirpollution</word>
<word lang="hin">kaise</word>
<word lang="hin">bhol</word>
<word lang="hin">gaye</word>
<word lang="hin">jo</word>
<word lang="eng">national</word>
<word lang="eng">emergency</word>
<word lang="hin">hai,</word>
<word lang="eng">play</word>
<word lang="eng">a</word>
<word lang="eng">fair</word>
<word lang="eng">game</word>
<word lang="hin">sirji</word>
</tweet>
<emotion>          <causal_language>
Sadness            Mixed
</emotion>         </causal_language>
```

Figure 1: Annotated Instance for tweet "*@sachin_rt sab cheezo ke bare main tweet kartey ho toh #delhiAirpollution kaise bhol gaye jo national emergency hai, play a fair game sirji*"

3.1 Annotation

The annotation step was carried out in following two phases:

Language Annotation : For each word, a tag was assigned to its source language. Three kinds of tags namely, 'eng', 'hin' and 'other' were assigned to the words by bilingual speakers. 'eng' tag was assigned to words which are present in English vocabulary, such as "successful", "series" used in **T2**. 'hin' tag was assigned to words which are present in the Hindi vocabulary such as "naye"(new), "hain"(is) used in **T3**. The tag 'other' was given to symbols, emoticons, punctuations, named entities, acronyms, and URLs.

Emotion and Causal Language Annotation : We annotated the tweets with six standard emotions, namely, Happiness, Sadness, Anger, Fear, Disgust and Surprise (Ekman, 1992, 1993). Hindi and English were annotated as the two causal languages. Since emotion in a statement can be expressed through the two languages separately, and also through mixed phrases like:

"mujhe fear hai", it is thus essential to annotate the data with four kinds of causal situations (Lee and Wang, 2015), i.e. Hindi, English, Mixed and Both. Next, we further discuss these situations in detail.

Hindi means the emotion of the given post is solely expressed through Hindi text. In the example, **T4** happiness is expressed through Hindi text.

T4 : *"Bahut badiya, ab sab okay hai surgical strike ke baad."*
Translation : "Very good, now everything is okay after the surgical strike."

English means the emotion of the given post is solely expressed through English text. **T5** is an example that expresses surprise through English text.

T5 : *"He is in complete shock, itni property waste ho gayi uski."*
Translation : "He is in complete shock that so much of his property has been wasted."

Both means the emotion of the given tweet is expressed through both Hindi and English text. Since a user can express a kind of emotion using multiple phrases, it is essential to incorporate the case when same emotion is expressed through both the languages. **T6** is an example where sadness is expressed through both Hindi and English texts.

T6 : *"Demonetisation ko Saal hogaye hai..ab toh chod do..these are the people jo har post ko @narendramodi NoteBandi aur Desh ki Sena se jod dete hai.. grow up man..have a life for Gods sake."*
Translation : "It has been one year of Demonetisation. Please Leave it now. These are the people who relates every post with @narendramodi, NoteBandi and Army of this country. Grow up man. Have a life for Gods sake."

Mixed means the emotion of the given tweet is expressed through one or multiple Hindi-English mixed phrases. **T7** is an example which expresses sadness through the mixed phrase 'dekhke sad lagta hai'.

T7 : *"In this country gareeb logo ki haalat dekhke sad lagta hai."*
Translation : "It is sad to see the condition of poor people in this country."

Annotation of this dataset is performed by two of the co-authors who are native Hindi speakers and have proficiency in both Hindi and English. Figure 1 shows an instance of annotation, where both the emotion and the caused language is annotated. In a given tweet, for each emotion, annotator marked whether it expresses that emotion along with it's caused language. The annotated dataset with the classification system is made available online[2].

3.2 Inter Annotator Agreement

Annotation of the dataset to identify emotion in the tweets was carried out by two human annotators having linguistic background and proficiency in both Hindi and English. In order to validate the quality of annotation, we calculated the inter-annotator agreement (IAA) between the two annotation sets of 2866 code-mixed tweets using Cohen's Kappa coefficient. Table 1 shows the results of agreement analysis. We find that the agreement is significantly high. This indicates that the quality of the annotation and presented schema is productive. Furthermore, the agreement of emotion annotation is lower than that of caused language, which probably is due to the fact that in some tweets, emotions are expressed indirectly.

	Cohen Kappa
Emotion	0.902
Caused Language	0.945

Table 1: Inter Annotator Agreement.

4   Data Statistics

We retrieved 3,55,448 tweets from Twitter. After manually filtering the tweets as described in Section 3, we found that only 5546 tweets were code-mixed tweets. Table 2 shows the distribution of data across different emotion categories. Out of 5546 code-mixed tweets, only 2866 tweets were expressing any emotion. The remaining tweets were removed from our dataset, thus keeping only

Emotion	Sentences
Happiness	595
Sadness	878
Anger	667
Fear	85
Disgust	291
Surprise	182
Multiple Emotions	168
Total sentences	2866

Table 2: Data Distribution.

Caused Language	Sentences
English	113 (3.7%)
Hindi	1301 (43%)
Mixed	1483 (49%)
Both	127 (4.1%)

Table 3: Caused Language Distribution.

those code-mixed tweets which were expressing any of the six emotions. Also, it is vital to note that some of the tweets contained multiple phrases depicting different emotions. These emotions could be caused by any of the four causal languages. As a result, total number of causal language annotations is more than the number of tweets in the dataset. Usually, a user while posting a tweet feels only one kind of emotion. Hence all such tweets are neglected to avoid any conflict between the literal depiction and the implicit conveyance of emotions in the tweets. This resulted in 2698 emotional code-mixed tweets. Table 3 shows the count of sentences in which emotion was expressed in English, Hindi, Both and Mixed. It clearly shows that in most of the sentences emotion is expressed through a mixed Hindi-English phrase.

5   System Architecture

After developing the annotated corpus, we try to detect emotion in the code-mixed tweets. We break down the process of emotion detection into three sub-processes: pre-processing of raw tweets, feature identification and extraction and finally, the classification of emotion as happiness, sadness, and anger. It is important to note that classification is carried out only for three classes i.e., 'happiness', 'sadness' and 'anger', as number of tweets which express 'fear', 'disgust' and 'surprise' are extremely limited. The steps have been discussed in sequential order.

5.1 Pre-processing of the code-mixed tweets

Following are the steps which were performed in order to pre-process the data prior to feature extraction.

1. **Removal of URLs:** All the links and URLs in the tweets are stored and replaced with "URL", as these do not contribute towards emotion of the text.

2. **Replacing User Names:** Tweets often contain mentions which are directed towards certain users. We replaced all such mentions with "USER."

3. **Replacing Emoticons :** All the emoticons used in the tweets are replaced with "Emoticon". Before replacing, the emoticons along with their respective counts are stored since we use them as one of the features for classification.

4. **Removal of Punctuations:** All the punctuation marks in a tweet are removed. However, before removing them we store the count of each punctuation mark since we use them as one of the features in classification.

5.2 Feature Identification and Extraction :

In our work, we have used the following feature vectors to train our supervised machine learning model.

1. **Character N-Grams (C):** Character N-Grams are language independent and have proven to be very efficient for classifying text. These are also useful in situations when the text suffers from errors such as misspellings (Cavnar et al., 1994; Huffman, 1995; Lodhi et al., 2002). Groups of characters can help in capturing semantic meaning, especially in the code-mixed language where there is an informal use of words, which vary significantly from the standard Hindi and English words. We use character n-grams as one of the features, where n varies from 1 to 3.

2. **Word N-Grams (W) :** Bag of word features have been widely used to capture emotion in a text (Purver and Battersby, 2012) and in detecting hate speech (Warner and Hirschberg, 2012). Thus we use word n-grams, where n varies from 1 to 3 as a feature to train our classification models.

3. **Emoticons (E) :** We also use emoticons as a feature for emotion classification since they often represent textual portrayals of a writer's emotion in the form of symbols. For example, ':o('and ':(' express sadness, ':)'and ';)' express happiness. We use a list of Western Emoticons from Wikipedia.[3]

4. **Punctuations (P):** Punctuation marks can also be useful for emotion classification. Users often use exclamation marks when they want to express strong feelings. Multiple question marks in the text can denote surprise, excitement, and anger. Usage of an exclamation mark in conjunction with the question mark indicates astonishment and annoyed feeling. We count the occurrence of each punctuation mark in a sentence and use them as a feature.

5. **Repetitive Characters (R) :** Users on social media often repeat some characters in a word to stress upon particular emotion. For example, 'lol' (abbreviated form of laughing out loud) can be written as 'loool', 'looool'. 'Happy' can be written as 'happppyyyy,' 'haaappyy'. We stored the count of all such words in a tweet in which a particular character is repeated more than two times in a row and use them as one of the features.

6. **Uppercase Words (U) :** Users often write some words in a text in capital letters to represent shouting and anger (Dadvar et al., 2013). Hence for every tweet, we count all such words which are completely written in capital letters and contain more than 4 letters and use it as a feature.

7. **Intensifiers (I):** Users often tend to use intensifiers for laying emphasis on sentiment and emotion. For example in the following code-mixed text,
"Wo kisi se baat nahi karega because he is too sad",
Translation : *"He will not talk to anyone because he is too sad".*
"too" is used to emphasize on the sadness of the boy. A list of English intensifiers was taken from wikipedia[4]. For creating the list of Hindi intensifiers, English intensifiers were

---

[3]https://en.wikipedia.org/wiki/List_of_emoticons
[4]https://en.wikipedia.org/wiki/Intensifier

Class	Weight
Happiness	4
Sadness	2
Anger	1

Table 4: Weights assigned to classes

transliterated to Hindi. Also Hindi words found in the corpus which are usually used as intensifiers were incorporated in the list. We count the number of intensifiers in a tweet and use the count as a feature.

8. **Negation Words (N) :** We select negation words to address variance from the desired emotion caused by negated phrases like "not sad" or "not happy". For example the tweet "It's diwali today and subah jaldi uthna padega!! Not happy" should be classified as a sad tweet, even though it has a happy unigram. To tackle this problem we define negation as a separate feature. A list of English negation words was taken from Christopher Pott's sentiment tutorial[5]. Hindi negation words were manually selected from the corpus. We count the number of negations in a tweet and use the count as a feature.

9. **Lexicon (L) :** It has been demonstrated in (Mohammad, 2012) that emotion lexicon features provide a significant gain in classification accuracy when combined with corpus-based features, if training and testing sets are drawn from the same domain. We used the (Mohammad and Turney, 2010, 2013) emotion lexicon containing 14182 unigrams both of English and Hindi. The words in Hindi emotion lexicon were written in the Devanagri[6] script and had to be transliterated into Roman Script by the authors. Each word in the lexicon is given a association score of 1 if it is related to a emotion otherwise the association score is 0. A weight was given to each word in a lexicon. The exact weight values are mentioned in the Table 4. This assignment of weight ensured that if a word is related to more than one emotion then we don't lose any information.

Feature Eliminated	Accuracy
None	58.2
Emoticons	58.1
Char N-Grams	42.9
Word N-Grams	57.6
Repetitive Characters	58.2
Punctuation Marks	57.4
Upper Case Words	58.2
Intensifiers	58.2
Negation Words	58.2
Lexicon	57.9

Table 5: Impact of each feature on the classification accuracy of emotion in the text calculated by eliminating one feature at a time.

6 Results and Discussions

This section presents the results for various feature experimentation.

6.1 Feature Experiments

In order to determine the effect of each feature on classification, we performed several experiments by elimination one feature at a time. In all the experiments, we carried out 10-fold cross-validation. We performed experiments using SVM classifier with radial basis function. The results of the experiments performed after eliminating one feature at a time (i.e., Ablation test to test interaction of feature sets) and using the above-mentioned classifier are mentioned in Table 5. Since the size of feature vectors formed are very large, we applied chi-square feature selection algorithm which reduces the size of our feature vector to 1600[7]. In our system, we have used SVM with RBF kernel as they perform efficiently in case of high dimensional feature vectors. For training our system classifier, we have used Scikit-learn(Pedregosa et al., 2011). The results from Table 5 shows that Character N-Grams, Punctuation Marks, Word N-Grams, Emoticons and Upper Case Words are the features which affect the accuracy most. We were able to achieve the best accuracy of 58.2% using the Character N-Grams, Word N-grams, Punctuation Marks and Emoticons as features trained with SVM classifier.

---

[5]http://sentiment.christopherpotts.net/lingstruc.html
[6]https://en.wikipedia.org/wiki/Devanagari

[7]The size of feature vector was decided after empirical fine tuning

7 Conclusion and Future Work

In this paper, we present a freely available corpus of Hindi-English code-mixed text, consisting of tweet ids and the corresponding annotations. We also present the supervised system used for classifying the emotion of the tweets. The corpus consists of 2866 code-mixed tweets annotated with 6 emotions namely happiness, sadness, anger, surprise and sadness and with the caused language, i.e., English, Hindi, Mixed and Both. The words in the tweets are also annotated with the source language of the words. Experiments clearly show that usage of punctuation marks and emoticons result in better accuracy. Char N-Grams feature vector is also important for classification. As it is clear from the results, in the absence of char n-grams, the classification accuracy drops nearly by 16%. This paper describes the initial efforts in emotion prediction in Hindi-English code-mixed social media texts.

As a part of future work, the corpus can be annotated with part-of-speech tags at word level which may yield better results. Moreover, the dataset contains very limited tweets expressing fear, disgust, and surprise as emotion. Thus it can be extended to include more tweets having these emotions. The annotations and experiments described in this paper can also be carried out for code-mixed texts containing more than two languages from multilingual societies, in future.

References

Cecilia Ovesdotter Alm, Dan Roth, and Richard Sproat. 2005. Emotions from text: machine learning for text-based emotion prediction. In *Proceedings of the conference on human language technology and empirical methods in natural language processing*, pages 579–586. Association for Computational Linguistics.

Kalika Bali, Jatin Sharma, Monojit Choudhury, and Yogarshi Vyas. 2014. " i am borrowing ya mixing?" an analysis of english-hindi code mixing in facebook. In *Proceedings of the First Workshop on Computational Approaches to Code Switching*, pages 116–126.

Utsab Barman, Amitava Das, Joachim Wagner, and Jennifer Foster. 2014. Code mixing: A challenge for language identification in the language of social media. In *Proceedings of the first workshop on computational approaches to code switching*, pages 13–23.

William B Cavnar, John M Trenkle, et al. 1994. N-gram-based text categorization. *Ann arbor mi*, 48113(2):161–175.

Ying Chen, Sophia Yat Mei Lee, Shoushan Li, and Chu-Ren Huang. 2010. Emotion cause detection with linguistic constructions. In *Proceedings of the 23rd International Conference on Computational Linguistics*, pages 179–187. Association for Computational Linguistics.

Maral Dadvar, Dolf Trieschnigg, Roeland Ordelman, and Franciska de Jong. 2013. Improving cyberbullying detection with user context. In *European Conference on Information Retrieval*, pages 693–696. Springer.

Dipankar Das and Sivaji Bandyopadhyay. 2010. Identifying emotional expressions, intensities and sentence level emotion tags using a supervised framework. In *Proceedings of the 24th Pacific Asia Conference on Language, Information and Computation*.

Luisa Duran. 1994. Toward a better understanding of code switching and interlanguage in bilinguality: Implications for bilingual instruction. *The Journal of Educational Issues of Language Minority Students*, 14(2):69–88.

Paul Ekman. 1992. An argument for basic emotions. *Cognition & emotion*, 6(3-4):169–200.

Paul Ekman. 1993. Facial expression and emotion. *American psychologist*, 48(4):384.

Souvick Ghosh, Satanu Ghosh, and Dipankar Das. 2017. Sentiment identification in code-mixed social media text. *arXiv preprint arXiv:1707.01184*.

Marjolein Gysels. 1992. French in urban lubumbashi swahili: Codeswitching, borrowing, or both? *Journal of Multilingual & Multicultural Development*, 13(1-2):41–55.

Stephen Huffman. 1995. Acquaintance: Language-independent document categorization by n-grams. Technical report, DEPARTMENT OF DEFENSE FORT GEORGE G MEADE MD.

Aditya Joshi, Ameya Prabhu, Manish Shrivastava, and Vasudeva Varma. 2016. Towards sub-word level compositions for sentiment analysis of hindi-english code mixed text. In *Proceedings of COLING 2016, the 26th International Conference on Computational Linguistics: Technical Papers*, pages 2482–2491.

Sophia Lee and Zhongqing Wang. 2015. Emotion in code-switching texts: Corpus construction and analysis. In *Proceedings of the Eighth SIGHAN Workshop on Chinese Language Processing*, pages 91–99.

Huma Lodhi, Craig Saunders, John Shawe-Taylor, Nello Cristianini, and Chris Watkins. 2002. Text classification using string kernels. *Journal of Machine Learning Research*, 2(Feb):419–444.

Saif Mohammad. 2012. Portable features for classifying emotional text. In *Proceedings of the 2012 Conference of the North American Chapter of the Association for Computational Linguistics: Human Language Technologies*, pages 587–591. Association for Computational Linguistics.

Saif M Mohammad and Peter D Turney. 2010. Emotions evoked by common words and phrases: Using mechanical turk to create an emotion lexicon. In *Proceedings of the NAACL HLT 2010 workshop on computational approaches to analysis and generation of emotion in text*, pages 26–34. Association for Computational Linguistics.

Saif M. Mohammad and Peter D. Turney. 2013. Crowdsourcing a word-emotion association lexicon. 29(3):436–465.

Pieter Muysken. 2000. *Bilingual speech: A typology of code-mixing*, volume 11. Cambridge University Press.

Carol Myers-Scotton. 1993. Dueling languages: Grammatical structure in code-switching. claredon.

Fabian Pedregosa, Gaël Varoquaux, Alexandre Gramfort, Vincent Michel, Bertrand Thirion, Olivier Grisel, Mathieu Blondel, Peter Prettenhofer, Ron Weiss, Vincent Dubourg, et al. 2011. Scikit-learn: Machine learning in python. *Journal of machine learning research*, 12(Oct):2825–2830.

Matthew Purver and Stuart Battersby. 2012. Experimenting with distant supervision for emotion classification. In *Proceedings of the 13th Conference of the European Chapter of the Association for Computational Linguistics*, pages 482–491. Association for Computational Linguistics.

Khyathi Chandu Raghavi, Manoj Kumar Chinnakotla, and Manish Shrivastava. 2015. Answer ka type kya he?: Learning to classify questions in code-mixed language. In *Proceedings of the 24th International Conference on World Wide Web*, pages 853–858. ACM.

Arnav Sharma, Sakshi Gupta, Raveesh Motlani, Piyush Bansal, Manish Srivastava, Radhika Mamidi, and Dipti M Sharma. 2016. Shallow parsing pipeline for hindi-english code-mixed social media text. *arXiv preprint arXiv:1604.03136*.

Yogarshi Vyas, Spandana Gella, Jatin Sharma, Kalika Bali, and Monojit Choudhury. 2014. Pos tagging of english-hindi code-mixed social media content. In *Proceedings of the 2014 Conference on Empirical Methods in Natural Language Processing (EMNLP)*, pages 974–979.

Zhongqing Wang, Yue Zhang, Sophia Lee, Shoushan Li, and Guodong Zhou. 2016. A bilingual attention network for code-switched emotion prediction. In *Proceedings of COLING 2016, the 26th International Conference on Computational Linguistics: Technical Papers*, pages 1624–1634.

William Warner and Julia Hirschberg. 2012. Detecting hate speech on the world wide web. In *Proceedings of the Second Workshop on Language in Social Media*, pages 19–26. Association for Computational Linguistics.

Ge Xu, Xinfan Meng, and Houfeng Wang. 2010. Build chinese emotion lexicons using a graph-based algorithm and multiple resources. In *Proceedings of the 23rd international conference on computational linguistics*, pages 1209–1217. Association for Computational Linguistics.

A Appendix

A.1 HashTags

Category	Hash Tags
Politics	#budget, #Trump, #swachhbharat, #makeinindia, #SupremeCourt, #RightToPrivacy, #RahulGandhi, #MannKiBaat, #ManmohanSingh, #MakeInIndia, #SurgicalStrike
Sports	#CWCU19, #U19CWC, #icc, #srt, #pvsindhu, #IndvsSA, #kohli, #dhoni
Social Events	#Festivals, #Holi, #Diwali
Others	#bitcoin, #Jio, #Fraud, #PNBScam, #MoneyLaundering, #Scam

Table 6: List of Hashtags used for mining the tweets.

Sensing and Learning Human Annotators
Engaged in Narrative Sensemaking

McKenna K. Tornblad,[1] Luke Lapresi,[2] Christopher M. Homan,[2]
Raymond W. Ptucha[3] and Cecilia Ovesdotter Alm[4]

[1]College of Behavioral and Health Sciences, George Fox University
[2]Golisano College of Computing and Information Sciences, Rochester Institute of Technology
[3]Kate Gleason College of Engineering, Rochester Institute of Technology
[4]College of Liberal Arts, Rochester Institute of Technology

`mtornblad14@georgefox.edu, lxl6996@rit.edu, cmh@cs.rit.edu,`
`rwpeec@rit.edu, coagla@rit.edu`

Abstract

While labor issues and quality assurance in crowdwork are increasingly studied, how annotators make sense of texts and how they are personally impacted by doing so are not. We study these questions via a narrative-sorting annotation task, where carefully selected (by sequentiality, topic, emotional content, and length) collections of tweets serve as examples of everyday storytelling. As readers process these narratives, we measure their facial expressions, galvanic skin response, and self-reported reactions. From the perspective of annotator well-being, a reassuring outcome was that the sorting task did not cause a measurable stress response, however readers reacted to humor. In terms of sensemaking, readers were more confident when sorting sequential, target-topical, and highly emotional tweets. As crowdsourcing becomes more common, this research sheds light onto the perceptive capabilities and emotional impact of human readers.

1 Introduction

A substantial sector of the gig economy is the use of crowdworkers to annotate data for machine learning and analysis. For instance, storytelling is an essential human activity, especially for information sharing (Bluvshtein et al., 2015), making it the subject of many data annotation tasks. Microblogging sites such as Twitter have reshaped the narrative format, especially through character restrictions and nonstandard language, elements which contribute to a relatively unexplored mode of narrative construction; yet, little is known about reader responses to such narrative content.

We explore reader reactions to narrative sensemaking using a new sorting task that varies the presumed cognitive complexity of the task and elicits readers' interpretations of a target topic and its emotional tone. We carefully and systematically extracted 60 sets of tweets from a 1M-tweet dataset and presented them to participants via an interface that mimicks the appearance of Twitter (Figure 1). We asked subjects to sort chronologically the tweets in each set, half with true narrative sequence and half without. Each set consisted of 3–4 tweets from a previously collected corpus, where each tweet was labeled using a framework by Liu et al. (2016) as work-related or not. In addition to sequentiality and job-relatedness, sets were evenly distributed across two other variables with two levels each, of interest for understanding narrative sensemaking (Table 1). We recorded readers' spoken responses to four questions (Figure 2) about each set, which involved the sorting task, reader confidence, topical content (job-relatedness), and emotional tone. We used galvanic skin response (GSR) and facial expression analysis to explore potentially quantifiable metrics for stress-based reactions and other aspects of reader-annotator response. Our results add understanding of how annotators react to and process everyday microblog narratives.

This study makes these contributions:
1) Opens a dialogue on annotator well-being;
2) Presents a method to study annotator reactions;
3) Indicates that narrative sorting (task with degrees of complexity) does not cause an increased stress response as task complexity increases;
4) Studies the role of topic saliency and emotional tone in narrative sense-making; and
5) Probes how features model annotator reactions.

2 Related Work

That annotation tasks cause fatigue is widely recognized (Medero et al., 2006), and crowdsourcing

Proceedings of NAACL-HLT 2018: Student Research Workshop, pages 136–143
New Orleans, Louisiana, June 2 - 4, 2018. ©2017 Association for Computational Linguistics

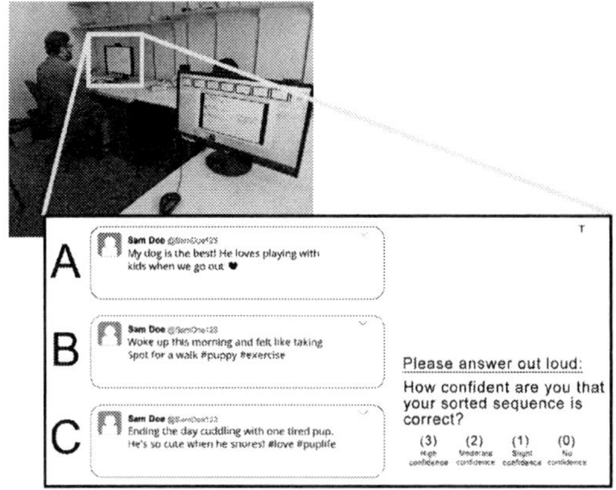

Figure 1: The experimental setup showing the experimenter's screen, a view of the participant on a second monitor, and a closeup view of the participant's screen. A fictional tweet set is shown to maintain privacy.

1. What is the correct chronological order of these tweets?

2. How confident are you that your sorted sequence is correct?

3. Are these tweets about work? [Target topic] If so, are they about starting or leaving a job?

4. What is the dominant emotion conveyed in this tweet set?

Figure 2: The four study questions that participants answered for each tweet set in both trials.

annotations has been critiqued for labor market issues, etc. (Fort et al., 2011). Another important concern is how stressful or cognitively demanding annotation tasks may adversely impact annotators themselves, a subject matter that has not yet been prominently discussed, despite its obvious ethical implications for the NLP community and machine learning research.

Microblogging sites raise unique issues around sharing information and interacting socially. Compared to traditional published writing, Twitter users must choose language that conveys meaning while adhering to brevity requirements (Barnard, 2016). This leads to new narrative practices, such as more abbreviations and nonstandard phraseology, which convey meaning and emotion differently (Mohammad, 2012). Tweets are also published in real time and the majority of users make their tweets publicly available, even when their subject matter is personal (Marwick and Boyd,

2011). Stories are shared among—and everyday narrative topics are explored by—communities, providing a window into the health and well-being of both online and offline networks at community levels.

We selected job-relatedness as our *Target Topic* variable. Employment plays a prominent role in the daily lives and well-being of adults and is a popular theme in the stories microbloggers share of their lives. One study reported that slightly more than a third of a sample of nearly 40,000 tweets by employed people were work-related (van Zoonen et al., 2015). Employees can use social media to communicate with coworkers or independently to share their experiences (Madsen, 2016; van Zoonen et al., 2014), providing many interesting job-related narratives. Because it is so common in on- and off-line storytelling, annotators can relate to narratives about work. Work is also a less stressful topic, compared to other ones (Calderwood et al., 2017). Tweets with high or low emotional content in general may also affect readers in ways that change how they understand texts (Bohn-Gettler and Rapp, 2011). We used the sentiment functionality of TextBlob[1] to distinguish high- and low-emotion tweets in the study.

Variable	Lvl 1	Abbr.	Lvl 2	Abbr.
Narrative Seq.	yes	seq+	no	seq-
Target Topic	yes	job+	no	job-
Emo. Content	high	emo+	low	emo-
Num. Tweets	3		4	

Table 1: Overview of the four study variables that characterize each tweet set. Lvl 1 indicates the first condition for a variable, and Lvl 2 indicates the second. The primary distinction is between sets in Trial 1 (all seq+) and 2 (all seq-).

3 Study Design

The study involved 60 total tweet sets across two trials, reflecting a presumed increase in the cognitive complexity of the narrative sorting task. Trial 1 consisted of sets with a true narrative order (seq+) and Trial 2 of sets without (seq-); with the assumption that the latter is more cognitively demanding. The tweets were evenly distributed across the other three study variables (Table 1).

[1]https://textblob.readthedocs.io

For selecting job+ sets in Trial 1, queries of the corpus combined with keywords (such as *coworker*, *interview*, *fired* and other employment-related terms) identified job-related seed tweets while additional querying expanded the set for the same narrator. For example, a 3-item narrative could involve interviewing for a job, being hired, and then starting the job. For the job- sets in Trial 1, queries for seed tweets focused on keywords for other life events that had the potential to contain narratives (such as *birthday*, *driver's license*, and *child*), continuing with the same method used for job+ sets. For each Trial 2 set, we conducted similar keyword queries, except that we chose the seed tweet without regard to its role in any larger narrative. We selected the rest of the tweets in the set to match and be congruent with the same user and job+/job- and emo+/emo- classes as the seed tweet. The final selection of 60 tweet sets was based on careful manual inspection.

4 Methods

Participants: Participants were nineteen individuals (21% women) in the Northeastern U.S. who ranged in age from 18 to 49 years ($M = 25.3$). 58% were native English speakers, and active Twitter users made up 42% of the sample.

Measures: *Galvanic Skin Response (GSR):* We used a Shimmer3 GSR sensor with a sampling rate of 128 Hz to measure participants' skin conductance in microsiemens (μS). More cognitively difficult tasks may induce more sweating, and higher μS, corresponding to a decrease in resistance and indicating cognitive load (Shi et al., 2007). We used GSR peaks, as measured by iMotions software (iMotions, 2016), to estimate periods of increased cognitive arousal.

Facial Expression: To also differentiate between positive and negative emotional arousal, we captured and analyzed readers' expressed facial emotions while interacting with the task using Affectiva's facial expression analysis in iMotions (McDuff et al., 2016; iMotions, 2016).

Procedure: Participants sat in front of a monitor with a Logitech C920 HD Pro webcam and were fitted with a Shimmer3 GSR sensor worn on their non-dominant hand. They then completed a demographic pre-survey while the webcam and GSR sensor were calibrated within the iMotions software. Next, participants completed a practice trial with an unsorted tweet set on the left-hand side of the screen and questions on the right (Figure 1).

Participants answered each question aloud, minimizing movement, and continued to the next question by pressing a key. We provided a visual of Plutchik's wheel of emotions (Plutchik, 2001) if the participant needed assistance in deciding on an emotion for Question 4 (Figure 2), although they were free to say any emotion word. After the practice trial, the participant completed Trial 1 (seq+), followed by a short break, then Trial 2 (seq-). Finally, we gave each participant a post-study survey on their self-reported levels of comfort with the equipment and of cognitive fatigue during each trial.

One experimenter was seated behind the participant in the experiment room with a separate video screen to monitor the sensor data and answer any questions. A second experimenter was in another room recording the participants' answers as they were spoken via remote voice and screen sharing.

Classifier: Pairing each tweet set with each participant's response data as a single item yields 1140 data items (19 subjects * 60 sets). We used the LIBSVM (Chang and Lin, 2011) support vector machine (SVM) classifier library, with a radial basis function kernel and 10-fold cross-validation, to predict variables of interest in narrative sensemaking. Table 2 lists observed and predicted features. When a feature served as a prediction target it was not used as an observed one. The mean value of the feature was used in cases of missing data points.

Study	Self-Report	Sensing
Narrative Seq.	Kendall τ Dist.	Facial Expression
Emo. Content	Confidence	Average GSR
Target Topic	Topic Judgment	Num. GSR Peaks
Num. Tweets .	Dom. Emotion	Time
	Twitter User	
	Soc. Media Use	

Table 2: Features used for a SVM classifier were put into three groups: 1) Study variables; 2) Subject self-reported measures from participants' answers to study questions and pre-survey responses related to social media use; and 3) Sensing attributes relating to collected sensor and time data.

5 Results and Discussion

Trial Question 1: Tweet Sorting To quantify how close participants' sorted orders were to the correct narrative sequence for each tweet set in Trial 1, we used the Kendall τ rank distance between the two, or the total number of pairwise swaps of adjacent items needed to transform one sequence into the other. An ANOVA revealed that participants were significantly closer to the correct narrative order when tweets were job-related (job+), compared to not job-related (job-), regardless of emotional content, $F(1, 566) = 13.30, p < .001$ (Figure 3a). This result indicates that the target topic was useful for temporally organizing parts of stories. Without this topic's frame to start from, readers were less accurate in the sorting task.

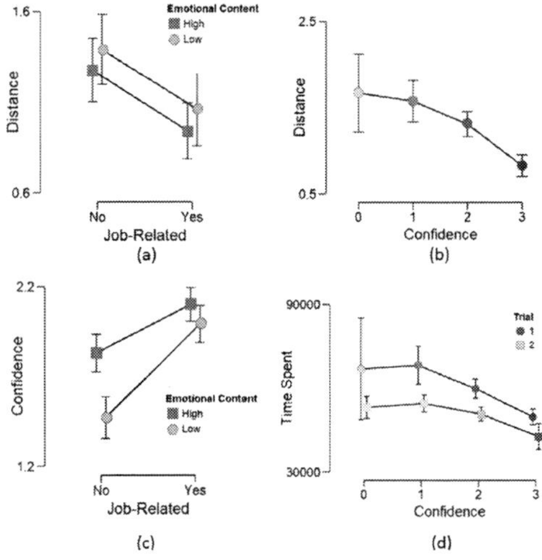

Figure 3: The four panels show: (a) Average Kendall τ rank distance between participants' orders and the correct order by job-relatedness (target topic) and emotional content in Trial 1 only. Participants were significantly more accurate with sets about the target topic, regardless of emotional content. (b) Average Kendall τ rank distance between participants' sorted orders and the correct order by confidence level in Trial 1. $0 = $ *No Confidence* and $3 = $ *High Confidence*. Participants tended to be closer to the correct order as their confidence increased. (c) Average confidence ratings across both trials by job-relatedness and emotional content. The only non-significant difference was between Job-Related (job+) x High Emotional Content (emo+), and Job-Related (job+) x Low Emotional Content (emo-) groups (see Table 3), indicating an interaction between target topic and emotional content. (d) Average time spent (ms) per tweet set by confidence and trial. Participants spent overall less time on sets in Trial 2 than Trial 1, and less time for sets in both trials as confidence increased.

Trial Question 2: Confidence An ANOVA showed that as participants became more confident

Grp 1	Grp 2	t	p	SE	d
Y × H	Y × L	1.646	.101	0.066	0.097
Y × H	N × H	4.378	<.001*	0.062	0.259
Y × H	N × L	10.040	<.001*	0.063	0.595
Y × L	N × H	2.541	.012†	0.064	0.151
Y × L	N × L	8.030	<.001*	0.065	0.476
N × H	N × L	5.750	<.001*	0.063	0.341

Table 3: Student's t-test indicates differences in confidence by job-relatedness and emotional content (visualized in Figure 3c) with df=284 for all conditions. Groups are named with the following convention: Job-Relatedness x Emotional Content. Y = Yes (job+), N = No (job-), H = High (emo+), and L = Low (emo-). (* $p < .001$ † $p < .05$).

in Trial 1, their sorted tweet orders were closer to the correct order, $F(3, 566) = 14.72, p < .001$. This demonstrated that readers are able to accurately estimate their correctness in the sorting task when tweets had a true narrative sequence (Figure 3b). This is an interesting result suggesting that participants were not under- or overconfident but self-aware of their ability to complete the sorting task. An ANOVA also showed that participants were significantly more confident in Trial 1 ($M = 2.20, SD = 0.79$) than Trial 2 ($M = 1.50, SD = 0.92$), $F(1, 1138) = 188.00, p < .001$, regardless of other study variables (Figure 4). This indicates that it was more difficult for participants to assign a sorted order when the tweets did not have one.

CONFIDENCE DISTRIBUTION

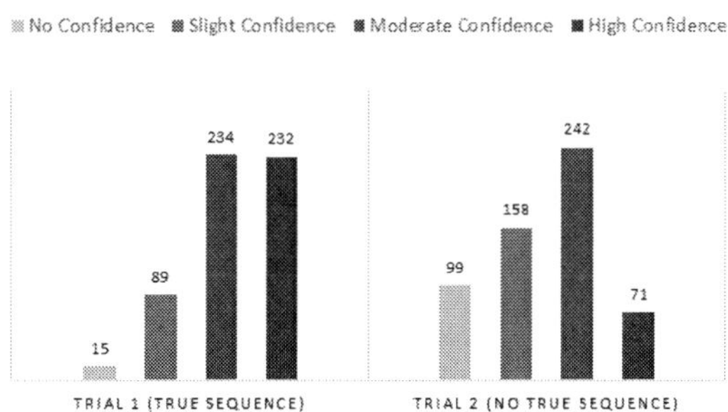

Figure 4: Total instances of each confidence level by trial (0 = *No Confidence* and 3 = *High Confidence*).

Because each participant's confidence scores for tweet sets in Trial 1 were not related to scores in Trial 2, we used an independent samples t-test and found that confidence was significantly higher for job+ tweets ($M = 2.05, SD = 0.84$) than job- tweets ($M = 1.65, SD = 0.97$), $t(1138) = -7.38, p < .001$. By including emotional content in an ANOVA, we also found that participants were significantly more confident about emo+ tweets compared to emo-, but only when the topic was not job-related (job-), $F(1, 1136) = 5.65, p = .018$. Comparisons among groups these groups can be seen in Table 3 and Figure 3c.

These findings suggest that the target topic, having a known narrative frame, was the most useful piece of information for participants in ordering tweets. When there was no job narrative to guide interpretation, emotional context was instead used as the primary sorting cue. This result agrees with previous work (Liu et al., 2016) by suggesting that the job life cycle involves a well-known narrative sequence that is used as a reference point for sorting tweets chronologically.

Confidence level could indicate cognitive load, which is supported by the ANOVA result that participants spent less time for each tweet set as their confidence increased, regardless of trial, $F(3, 1103) = 16.71, p < .001$ (Figure 3d). This suggests that participants spent less time on sets that appeared to be easier to sort and more time on sets that were perceived as more difficult. This could be a promising factor to predict how straightforward sorting different texts will be based on readers' confidence and time spent.

However, participants also spent significantly more time for each tweet set in Trial 1 than Trial 2 regardless of confidence level, $F(1, 1103) = 29.53, p < .001$ (Figure 3d), even though Trial 2 was expected to be more difficult and thus time-consuming. This contrary result could be for several reasons. First, participants may have simply got faster through practice. Second, they may have been fatigued from the task and sped up to finish. Lastly, participants could have given up on the task more quickly because it was more difficult, an indicator of cognitive fatigue.

Trial Question 3: Target Topic Participants correctly inferred the topic as job-related 97.5% of the time (true positive rate) and not job-related 96.3% (true negative rate) of the time. For more ambiguous sets, we observed that participants added qualifiers to their answers more often, such as *"these tweets could be about starting a job,"* but were still able to determine the topic. These observations indicate that readers perform well when determining the topical context of tweets despite the format peculiarities that accompany the text.

Trial Question 4: Dominant Emotion If participants gave more than one word to answer this question, we used only the first to capture the participant's initial reaction to the text. We categorized words according to Plutchick's wheel of emotions (2001), and used the fundamental emotion in each section of the wheel (such as *joy* and *sadness*) as the category label. Emotion words in between each section were also used as labels and a neutral category was added, resulting in 17 categories explored in classification (below).

Sensor Data Analysis We averaged GSR readings across all four study questions for each tweet set. Because participants spent minutes answering questions 1 and 4 compared to mere seconds on 2 and 3, we chose to examine overall readings for each set instead of individual questions. An extremely short timeframe yields fewer data points and more impact in the event of poor measurement. We were also more interested in differences between the study variables of the tweet sets (Table 1) rather than differences by question, although this could be a direction for future data analysis and research.

Interestingly, an ANOVA indicated no differences in overall normalized GSR levels or number of peaks across any of the four study variables, which leads to important insights. First, it suggests that annotators may not feel more stressed when trying to sort texts that have no true narrative sequence. This could be because piecing together narratives is so fundamental and natural in human interaction and cognition. Second, when the focus is the sorting task, it appears that engaging with tweet sets with high emotional content—whether about or not about the target topic—did not elicit a greater stress response in readers. This adds more understanding to previous research (Calderwood et al., 2017) on emotional and physiological responses to texts.

We analyzed facial expressions using Affectiva (McDuff et al., 2016), obtaining the total number of instances per minute of each facial expression (anger, contempt, disgust, fear, joy, sadness, and surprise) for each tweet set by participant. We recorded the emotion that was displayed most often by a participant for a given tweet set (*neutral* if no emotion registered over Affectiva's threshold of 50). Disgust and contempt appeared to be the primary emotions displayed across all narratives regardless of topic or emotional content.We observed that participants' neutral resting faces tended to be falsely registered as disgust and contempt. Other factors such as skin tone and glasses influenced facial marker tracking.

By observation it was clear that participants had reactions (Figure 5) to tweet sets that were funny, including complex forms of humor such as irony and sarcasm. This is an important finding because annotating humor is a task that human readers are very good at compared to machines. The facial response to humor when reading texts could be used in a machine learning-based model to identify and classify humorous content.

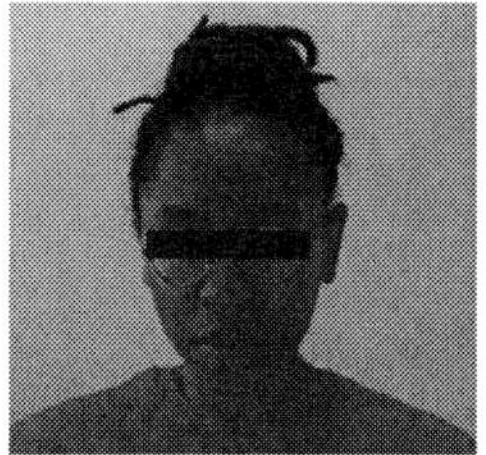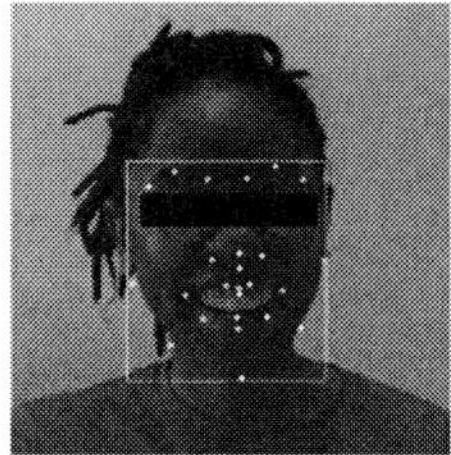

Figure 5: Participant displaying a neutral facial expression followed by a joy reaction to a humorous tweet.

Classification Results To further study the collected human data and explore patterns of interest in the data, we used SVMs to model a tweet set's *Emotional Content* (emo+/-) and *Narrative Sequence* (seq+/-); and a participant's *Confidence* and self-reported *Dominant Emotion* (Dom. Emo.) (see Table 4). The label set differed for each classification problem, ranging from binary (emo+/- and seq+/-) to multiple, less balanced classes (4 for confidence and 17 for dominant emotion). When the label being predicted was also part of the observed feature group used to build the classifier, it was excluded from the feature set.

Table 4 displays the accuracy for these classifiers, using various combinations of the features sets from Table 2. It also shows, for each variable modeled, results from a *Good-3* selection of features. This approach uses top-performing features via exhaustive search over all valid combinations of three. The same Good-3 features (Table 5) were used for all trials for a classification problem in Table 4.

Often, either All or Good-3 sets result in higher performance. Confidence and emo+/- classification improves performance with Trial 1 classification; however, since the dataset is modest in size,

Feat.	Conf.			Emo+/-			Dom. Emo.			Seq+/-
	T1	T2	C	T1	T2	C	T1	T2	C	C
Leave 1-subject out cross-validation										
Study	**49**	41	**45**	53	53	53	32	**34**	33	53
Rep.	48	35	43	65	62	59	28	28	26	67
Sens.	43	39	37	54	56	52	26	22	25	49
All	46	38	42	62	**64**	62	**35**	32	**34**	68
Good-3	**49**	**42**	**45**	**71**	62	**66**	34	30	32	**70**
Leave 1-question out cross-validation										
Study	46	41	44	27	27	53	23	19	21	53
Rep.	47	40	42	**63**	**58**	43	21	22	20	64
Sens.	45	**43**	39	45	52	44	24	21	25	51
All	47	41	45	39	44	42	26	19	23	63
Good-3	**50**	41	**46**	55	31	**57**	**34**	**25**	**30**	**67**
Leave 1-subject-and-question out cross-validation										
Study	49	**45**	**47**	27	27	27	**35**	**36**	**34**	27
Rep.	46	41	43	64	57	56	24	27	25	68
Sens.	46	42	39	52	55	50	26	24	25	59
All	50	42	**47**	57	61	60	**35**	31	**34**	**74**
Good-3	**51**	42	46	**71**	**62**	**66**	34	33	33	70

Table 4: Classification accuracies rounded to nearest percent for Trial 1 (T1), Trial 2 (T2) and both trials combined (C). Bold values indicate the most accurate feature set's prediction percentage per trial or combined. Because trials 1 and 2 differed in having a true narrative sequence, no seq+/- prediction is reported by trial.

it is difficult to make a judgment as to whether or not presenting users with chronologically ordered tweets yield better classifiers for narrative content. As expected, regardless of which set of features is being used, simpler boolean problems outperform the more difficult multiclass ones.

6 Conclusion and Future Work

This study adds understanding of how annotators make sense of microblog narratives and on the importance of considering how readers may be impacted by engaging with text annotation tasks.

The narrative sorting task—and the self-evaluated confidence rating—appears useful for understanding how a reader may frame and interpret a microblog narrative. Confidence displayed a strong relationship with several factors, including target topic, time spent, Kendall τ distance, and cognitive complexity between trials. This points to the importance of considering confidence in an-

Confidence	Emo+/-	Dom. Emo.	Seq+/-
Seq+/-	# of Tweets	# of Tweets	Job+/-
Kendall τ dist.	Job+/-	Emo+/-	K. τ dist.
Soc. Med. use	Dom. Emo.	Seq+/-	Confid.

Table 5: Good-3 features used for each SVM classifier.

notation. Confidence ratings can also help identify outlier narratives that are more challenging to process and interpret. The increase in cognitive complexity in Trial 2 did not appear to cause a potentially unhealthy stress response in annotators.

Despite generating interesting results, this study had limitations. For example, the sample size was modest and trial order was not randomized. Additionally, the topics of tweets were not overly stressful, and we avoided including tweets we thought could trigger discomfort. As an exploratory study, the quantitative results presented represent preliminary findings. More nuanced and advanced statistical analysis is left for future work.

Future work could benefit from developing classifiers for predicting whether a microblog post is part of a narrative; a useful filtering task completed by careful manual inspection in this study. Additional development of classifiers will focus on further aspects related to how readers are likely to interpret and annotate microblog narratives.

Acknowledgments

This material is based upon work supported by the National Science Foundation under Award No. IIS-1559889. Any opinions, findings, and conclusions or recommendations expressed in this material are those of the author(s) and do not necessarily reflect the views of the National Science Foundation.

References

Josie Barnard. 2016. Tweets as microfiction: On Twitter's live nature and 140-character limit as tools for developing storytelling skills. *New Writing: The International Journal for the Practice and Theory of Creative Writing*, 13(1):3–16.

Marina Bluvshtein, Melody Kruzic, and Victor Massaglia. 2015. From netthinking to networking to netfeeling: Using social media to help people in job transitions. *The Journal of Individual Psychology*, 71(2):143–154.

Catherine M Bohn-Gettler and David N Rapp. 2011. Depending on my mood: Mood-driven influences on text comprehension. *Journal of Educational Psychology*, 103(3):562.

Alexander Calderwood, Elizabeth A Pruett, Raymond Ptucha, Christopher Homan, and Cecilia O Alm. 2017. Understanding the semantics of narratives of interpersonal violence through reader annotations and physiological reactions. In *Proceedings of the Workshop on Computational Semantics beyond Events and Roles*, pages 1–9.

Chih-Chung Chang and Chih-Jen Lin. 2011. LIBSVM: A library for support vector machines. *ACM Transactions on Intelligent Systems and Technology*, 2:27:1–27:27.

Karën Fort, Gilles Adda, and K Bretonnel Cohen. 2011. Amazon Mechanical Turk: Gold mine or coal mine? *Computational Linguistics*, 37(2):413–420.

iMotions. 2016. iMotions Biometric Research Platform 6.0.

Tong Liu, Christopher Homan, Cecilia Ovesdotter Alm, Megan C Lytle, Ann Marie White, and Henry A Kautz. 2016. Understanding discourse on work and job-related well-being in public social media. In *Proceedings of the 54th Annual Meeting of the Association for Computational Linguistics*, pages 1044–1053.

Vibeke Thøis Madsen. 2016. Constructing organizational identity on internal social media: A case study of coworker communication in Jyske Bank. *International Journal of Business Communication*, 53(2):200–223.

Alice E Marwick and Danah Boyd. 2011. I tweet honestly, I tweet passionately: Twitter users, context collapse, and the imagined audience. *New Media & Society*, 13(1):114–133.

Daniel McDuff, Abdelrahman Mahmoud, Mohammad Mavadati, May Amr, Jay Turcot, and Rana el Kaliouby. 2016. AFFDEX SDK: A cross-platform real-time multi-face expression recognition toolkit. In *Proceedings of the 2016 CHI Conference Extended Abstracts on Human Factors in Computing Systems*, CHI EA '16, pages 3723–3726, New York, NY, USA. ACM.

Julie Medero, Kazuaki Maeda, Stephanie Strassel, and Christopher Walker. 2006. An efficient approach to gold-standard annotation: Decision points for complex tasks. In *Proceedings of the Fifth International Conference on Language Resources and Evaluation*, volume 6, pages 2463–2466.

Saif M Mohammad. 2012. #Emotional tweets. In *Proceedings of the First Joint Conference on Lexical and Computational Semantics*, pages 246–255. Association for Computational Linguistics.

Robert Plutchik. 2001. The Nature of Emotions. *American Scientist*, 89:344.

Yu Shi, Natalie Ruiz, Ronnie Taib, Eric Choi, and Fang
Chen. 2007. Galvanic skin response (GSR) as an in-
dex of cognitive load. In *Proceedings of CHI '07
Extended Abstracts on Human Factors in Comput-
ing Systems*, CHI EA '07, pages 2651–2656, New
York, NY, USA. ACM.

Ward van Zoonen, Toni GLA van der Meer, and
Joost WM Verhoeven. 2014. Employees work-
related social-media use: His master's voice. *Public
Relations Review*, 40(5):850–852.

Ward van Zoonen, Joost WM Verhoeven, and Rens
Vliegenthart. 2015. How employees use Twitter to
talk about work: A typology of work-related tweets.
Computers in Human Behavior, 55:329–339.

Generating Image Captions in Arabic using Root-Word Based Recurrent Neural Networks and Deep Neural Networks

Vasu Jindal
University of Texas at Dallas
Texas, USA
vasu.jindal@utdallas.edu

Abstract

Image caption generation has gathered widespread interest in the artificial intelligence community. Automatic generation of an image description requires both computer vision and natural language processing techniques. While, there has been advanced research in English caption generation, research on generating Arabic descriptions of an image is extremely limited. Semitic languages like Arabic are heavily influenced by root-words. We leverage this critical dependency of Arabic to generate captions of an image directly in Arabic using root-word based Recurrent Neural Network and Deep Neural Networks. Experimental results on datasets from various Middle Eastern newspaper websites allow us to report the first BLEU score for direct Arabic caption generation. We also compare the results of our approach with BLEU score captions generated in English and translated into Arabic. Experimental results confirm that generating image captions using root-words directly in Arabic significantly outperforms the English-Arabic translated captions using state-of-the-art methods.

1 Introduction

With the increase in the number of devices with cameras, there is a widespread interest in generating automatic captions from images and videos. Automatic generation of image descriptions is a widely researched problem. However, this problem is significantly more challenging that the image classification or image recognition tasks which gained popularity with ImageNet recognition challenge (Russakovsky et al., 2015). Automatic generation of image captions have a huge impact in the fields of information retrieval, accessibility for the vision impaired, categorization of images etc. Additionally, the automatic generation of the descriptions of images can be used as

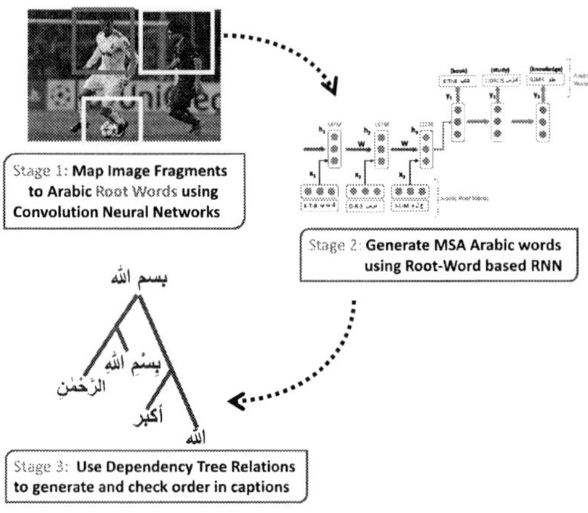

Figure 1: Overview of Our Approach

a frame by frame approach to describe videos and explain their context.

Recent works which utilize large image datasets and deep neural networks have obtained strong results in the field of image recognition (Krizhevsky et al., 2012; Russakovsky et al., 2015). To generate more natural descriptive sentences in English, (Karpathy and Fei-Fei, 2015) introduced a model that generates natural language descriptions of image regions based on weak labels in form of a dataset of images and sentences.

However, most visual recognition models and approaches in the image caption generation community are focused on Western languages, ignoring Semitic and Middle-Eastern languages like Arabic, Hebrew, Urdu and Persian. As discussed further in related works, almost all major caption generation models have validated their approaches using English. This is primarily due to two major reasons: i) lack of existing image corpora in languages other than English ii) the significant di-

Proceedings of NAACL-HLT 2018: Student Research Workshop, pages 144–151
New Orleans, Louisiana, June 2 - 4, 2018. ©2017 Association for Computational Linguistics

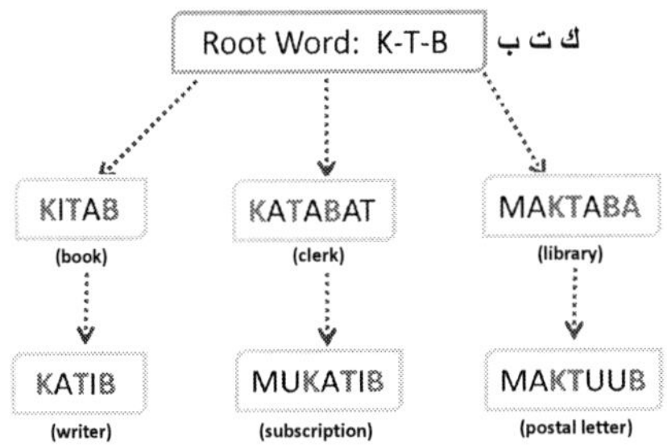

Figure 2: Leveraging Root-Word in Arabic, Constants and Vowels are filled using Recurrent Neural Network

Figure 3: State-of-the-Art: Man studying with books
Ours (translated from Arabic for reader's readability): Writer writing on notebook

alects of Arabic and the challenges in translating images to natural sounding sentences. Translation of English generated captions to Arabic captions may not always be efficient due to the various Arabic morphologies, dialects and phonologies which results in losing the descriptive nature of the generated captions. A cross-lingual image caption generation approach in Japanese concluded that a bilingual comparable corpus has better performance than a monolingual corpus in image caption generation (Miyazaki and Shimizu, 2016).

Arabic is ranked as the fifth most widely spoken native language among the population. Furthermore, Arabic has tremendous impact on the social and political aspects in the current community and is listed as one of the six official languages of the United Nations. Given the high influence of Arabic, it is necessary for a robust approach for Arabic caption generation.

1.1 Novel Contributions

Semitic languages like Arabic are significantly influenced by their original root-word. Figure 2 explains how simple root-words can form new words with similar context. We leverage this critical aspect of Arabic to formalize a three stage approach integrating root-word based Deep Neural Networks and root-word based Recurrent Neural Network and dependency relations between these root words to generate Arabic captions. Fragments of images are extracted using pre-trained deep neural network on ImageNet, however, unlike other published approaches for English caption generation (Socher et al., 2014; Karpathy and Fei-Fei, 2015; Vinyals et al., 2015), we map these fragments to a set of root words in Arabic rather than actual words or sentences in English. *Our main contribution in this paper is three-fold:*

- Mapping of image fragments onto root words in Arabic rather than actual sentences or words/fragments of sentences as suggested in previously proposed approaches.
- Finding the most appropriate words for an image by using a root-word based Recurrent Neural Network.
- Finally, using dependency tree relations of these obtained words to check order in sentences in Arabic

To the best of our knowledge, this is the first work that leverage root words to generate captions in Arabic (Jindal, 2017). We also report the first BLEU scores for Arabic caption generation. *Additionally, this opens a new field of research to use root-words to generate captions from images in Semitic languages.* For the purpose of clarity, we use the term "root-words" throughout this paper to represent the roots of an Arabic word.

2 Background

2.1 Previous Works

The adoption of deep neural networks (Krizhevsky et al., 2012; Jia et al., 2014; Sharif Razavian et al., 2014) has tremendously improved both image recognition and natural language processing tasks. Furthermore, machine translation using recurrent neural networks have gained attention with sequence-to-sequence training approaches (Cho et al., 2014; Bahdanau et al., 2014; Kalchbrenner and Blunsom, 2013).

Recently, many researchers, have started to combine both a convolutional neural network and a recurrent neural network. Vinyals et al. used a convolutional neural network (CNN) with inception modules for visual recognition and long short-term memory (LSTM) for language modeling (Vinyals et al., 2015).

However, to the best of our knowledge most caption generation approaches were performed on English. Recently, authors in (Miyazaki and Shimizu, 2016) presented results on the first cross-lingual image caption generation on the Japanese language. (Peng and Li, 2016) generated Chinese captions on the Flickr30 dataset. There has been no single work addressing to the generation of captions in Semitic languages like Arabic. Furthermore, all previously proposed approaches map image fragments to actual words/phrases. We rather propose to leverage the significance of root-words in Semitic languages and map image fragments to root-words and use these root-words in a root-word based recurrent neural network.

2.2 Arabic Morphology and Challenges

Arabic belongs to the family of Semitic languages and has significant morphological, syntactical and semantic differences from other languages. It consists of 28 letters and can be extended to 90 by adding shapes, marks, and vowels. Arabic is written from right to left and letters have different styles based on the position in the word. The base words of Arabic inflect to express eight main features. Verbs inflect for aspect, mood, person and voice. Nouns and adjectives inflect for case and state. Verbs, nouns and adjectives inflect for both gender and number.

Furthermore, Arabic is widely categorized as a diglossia (Ferguson, 1959). A diglossia refers to a language where the formal usage of speech in written communication is significantly different in grammatical properties from the informal usage in verbal day to day communication. Arabic morphology consists of a bare root verb form that is trilateral, quadrilateral, or pentalateral. The derivational morphology can be lexeme = Root + Pattern or inflection morphology (word = Lexeme + Features) where features are noun specific, verb specific or single letter conjunctions. In contrast, in most European languages words are formed by concatenating morphemes.

Stem pattern are often difficult to parse in Arabic as they interlock with root consonants (Al Barrag, 2014). Arabic is also influenced by infixes which may be consonants and vowels and can be misinterpreted as root-words. One of the major problem is the use of a consonant, hamza. Hamza is not always pronounced and can be a vowel. This creates a severe orthographic problem as words may have differently positioned hamzas making them different strings yet having similar meaning.

Furthermore, diacritics are critical in Arabic. For example, two words formed from "zhb" meaning "to go" and "gold" differ by just one diacritic. The two words can only be distinguished using diacritics. The word "go" may appear in a variety of images involving movement while "gold" is more likely to appear in images containing jewelry.

3 Methodology

Our methodology is divided into three main stages. Figure 1 gives an overview of our approach. In Stage 1, we map image fragments onto root words in Arabic. Then, in Stage 2, we used root word based Recurrent Neural Networks with LSTM memory cell to generate the most appropriate words for an image in Modern Standard Arabic (MSA). Finally, in Stage 3, we use dependency tree relations of these obtained words to check the word order of the RNN formed sentences in Arabic. Each step is described in detail in following subsections.

3.1 Image Fragments to Root-Words using DNN

We extract fragments from images using the state-of-the-art deep neural networks. According to (Kulkarni et al., 2011; Karpathy et al., 2014), objects and their attributes are critical in generating sentence descriptions. Therefore, it is important to efficiently detect as many objects as possible in the image.

We apply the approach given in (Jia et al., 2014; Girshick et al., 2014) to detect objects in every image with a Region Convolutional Neural Network (RCNN). The CNN is pre-trained on ImageNet (Deng et al., 2009) and fine-tuned on the 200 classes of the ImageNet Detection Challenge. We also use the top 19 detected locations as given by Karpathy et al in addition to the whole image and compute the representations based on the pixels inside each bounding box as suggested in (Karpathy and Fei-Fei, 2015). It should be noted that the output of the convolutional neural network are Arabic root-words. To achieve this, at any given time when English labels of objects were

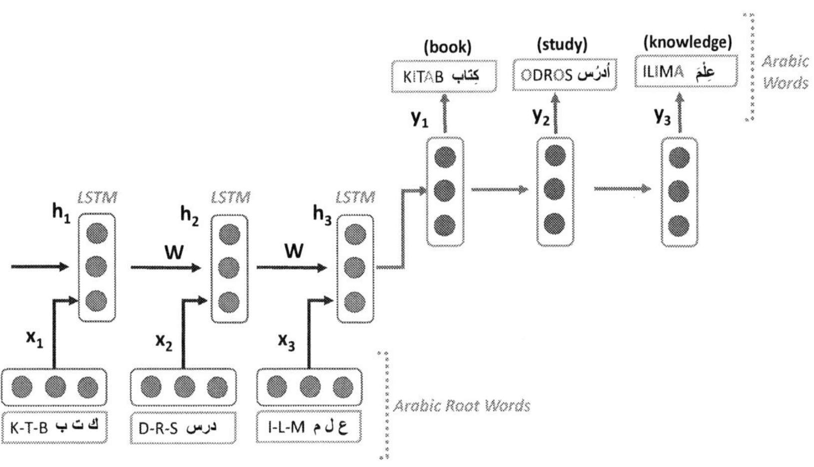

Figure 4: Our Root-Word based Recurrent Neural Network

used in training of the convolution neural network, **Arabic root-words of the object were also given as input** in the training phase. (Yaseen and Hmeidi, 2014; Yousef et al., 2014) proposed the well-known transducer based algorithm for Arabic root extraction which is used to extract root-words from an Arabic word in the training stage. Given the Arabic influence on root-words and the limited 4 verb prefixes, 12 noun prefixes and 20 common suffixes, the approach is optimized for initial training. Briefly, the algorithm has following steps given the morphology of Arabic.

1. Construct all noun/verb transducer
2. Construct all noun/verb patterns transducer
3. Construct all noun/verb suffixes transducer
4. Concatenate noun transducers/verb transducers obtained in steps 1, 2 and 3.
5. Sum the two transducers obtained in step 4.

Similar to (Vinyals et al., 2015), we used a discriminative model to maximize the probability of the correct description given the image. Formally, this can be represented using:

$$\theta^\star = \arg\max_\theta \sum_{(I,S)} \sum_{t=0}^{N} \log p(S_t|I, S_0, \ldots, S_{t-1}; \theta)$$

(1)

where θ are the parameters of our model, I is an image, and S its correct transcription and N is a particular length of a caption. This $p(S_t|I, S_0, \ldots, S_{t-1}; \theta)$ is modeled using a root-word based Recurrent Neural Network (RNN).

3.2 Root-Word Based Recurrent Neural Network and Dependency Relations

We propose a root-word based recurrent neural network (rwRNN). The model takes different root-words extracted from text, and predicts the most appropriate words for captions in Arabic, essentially also learning the context and environment of the image. The structure of the rwRNN is based on a standard many-to-many recurrent neural network, where current input (x) and previous information is connected through hidden states (h) by applying a certain (e.g. sigmoid) function (g) with linear transformation parameters (W) at each time step (t). Each hidden state is a long short-term memory (LSTM) (Hochreiter and Schmidhuber, 1997) cell to solve the vanishing gradient issue of vanilla recurrent neural networks and inefficiency in learning long distance dependencies.

While a standard input vector for RNN derives from either a word or a character, the input vector in rwRNN consists of a root-word specified with 3 letters (r_{1n}, r_{2n}, r_{3n}) that correspond to the characters in root-words' position. Most root-words in Arabic are trilateral very few being quadilateral or pentalateral. If a particular root-word is quadilateral (pentalateral) then the r_{2n} represents the middle three (four) letters of the root-word. Formally:

$$x_n = \begin{bmatrix} r_{1n} \\ r_{2n} \\ r_{3n} \end{bmatrix}$$

(2)

The final output (i.e. the predicted actual Arabic word y_n), the hidden state vector (h_n) of the

Figure 5: Arabic-English: Dog playing with ball
Ours: Dog plays with a ball

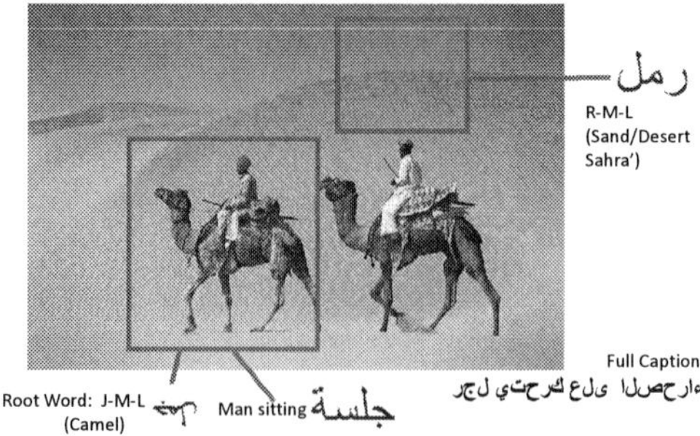

Figure 6: Arabic-English: Man sitting on camel
Ours: Man moving on camel in desert

Figure 7: Arabic-English: Woman standing in city
Ours: Woman with crown standing in front of skysrapers

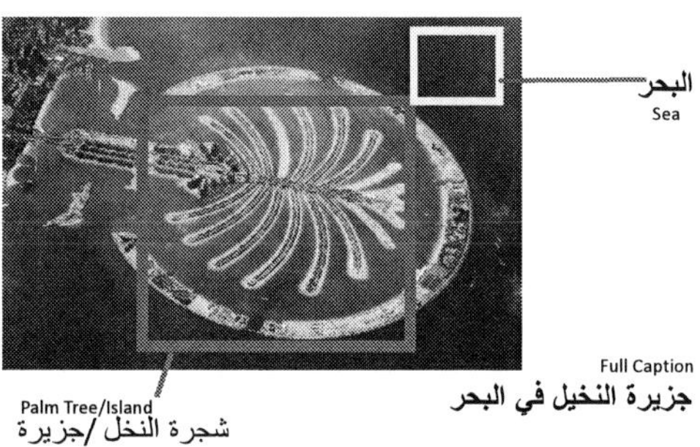

Figure 8: Arabic-English: Island in Sea
Ours: Palm Shaped Islands in the Sea

LSTM is taken as input to the following softmax function layer with a fixed vocabulary size (v).

$$y_n = \frac{\exp\left(W_h \cdot h_n\right)}{\sum_v \exp\left(W_h \cdot h_n\right)} \quad (3)$$

Cross-entropy training criterion is applied to the output layer to make the model learn the weight matrices (W) to maximize the likelihood of the training data. Figure 4 gives an overview of our root-word based Recurrent Neural Network. The dependency tree relations are used to check if the order of Recurrent Neural Network is correct.

Dependency tree constraints (Kuznetsova et al., 2013) checks the caption generated from RNN to be grammatically valid in Modern Standard Arabic and robust to different diacritics in Arabic. The model also ensures that the relations between image-text pair and verbs generated from RNN are still maintained. Formally, the following objective function is maximized:

$$\text{Maximize} \quad F(y;x) = \Phi(y;x,v) + \Psi(y;x)$$
$$\text{subject to} \quad \Omega(y;x,v) \quad (4)$$

where $x = x_i$ is the input caption from RNN (a sentence), v is the accompanying image, $y = y_i$ is the output sentence, $\Phi(y;x,v)$ is the content selection score, $\Phi(y;x)$ is the linguistic fluency score, and $\Omega(y;x,v)$ is the set of hard dependency tree constraints. The most popular Prague Arabic Dependency Treebank (PADT) consisting of multi-level linguistic annotations over Modern Standard Arabic is used for the dependency tree constraints (Hajic et al., 2004).

4 Experimental Results

Figure 3, 5-8 gives a sample of our approach in action. *For the convenience of our readers who are not familiar with Arabic, Figure 5, 6, 7, 8 have the English caption generated using (Xu et al., 2015) denoted as "Arabic-English" and "Ours" denote a professional English translation of the Arabic caption generated from our approach.* We evaluate our technique using two datasets: Flickr8k dataset with manually written captions in Arabic by professional Arabic translators and 405,000 im-

Table 1: BLEU-1,2,3,4/METEOR metrics compared to other methods, (—) indicates an unknown metric

| Dataset | Model | BLEU | | | | METEOR |
		BLEU-1	BLEU-2	BLEU-3	BLEU-4	
Flickr8k	BRNN (Karpathy and Fei-Fei, 2015)	48.2	45.1	29.4	15.5	—
	Google (Vinyals et al., 2015)	52.4	46.1	34.8	18.6	—
	Visual Attention (Xu et al., 2015)	54.2	48.4	36.2	19.4	—
	Ours	**65.8**	**55.9**	**40.4**	**22.3**	**20.09**
Middle Eastern News Websites	MS Research (Fang et al., 2015)	44.1	33.9	26.8	13.7	9.25
	BRNN (Karpathy and Fei-Fei, 2015)	45.4	34.8	27.6	13.9	12.11
	Google (Vinyals et al., 2015)	46.2	36.4	28.5	14.3	15.18
	Visual Attention (Xu et al., 2015)	48.5	38.1	30.9	15.4	16.82
	Ours	**55.6**	**43.3**	**34.5**	**18.9**	**18.01**

ages with captions from various Middle Eastern countries' newspapers. All these newspapers publish articles with images and their captions in both Arabic and English.

We also compare the results of our approach with generating English captions using previously proposed approaches and translating them to Arabic using Google translate. To evaluate the performance, automatic metrics are computed using human generated ground-truth captions. All our images in the dataset were translated using professional Arabic translations as ground-truth. The most commonly used metric to compare generated image captions is BLEU score (Papineni et al., 2002). BLEU is the precision of word n-grams between generated and reference sentences. Additionally, scores like METEOR (Vedantam et al., 2015) which capture perplexity of models for a given transcription have gained widespread attention. Perplexity is the geometric mean of the inverse probability for each predicted word. We report both the BLEU and METEOR score for Arabic captions using root-words. Additionally, this opens a new field of research to use root-words to generate captions from images in Semitic languages and may also be applied to English for words originating from Latin. To the best of our knowledge, our scores are the first reported score for Arabic captions. *Furthermore, the results also show that generating captions directly in Arabic attains a much better BLEU scores compared to generating captions in English and translating them to Arabic.* All results shown in Table 1 are captions generated using the corresponding approaches in English and translating them to Arabic using Google Translate. According to Table 1, we can see that our root-word based approach outperforms all current English based approaches and translated to Arabic using Google Translate.

An interesting observation is in Figure 8. While all current approaches fail to describe the actual "Palm Jumeriah Island" which is a man-made island in shape of Palm tree in Dubai, our approach learns the context of "sea", "island" and "palm" and produces the correct result. Most inefficient cases in our algorithm are due to random outliers like some recent words which are not influenced by root-words. This can be further improved by using a larger dataset and using new dialectal captions in the training phase.

5   Conclusion and Future Work

This paper presents a novel three-stage technique for automatic image caption generation using a combination of root-word based recurrent neural network and root-word based deep convolution neural network. This is the first reported BLEU score for Arabic caption generation and the experimental results show a promising performance. We propose to directly generate captions in Arabic as opposed to generating in English and translating to a target language. However, our research proves, using the BLEU metric, that generating captions directly in Arabic has much better results rather than generating captions in English and translating them to Arabic. Our technique is robust against different diacritics, many dialects and complex morphology of Arabic. Furthermore, this procedure can be extended other Semitic languages like Hebrew which intensively depend on root-words. Future work includes exploring other Arabic morphologies like lemmas used in Arabic dependency parsing (Marton et al., 2010; Haralambous et al., 2014). We also plan to apply this approach to other Semitic languages and release appropriate datasets for the new Semitic languages.

References

Thamir Al Barrag. 2014. Noun phrases in urban hijazi arabic: A distributed morphology approach.

Dzmitry Bahdanau, Kyunghyun Cho, and Yoshua Bengio. 2014. Neural machine translation by jointly learning to align and translate. *arXiv preprint arXiv:1409.0473*.

Kyunghyun Cho, Bart Van Merriënboer, Dzmitry Bahdanau, and Yoshua Bengio. 2014. On the properties of neural machine translation: Encoder-decoder approaches. *arXiv preprint arXiv:1409.1259*.

Jia Deng, Wei Dong, Richard Socher, Li-Jia Li, Kai Li, and Li Fei-Fei. 2009. Imagenet: A large-scale hierarchical image database. In *Computer Vision and Pattern Recognition, 2009. CVPR 2009. IEEE Conference on*, pages 248–255. IEEE.

Hao Fang, Saurabh Gupta, Forrest Iandola, Rupesh K Srivastava, Li Deng, Piotr Dollár, Jianfeng Gao, Xiaodong He, Margaret Mitchell, John C Platt, et al. 2015. From captions to visual concepts and back. In *Proceedings of the IEEE Conference on Computer Vision and Pattern Recognition*, pages 1473–1482.

Charles A Ferguson. 1959. Diglossia. *word*, 15(2):325–340.

Ross Girshick, Jeff Donahue, Trevor Darrell, and Jitendra Malik. 2014. Rich feature hierarchies for accurate object detection and semantic segmentation. In *Proceedings of the IEEE conference on computer vision and pattern recognition*, pages 580–587.

Jan Hajic, Otakar Smrz, Petr Zemánek, Jan Šnaidauf, and Emanuel Beška. 2004. Prague arabic dependency treebank: Development in data and tools. In *Proc. of the NEMLAR Intern. Conf. on Arabic Language Resources and Tools*, pages 110–117.

Yannis Haralambous, Yassir Elidrissi, and Philippe Lenca. 2014. Arabic language text classification using dependency syntax-based feature selection. *arXiv preprint arXiv:1410.4863*.

Sepp Hochreiter and Jürgen Schmidhuber. 1997. Long short-term memory. *Neural computation*, 9(8):1735–1780.

Yangqing Jia, Evan Shelhamer, Jeff Donahue, Sergey Karayev, Jonathan Long, Ross Girshick, Sergio Guadarrama, and Trevor Darrell. 2014. Caffe: Convolutional architecture for fast feature embedding. In *Proceedings of the 22nd ACM international conference on Multimedia*, pages 675–678. ACM.

Vasu Jindal. 2017. A deep learning approach for arabic caption generation using roots-words. In *AAAI*, pages 4941–4942.

Nal Kalchbrenner and Phil Blunsom. 2013. Recurrent continuous translation models. In *EMNLP*, 39, page 413.

Andrej Karpathy and Li Fei-Fei. 2015. Deep visual-semantic alignments for generating image descriptions. In *Proceedings of the IEEE Conference on Computer Vision and Pattern Recognition*, pages 3128–3137.

Andrej Karpathy, Armand Joulin, and Fei Fei F Li. 2014. Deep fragment embeddings for bidirectional image sentence mapping. In *Advances in neural information processing systems*, pages 1889–1897.

Alex Krizhevsky, Ilya Sutskever, and Geoffrey E Hinton. 2012. Imagenet classification with deep convolutional neural networks. In *Advances in neural information processing systems*, pages 1097–1105.

Girish Kulkarni, Visruth Premraj, Sagnik Dhar, Siming Li, Yejin Choi, Alexander C Berg, and Tamara L Berg. 2011. Baby talk: Understanding and generating image descriptions. In *Proceedings of the 24th CVPR*.

Polina Kuznetsova, Vicente Ordonez, Alexander C Berg, Tamara L Berg, and Yejin Choi. 2013. Generalizing image captions for image-text parallel corpus. In *ACL (2)*, pages 790–796.

Yuval Marton, Nizar Habash, and Owen Rambow. 2010. Improving arabic dependency parsing with lexical and inflectional morphological features. In *Proceedings of the NAACL HLT 2010 First Workshop on Statistical Parsing of Morphologically-Rich Languages*, pages 13–21. Association for Computational Linguistics.

Takashi Miyazaki and Nobuyuki Shimizu. 2016. Cross-lingual image caption generation. In *Proceedings of the 54th Annual Meeting of the Association for Computational Linguistics*, volume 1, pages 1780–1790.

Kishore Papineni, Salim Roukos, Todd Ward, and Wei-Jing Zhu. 2002. Bleu: a method for automatic evaluation of machine translation. In *Proceedings of the 40th annual meeting on association for computational linguistics*, pages 311–318. Association for Computational Linguistics.

Hao Peng and Nianhen Li. 2016. Generating chinese captions for flickr30k images.

Olga Russakovsky, Jia Deng, Hao Su, Jonathan Krause, Sanjeev Satheesh, Sean Ma, Zhiheng Huang, Andrej Karpathy, Aditya Khosla, Michael Bernstein, et al. 2015. Imagenet large scale visual recognition challenge. *International Journal of Computer Vision*, 115(3):211–252.

Ali Sharif Razavian, Hossein Azizpour, Josephine Sullivan, and Stefan Carlsson. 2014. Cnn features off-the-shelf: an astounding baseline for recognition. In *Proceedings of the IEEE Conference on Computer Vision and Pattern Recognition Workshops*, pages 806–813.

Richard Socher, Andrej Karpathy, Quoc V Le, Christopher D Manning, and Andrew Y Ng. 2014. Grounded compositional semantics for finding and describing images with sentences. *Transactions of the Association for Computational Linguistics*, 2:207–218.

Ramakrishna Vedantam, C Lawrence Zitnick, and Devi Parikh. 2015. Cider: Consensus-based image description evaluation. In *Proceedings of the IEEE Conference on Computer Vision and Pattern Recognition*, pages 4566–4575.

Oriol Vinyals, Alexander Toshev, Samy Bengio, and Dumitru Erhan. 2015. Show and tell: A neural image caption generator. In *Proceedings of the IEEE Conference on Computer Vision and Pattern Recognition*, pages 3156–3164.

Kelvin Xu, Jimmy Ba, Ryan Kiros, Kyunghyun Cho, Aaron C Courville, Ruslan Salakhutdinov, Richard S Zemel, and Yoshua Bengio. 2015. Show, attend and tell: Neural image caption generation with visual attention. In *ICML*, volume 14, pages 77–81.

Qussai Yaseen and Ismail Hmeidi. 2014. Extracting the roots of arabic words without removing affixes. *Journal of Information Science*, 40(3):376–385.

Nidal Yousef, Aymen Abu-Errub, Ashraf Odeh, and Hayel Khafajeh. 2014. An improved arabic word's roots extraction method using n-gram technique. *Journal of Computer Science*, 10(4):716.

Author Index

Association for Computational Linguistics
209 N. Eighth Street
Stroudsburg, Pennsylvania 18360

ISBN 978-1-5108-6349-1